The Pathways to Sobriety Workbook

Praise for The Pathways to Sobriety Workbook

"*The Pathways to Sobriety Workbook* opened my eyes. It helped me understand my addiction better than anything else I've ever read on the subject. It helped me get beyond my denial and gave me new ways to deal with cravings. My counselor said it's the best new chemical dependency workbook she's seen."

— Angie B., Rochester, NY

Praise for The Pathways to Peace Anger Management Workbook

"Anger is a major contributor to society and family ills. This book is non-shaming, non-blaming and comprehensive in its focus. It will be life-giving to the reader who is looking for answers to problems with anger."

— Claudia A. Black, MSW, Ph.D.,
author of *It Will Never Happen to Me* and other books

"It would be hard to imagine a more timely work than the Pathways to Peace workbook.... It is one thing to read a truth. It is another thing to integrate that truth into one's life so there is concrete change. Would that everyone in the violent, angry time would read and use *Pathways to Peace*."

— Earnie Larsen, author of *Anger to Forgiveness*

"*The Pathways to Peace Anger Management Workbook* and program saved me from relapsing back into alcoholism after the 9/11 attacks on New York City. The workbook helped me overcome a major block—anger and rage. It saved my recovery."

— Ken Q., New York City fireman

"The *Pathways to Peace* workbook on anger management and violence prevention is the best material on the subject that I have seen. This is solid material written by a stellar individual from whom we all have a lot to learn. We are fortunate to be using the materials. In short…the program works!"

— Dr. Anthony Evans, Executive Director,
Cattaraugus County, NY Youth Bureau

∾ Important Note ∾

The material in this book is intended to provide a guide for recovery from addiction to alcohol or other drugs. Every effort has been made to provide accurate and dependable information. However, professionals in the field may have differing opinions, and change is always taking place. The author, publisher, and editors cannot be held responsible for any error, omission, professional disagreement, outdated material, or adverse outcomes that derive from use of any of the activities or information provided in this book.

If you have questions concerning recovery from addiction to alcohol or other drugs, or about applying the information described in this book, please consult a qualified mental-health professional, licensed therapist, or certified alcohol and drug abuse counselor.

Dedication

I cannot list the names of everyone who in some way, large or small, directly or indirectly, played a part in the creation of this book. There are too many. Yet, a few names stand out which I am compelled to write down.

Bill L., who supported me as I took my first shaky steps on the road to recovery;

Frank R., who put down the gun for the poem, then the needle for the Muse;

Toni U., who suffered more than most, then went on to help so many recover;

Shanna M., who, like thousands of others, lost a loved one to drugs and was left with an empty place in her heart;

Tamboo, a.k.a. Curtis S., from back in Venice Beach days, who taught me acceptance;

Bill C., my Canadian brother from across the creek, who has done so much for Pathways.

Thank you, all of you. I honor you.

This book is especially dedicated to my wife, Jan, not only for her editorial expertise (as demonstrated on two successful book projects), but for her humanity. Eventually, like her, I may know instinctively what is right and what is true and what is good, rather than having to work so hard at it so much of the time.

Ordering

Trade bookstores in the U.S. and Canada please contact:

Publishers Group West
1700 Fourth Street, Berkeley CA 94710
Phone: (800) 788-3123   Fax: (510) 528-3444

Hunter House books are available at bulk discounts for textbook course adoptions; to qualifying community, health-care, and government organizations; and for special promotions and fund-raising. For details please contact:

Special Sales Department
Hunter House Inc., PO Box 2914, Alameda CA 94501-0914
Phone: (510) 865-5282   Fax: (510) 865-4295
E-mail: sales@hunterhouse.com

Individuals can order our books from most bookstores, by calling **(800) 266-5592**, or from our website at **www.hunterhouse.com**

The Pathways to Sobriety Workbook

William Fleeman

Director and Founder
of *Pathways to Peace*

Hunter House
PUBLISHERS

Copyright © 2004 by William Fleeman

All rights reserved. No part of this publication may be reproduced or transmitted in any form or by any means, electronic or mechanical, including photocopying and recording, or introduced into any information storage and retrieval system without the written permission of the copyright owner and the publisher of this book. Brief quotations may be used in reviews prepared for inclusion in a magazine, newspaper, or for broadcast. For further information please contact:

Hunter House Inc., Publishers
PO Box 2914
Alameda CA 94501-0914

Library of Congress Cataloging-in-Publication Data

Fleeman, William
　　The Pathways to sobriety workbook / William Fleeman.– 1st ed.
　　　　p. cm.
　　ISBN 0-89793-427-X (pbk.) — ISBN 0-89793-428-8 (spiral)
　　1. Addicts—Rehabilitation. 2. Substance abuse. 3. Self-help techniques. 4. Self-help groups—Activity programs. 5. Recovering addicts—Life skills guides. I. Title.
HV4998.F54 2004
613.8–dc22   2003024060

Project Credits

Cover Design: Brian Dittmar Graphic Design
Book Design and Production: Jinni Fontana Graphic Design
Copy Editor: Kelley Blewster
Proofreader: Lee Rappold
Acquisitions Editor: Jeanne Brondino
Editor: Alexandra Mummery
Publicist: Lisa E. Lee
Foreign Rights Assistant: Elisabeth Wohofsky
Customer Service Manager: Christina Sverdrup
Order Fulfillment: Washul Lakdhon
Administrator: Theresa Nelson
Computer Support: Peter Eichelberger
Publisher: Kiran S. Rana

Printed and Bound by Bang Printing, Brainerd, Minnesota

Manufactured in the United States of America

9 8 7 6 5 4 3 2 1   First Edition   04 05 06 07 08

Contents

Introduction

∽ The Problem ∽

Millions of people all over the world suffer the consequences of addiction. Individuals suffer, children and families suffer, society suffers. Many die as a direct result of the deadly effects of alcohol and other drugs, either from drug overdoses or from physical illnesses caused by or related to addiction to alcohol or other drugs. It has been estimated that 20 percent of civilian hospital beds in the United States, and up to 45 percent of Veterans Administration hospital beds, are occupied by people with alcoholism or other drug-related disorders. Many others die accidental deaths in which alcohol or other drugs are the main cause. Twenty-three thousand people die every year in the United States alone as a result of drunk driving. Many other people lose their lives as a result of violent acts at the hands of intoxicated people. More than half of all murders and more than half of all suicides are committed by people under the influence of alcohol or other drugs. Addiction to alcohol or other drugs is the cause of more than half of all divorces. The monetary cost of addiction in the United States alone is counted in the billions of dollars.

∽ Pathways to Sobriety: A Solution ∽

The Pathways to Sobriety program and workbook offer a solution to the problem of addiction. Notice that I said *a* solution, not *the* solution. Pathways to Sobriety is only one of many programs available to help solve this enormous worldwide problem. We offer no shortcuts or silver bullets. We do offer a program of recovery that has the potential to work for many people who have failed, until now, to find their pathway to sobriety. Pathways to Sobriety can work for you, as it has in one form or another for the many who have come before you.

∽ What Is Pathways to Sobriety?
What Is *The Pathways to Sobriety Workbook?* ∽

Pathways to Sobriety is a self-help program for people in recovery from alcohol and other drugs. *The Pathways to Sobriety Workbook* is the official guide for Pathways to Sobriety groups.

The Pathways to Sobriety Workbook is an interactive guide to help you understand the nature of addiction, to help you stop using alcohol or other drugs, and to help you learn how to live contentedly clean and sober. The lessons and exercises in the workbook follow a logical sequence, which is especially useful in situations where structured learning is desirable. The readability level of *The Pathways to Sobriety Workbook* makes the material accessible to most people.

∾ How Should You Use This Workbook? ∾

The Pathways to Sobriety Workbook can be used by individuals as a hands-on tool for learning and recovery, or by agencies, institutions, schools, social workers, or counselors as a structured chemical-dependency treatment program for individual clients or groups. It can also be used by Pathways to Sobriety self-help groups as a step-by-step guidebook for learning how to stay contentedly clean and sober.

This workbook contains writing exercises to help you look at your own experiences and at your addiction to alcohol or other drugs. These exercises are not tests; they don't have right or wrong answers. Their purpose is to help you understand yourself. You write the answers down, instead of just thinking about them, so that you can later look back at your answers and remember them. Write your answers in this workbook or in a special notebook or journal. Wherever you write them down, keep all the answers together, because some exercises later in the workbook ask you to look back at your answers from earlier exercises.

It's always okay to reread a section or a chapter while you're answering the exercises. In fact, you're encouraged to reread the material as often as you want or need to, because repetition is one of the best ways to understand something. Remember, it's not a test. The important thing is that you understand every chapter well, and that you understand how it applies to your life.

Those who have read and used my earlier book, *The Pathways to Peace Anger Management Workbook*, will find *The Pathways to Sobriety Workbook* similar in structure and content. These similarities should make it easy for the reader to understand and use both workbooks, since they complement each other.

∾ Compatible with Twelve-Step Programs ∾

The information contained in *The Pathways to Sobriety Workbook* is compatible with twelve-step program philosophy. Therefore, the workbook can be used by people involved in twelve-step groups such as Alcoholics Anonymous or Narcotics Anonymous. If you are now involved in a twelve-step program and find it helpful to your recovery, you are strongly encouraged to continue your participation in the program. Pathways to Sobriety is only one of many self-help programs available to people who want to stop using alcohol or other drugs, and *The Pathways to Sobriety Workbook* is only one of many useful guides.

∽ How Long Will It Take to Complete the Workbook? ∽

The workbook is designed to be completed in a minimum of sixteen to eighteen weeks, with at least one or two hours of study per week. Some people may take much longer to complete it. A Pathways to Sobriety program of almost any length could be designed; for example, a program plan could be designed with a completion target of one year or more.

However long it takes you to complete the workbook, it is recommended that you reread the material periodically and redo any of the exercises that you feel you haven't adequately responded to. Each time you read *The Pathways to Sobriety Workbook* and complete the exercises, your understanding of the concepts and techniques presented will increase.

∽ How Long Will It Take to Heal from Your Addiction? ∽

This workbook is only a beginning. Healing from addiction takes longer than a few months, since healing requires more than a change in behavior. Changing addictive behavior is the easy part. Making changes in the part of the self—sometimes called the *character*—that will lead to long-term, contented sobriety takes much longer and is much more difficult. True healing from addiction will not happen until a person's character has been transformed.

Full recovery from a long-standing pattern of addiction takes a minimum of two to three years. *Maintaining recovery is an ongoing, lifelong process.* Work hard, have patience, and be forgiving of yourself.

∽ What You Should Do First ∽

According to the American Medical Association, addiction (whether to alcohol or other drugs such as crack cocaine or heroin) is a potentially fatal progressive disease or disorder. The physical complications you may be suffering now as a result of alcohol or other drug use must be treated by medical doctors. Whether you are still using chemicals or have been clean and sober for awhile, before using this workbook you are strongly urged to see a qualified alcohol or chemical dependency counselor for a professional assessment and to make an appointment with your physician to determine the present status of your health.

∽ What You Need to Know about the Withdrawal Syndrome ∽

In 1972 legislation was passed by the U.S. Congress that officially guaranteed medical attention for people suffering from the acute stages of intoxication or withdrawal. Prior to that, many alcoholics and drug addicts died unnecessarily from the medical consequences of addiction. If and when addicted people showed up at hospitals complaining of symptoms, they sometimes were refused medical care. Some alcoholics were put in jail because of a crime committed while intoxicated, and some ended up committing suicide in their cells or dying while in jail from complications of alcohol withdrawal.

Things have changed, but people still suffer unnecessarily and occasionally die from the physical complications of addiction because of a lack of information or because of improper advice. Therefore, it is extremely important to know that withdrawal from certain classes of drugs can be fatal. Although this fact is still not widely known, the withdrawal syndrome that occurs with full-blown addiction to alcohol, a powerful central-nervous-system depressant, when left medically untreated includes convulsions and seizures and can lead to death. In fact, *full-blown alcoholics who go through abrupt withdrawal from alcohol without medical attention have a 50 percent chance of dying as a result of the withdrawal syndrome.* Other central-nervous-system drugs, most notably barbiturates (sleeping pills) and some of the other addictive sedatives, also lead to withdrawal syndromes that are potentially fatal. Even drugs that do not, in themselves, lead to potentially fatal withdrawal syndromes may be life-threatening in another way. For example, although full-blown addiction to cocaine or heroin rarely produces potentially fatal physiological withdrawal symptoms, the cocaine or heroin addict may experience profound mental depression during withdrawal, which, if left medically untreated, may result in death by suicide.

Once again, you are urged to undergo a professional addiction assessment and to make an appointment with a medical doctor before abruptly stopping the use of alcohol or other drugs, and before you begin any self-help addiction-recovery program, including Pathways to Sobriety.

∾ To the Person Struggling to Recover from Addiction ∾

When people begin the difficult struggle to overcome addiction, they often feel alone in their struggle. They feel that everyone has given up on them. If you feel alone in your struggle and that everyone has given up on you, know that you are not alone and that not everyone has given up. You may have suffered painful consequences because of your addiction to or abuse of alcohol or other drugs. You may feel so overwhelmed by guilt and shame that you have come to believe that no one could possibly care whether you live or die. But there are those who care.

You will find scattered throughout this workbook brief stories just like yours, written by men and women just like you. They have shared their personal histories with you in order to make it easier for you to understand and relate to the material in this workbook. Writing down their stories was often painful for them because it required them to recall things and events they would rather not think about. They struggled through the pain because they want to help you.

Like you, these men and women struggled with addiction. Like you, they felt alone and powerless. Like you, they suffered painful consequences because of their addiction. At one time they too were filled with overwhelming guilt and shame, and they too felt that no one cared.

But the people who have shared their personal stories in this workbook didn't struggle in vain; they struggled and won. They found acceptance and support from others, and they learned ways to help them deal with their addiction triggers. They learned how to live contented clean and sober lives with their families, their friends, their employers, and their coworkers. For the people who wrote down their stories, the struggle wasn't easy, but they did succeed. They changed their behavior, stopped using alcohol and other drugs once and for all, and are now reaping the rewards. They are living reasonably happy, productive lives. Most of these people continue to learn and to grow by participating in self-help groups in their community. These people care about you, because they understand. They sincerely hope that you find your pathway to sobriety.

⤳ To Family Members and Significant Others ⤳

Abuse of or addiction to alcohol or other drugs has a negative effect on almost everyone in the addict's life, especially those closest to the addict. Spouses and children are affected most. Siblings and extended family members may also be affected, even if they don't live under the same roof as the addict. The addict's friends, employers, coworkers, and even strangers may be affected.

If someone close to you abuses or is addicted to alcohol or other drugs, you are strongly urged to seek help for yourself. Even if the person who abuses or is addicted to alcohol or other drugs has stopped using chemicals and is working a recovery program, you may need counseling and support to help yourself cope. In some ways you may suffer more mental and emotional pain than the one who abuses or is addicted to alcohol or other drugs. You may even have some of the same symptoms. For example, even though you don't use alcohol or other drugs, you may suffer serious bouts of depression or anxiety. But help and hope do exist for loved ones of alcoholics and drug addicts, and I encourage you to seek them out.

◆ ◆ ◆

If you have picked up this workbook because you are struggling with addiction, my hope is that it will help you to understand the nature of addiction, empower you to stop using alcohol or other drugs once and for all, and inspire you to live the kind of happy clean and sober life you deserve.

> The author of this book sometimes uses the first person designation "I" and sometimes the third person "Bill." Using the first person helps him to connect and relate with the reader on a deeper, more personal level. It also aids him in the process of self-disclosure. The use of the third person, on the other hand, assists him in navigating the ideas and concepts covered in the text and helps him convey lessons to be learned in a more objective fashion.

PART ONE

Understanding
the Problem

1

The Basics

This chapter will provide you with some basic information about alcohol and other drugs and will help you begin to understand the nature of addiction and recovery from addiction.

❧ Why People Use Alcohol and Other Drugs ❧

People use alcohol or other drugs to change their emotional state—that is, to change how they feel. It's as simple as that. People use various drugs such as alcohol, cocaine, heroin, caffeine, Ecstasy, and nicotine in order to change painful feelings such as anxiety or depression into more pleasurable feelings such as relaxation or joy. Sometimes people use chemicals to increase the intensity of pleasurable feelings, such as excitement or confidence, that they are already experiencing. The reason that people continue to use alcohol or other drugs to change how they feel is because it works, at least for a while.

While it is true that people use alcohol or other drugs to change how they feel—even if only to feel more relaxed or more included in a social situation—it is also true that not all people become addicted. In fact, in the case of alcohol, some people seem to enjoy the taste as much as anything else.

❧ History of Alcohol and Other Drug Use ❧

People have been using alcohol or other drugs to alter their emotional state for at least five thousand years. There are written accounts of the use and abuse of alcohol from as early as 3000 B.C. The chewable form of cocaine was probably in use in South America at least two thousand years ago. People in Asia have been using opium for several thousand years.

Alcohol, the most widely used and abused drug of all, may have been in use in prehistoric times. Imagine a Neanderthal hunter shambling dejectedly along a path on the way home from an unsuccessful hunt, dragging the end of his stone-tipped spear in the dust. He not only feels like a failure, but also it is a very hot day under a boiling sun and so he feels thirsty as well. He notices a shallow pool of reddish bubbling liquid off to one side of the path. The liquid is made up of the fermenting juices of common berries that have fallen from a bush and lain in the sun for several days. The hunter recognizes the berry bush and recalls eating the red berries in the past without experiencing pain. Stopping to investigate, he kneels down and sniffs the reddish liquid. Then he sticks a finger into the mash and tastes it.

Cupping his hand, he scoops up some of the liquid and drinks it down. "Not bad," he grunts, experiencing a slight buzz. He drinks more. "Not bad at all," he grunts again, slurring his words slightly. Getting down on his hands and knees, he makes like a human wet-vac and sucks up the entire alcohol-laden pool. He becomes the very first person in history to get drunk, and he then proceeds to suffer the world's first hangover the next day.

∾ Classes of Drugs ∾

There are essentially two classes of drugs: central-nervous-system (CNS) depressants and central-nervous-system stimulants. CNS depressants include alcohol, nicotine (also a stimulant), cannabis (marijuana), and heroin. CNS depressants have a sedative effect on the brain. CNS depressants are more likely to produce serious withdrawal symptoms.

CNS stimulants include caffeine, amphetamines (diet pills, sometimes called "speed"), ephedra, and cocaine. The effect on the brain produced by CNS stimulants is, of course, the opposite of that of sedative drugs.

Another class of drugs deserves mention. Often called *psychedelic drugs*, they include LSD, peyote, and various forms of mushrooms (both foreign and domestic) that produce marked changes in perception. These drugs are sometimes referred to as *psychotomimetic drugs* because they have been known to produce effects that imitate the symptoms of major mental disorders such as schizophrenia. Psychedelic drugs fall into the two classifications described above. In their action on the central nervous system, they are classed as either depressants or stimulants. The drug Ecstasy, for example, is classified as both a psychedelic and a stimulant.

There are many more examples of drugs in each of the three categories—depressants, stimulants, and psychedelics. This is only a brief list of some of the more common drugs of abuse. All drugs change how people feel emotionally by interacting with brain chemistry.

∾ Signs and Symptoms of Physiological Addiction ∾

Bearing in mind the information given above, it is important to be on the lookout for signs and symptoms that may indicate a need to seek immediate medical attention. They include: excessive nervousness, sweats, tremors or shakes, rapid or irregular pulse, shortness of breath or irregular breathing, crying spells, laughing spells, rapid-fire speech, slow or slurred speech, unsteady gait, slow reflexes, depression, anxiety.

∾ History of Addiction Counseling ∾

In the United States and most other countries prior to about 1970, what later became known as addiction counseling was done by clergy and by volunteers who were members of Alcoholics Anonymous. Most physicians, psychologists, and psychiatrists would not treat alcoholism or drug addiction. They treated the medical complications that alcoholics and drug addicts invariably suffered, but they usually would not attempt to treat the disorder itself. In fact, the medical and psychiatric fields did not consider alcoholism and drug addiction, in themselves, to be diseases. Many of the top experts in the medical and psychiatric professions believed that alcoholism and drug addiction were moral afflictions. After treating them for medical complications, doctors often sent their alcoholic and drug-addicted patients to ministers, rabbis, or priests. Sometimes alcoholics ended up on psychiatric hospital back wards and died there. Their diagnosis: dipsomania. The dictionary defines *dipsomania* as an irresistible craving for intoxicants.

ᖚ Recovery Models: Abstinence vs. Controlled Use ᖚ

There are two very different recovery models: abstinence models and controlled-use models. *Abstinence models* maintain that recovery from addiction to alcohol or other drugs requires the addicted person to abstain completely. *Controlled-use models* suggest that the addicted person can learn how to use alcohol or other drugs in moderation and avoid consequences.

Alcoholics Anonymous

Alcoholics Anonymous (AA), which began in Akron, Ohio, in 1935 and was cofounded by William Wilson, a New York City stockbroker, and Robert Smith, an Akron physician, uses the abstinence model. Both Wilson and Smith were addicted to alcohol. Dr. Smith was said to have been addicted to barbiturates as well.

AA suggests that the alcoholic follow twelve specific steps in order to get sober and stay sober. For that reason, AA is often called a *twelve-step recovery program*. The steps ask the alcoholic to take responsibility for his or her addiction and for the consequences of his or her addiction; to turn to a "higher power" for strength, support, and guidance; and to make amends to people he or she may have harmed.

Largely because of the influence of Wilson and Smith and of AA as a whole, opinions about alcoholism and addiction began to change over the decades. Eventually (around 1970), the medical profession officially recognized alcoholism as a disease. When that happened, psychologists, psychiatrists, and other professional caregivers began to more actively treat addicted persons. Ultimately, a whole new field opened up: chemical-dependency counseling.

Narcotics Anonymous

Narcotics Anonymous (NA) was started around 1955 as a program specifically for people recovering from addiction to drugs other than alcohol. NA uses essentially the same format as AA, including a focus on the twelve steps. Like AA it encourages total abstinence from the use of drugs, and like AA it enjoys a very high success rate.

Controlled-Use Models

There are those who believe that people who are addicted to alcohol can learn how to use alcohol responsibly, whatever that means. It may be true that some people who are addicted to alcohol or other drugs can somehow learn to control their alcohol or other drug use. However, for the "true" alcohol addict or drug addict, this is a potentially dangerous idea. One of the symptoms of addiction is loss of control. This means the addicted person is at times unable to stop after just one or two drinks or after one or two puffs on the crack pipe.

Pathways to Sobriety believes that alcohol addicts or drug addicts who use the controlled-use model are likely to fail. They are more likely than not to return eventually to abusive use of alcohol or other drugs. The consequences for them as well as for their families could be lethal. Although people who use the abstinence model sometimes also relapse, Pathways to Sobriety believes that people who use the abstinence model are less likely to relapse into full-blown addiction.

Message from Jack

My name is Jack. I'm recovering from alcohol addiction. I loved the alcohol high and really didn't want to stop using alcohol to change how I feel. I tried AA but rejected that program because I'd have had to quit drinking entirely. I thought I could learn to control my intake so that I could still cop a buzz now and then but avoid getting into trouble. I read some books about how to control one's use of alcohol. I even found a counselor who said he could help me learn how to drink safely and responsibly. I did alright—at first. After about three months I was able to stop after just a few and could choose where and when to drink. I limited myself to three drinks in an evening if I went out and drove my car. I limited myself to four or five if I stayed home.

Then one night I went out to my favorite bar to have a couple of drinks with my friends. It was one of those times when I was having a lot of fun and didn't notice the effects of the alcohol. I ended up having about six drinks, twice the number I'd set as my limit. When I left the place around 10:00 P.M., I was feeling a little high but not drunk. I got home fine. Safe and sound at home, I decided to have another drink before going to bed. I ended up finishing the rest of a bottle of scotch that I'd had in the cupboard for a couple of months. The scotch went down easy, and I drank the equivalent of about six drinks. After finishing the scotch, I felt like having more. By then I was definitely impaired. I checked my watch. It said 11:35 P.M. The liquor store was only ten minutes away. I could easily make it without speeding. I felt totally confident. I walked from the kitchen cupboard to the kitchen table on the other side of the room. No problem. Straight as an arrow.

I went out and got into my car and headed for the liquor store. A few minutes later, I started feeling the effects of the scotch more than I wanted to. My eyesight got a little blurry. I could also tell that my reflexes weren't the best. About a block from the liquor store, I came to a stoplight. I stopped at the white line and waited. Looking to my left, I saw a car approaching from the cross street and saw it slow down. The light changed and I entered the intersection at a prudent speed. All of a sudden, the car on my left that I thought had stopped came barreling through the red light and smashed into my left front fender. I saw the car at the last second but it was too late. Drunk or sober, I couldn't have avoided a collision. There were two people in the other car, the driver and someone in the passenger seat. Neither of them was hurt. Nor was I.

The driver of the other car had called the police on his cell phone even before he got out of the car, and before I knew it the police were there. The cop Breathalyzed both of us. The other guy had been drinking but blew under the limit. I blew one point over. The other guy had run a red light and was clearly in the wrong. But there were no witnesses, other than me and the two guys in the other car. Naturally, the driver of the other car told the cops that I was the one who ran the red light, and the passenger backed up the driver's story. I'd had a DWI a few years before, so guess who got the ticket? Guess who lost his license? And guess who doesn't use the controlled-drinking model anymore?

❧ Pathways to Sobriety ❧

Like AA and NA, Pathways to Sobriety uses the abstinence model. But Pathways to Sobriety is not a twelve-step program. Pathways to Sobriety groups are structured in a way that is similar to the way twelve-step groups are structured. Pathways to Sobriety groups are facilitated by peer volunteers, charge no fees, and are open-ended and ongoing. However, Pathways to Sobriety groups do not use the twelve steps as guides for recovery. Instead, Pathways to Sobriety uses a set of eight principles.

❧ Relapse Prevention ❧

It is assumed that you have made a decision to stop using alcohol or other nonprescribed drugs, and to learn how to live happily clean and sober. Once you start on the road to recovery, from then on the name of the game is relapse prevention. In fact, you could say that the rest of this workbook is devoted to that single, extremely important end—relapse prevention.

If you abuse or are addicted to alcohol or other drugs, you have probably spent many years conditioning yourself to be a drinking or drugging machine. This conditioning process is now a permanent part of your subconscious mind. Your addiction program is hardwired into your subconscious and will remain potentially very powerful. What you need to do as a person in recovery from addiction is to saturate your subconscious with new material through a conscious application of the tools of recovery. *The Pathways to Sobriety Workbook* aims to help you do just that.

2

Bill's Story

Writing down my story was an important part of my recovery from addiction to alcohol and other drugs. Writing it helped me understand why I became addicted. It helped motivate me to stop drinking and using drugs and helped me find out how to stop. Writing my story was an important part of my self-assessment.

In addition to my addiction to alcohol and other drugs, I had another serious problem. I used anger like a drug as well. In my book *The Pathways to Peace Anger Management Workbook*, my story focused on my addiction to anger and rage. My story here focuses on my addiction to alcohol and other drugs. But the reader should understand that my addiction to alcohol and other drugs is closely related to my addiction to anger. I cannot talk about one without mentioning the other. Maybe it is that way for you too.

When I wrote my story in *The Pathways to Peace Anger Management Workbook*, I wrote down only the bare essentials. It was brief, only seven or eight pages. The story you are about to read here is a much more detailed and much longer version. I call it the whole story. My hope is that you will relate at a deep, personal level.

Exercises have been included after each main part of my story to encourage you to pause and reflect so you can see whether any of the events described in my story connect to similar events in your personal history.

❧ A Special Note ❧

In order to understand yourself as deeply as possible, and to heal as completely as possible from your addiction to alcohol or other drugs, you need to write down your story. Appendix A, located in the back of the workbook, has been set aside for you to write down your story. It is located in the back of the book because you will need time to think and reflect as you work on this very important part of your recovery from addiction to alcohol or other drugs. You are encouraged to begin work on your story as soon as you feel comfortable doing so, but you are not expected to finish writing down your story before you finish the rest of this workbook. There may be parts of your story that you will not want to write down or even think about before you have been clean and sober for a period of time. You may want to have the support of a professional counselor when you decide to write down some of the more emotionally charged events of your life. You can skip over these sensitive areas at first, but as you grow stronger you are encouraged to write down everything. Of course, you will not want to write down anything if making a record of it on paper would injure yourself or other people. Use discretion, but don't hold back unnecessarily.

Ten pages have been set aside for you in Appendix A. You may find that this is not enough and may want to add pages. Or you may feel more comfortable using a special journal or notebook for your story. A loose-leaf binder works well, because then you can easily add pages and rearrange the sequence of pages. Chances are, writing down your story will be a work in progress, as was mine. You may end up working at writing down your story a little at a time over the course of several years.

As your story unfolds on paper, find a person you can trust and share your story with that person. Choose someone who will take you seriously. Choose someone who will understand the purpose you have in mind. Tell him or her that you want to share your story in order to increase your understanding of yourself, so that you can more fully heal from your addiction to alcohol or other drugs. Share only what you feel comfortable sharing. You may want to share your story with a professional counselor. It would not be a good idea to share your story with anyone you have hurt in the past because of your addiction to alcohol or other drugs. You may also decide that it's best to choose someone else to share your story with other than your spouse or partner.

∼ Childhood Years: Birth to Age Twelve ∼

My father was a career soldier in three different branches of the military and was addicted to alcohol. Most people addicted to alcohol or other drugs come from families where one or both parents were addicted. There does appear to be a hereditary predisposition to addiction. That means genetics plays a part in the process of addiction to alcohol or other drugs, and people who come from families where there is a history of addiction are more likely to develop an addiction themselves. Here are some interesting statistics: If one of your parents is addicted to alcohol or other drugs, you have a 50 percent chance of developing an addiction if you use alcohol or other drugs. If both of your parents are addicted, you have a 90 percent chance of developing an addiction if you use alcohol or other drugs.

My father left my mother and me when I was a baby. My mother took me to live with my maternal grandparents in Upper Michigan. We were poor. My grandfather, like my father, was addicted to alcohol. He worked part-time on weekend nights as a taxicab dispatcher. He drank up most of what he earned at his dispatcher job, so in order to support us all, my mother had to work two jobs most of the time. My grandmother stayed home and took care of me.

When I got older, I tried to figure out why my father had abandoned me and my mother. I decided it must have been my fault. I don't know why I thought their separation and divorce was my fault, but I did. That made me think there must have been something basically wrong with me as a person. Otherwise, I reasoned, my father wouldn't have abandoned me.

I can remember feeling angry at my father for walking out of my life. I also remember wishing that he would come back. He never did, and soon I stopped thinking about him so much. But I never got over how I felt about his leaving. I felt worthless and defective, unloved and unwanted, angry and rejected. My father's leaving led me to believe you can't trust people to stick by you. If your own father leaves you, who can you trust? Nobody—period. That's what I came to believe.

Besides feeling angry, I also felt sad a lot of the time. In fact, as a child I could identify having only two specific feelings: anger and sadness. When I wasn't feeling angry or sad, I was vaguely aware of an ongoing sensation of inner tension that at times felt overwhelming. The inner tension became more and more intense as I grew older.

There was verbal and physical violence in my home. My grandfather was often violent when drinking, and he drank often. My mother and grandfather had physical fights. My grandmother spent a lot of time crying and wringing her hands in despair. My grandfather died when I was five years old. Although he was sometimes abusive towards me, his death saddened me deeply. Once again, I felt abandoned and rejected. Once again, I blamed myself for the loss. I must be a very bad child indeed, I thought, to have lost both my father and my grandfather.

When I was seven, my mother remarried. Now there was a stepfather around, a stranger to me. He resented me, I think, because I wasn't his real son. And I resented him, too, because he wasn't my real dad. My stepdad was a World War II veteran. Like many combat veterans, he came home from the war traumatized and with a terrible thirst; he was addicted to alcohol, like my father and grandfather. He also abused other drugs, mainly amphetamines (speed). Although at times I think he resented me, my stepdad also tried hard to give me love and guidance. He tried to be an example of kindness and respect, but I was resentful and resistant.

◆ **EXERCISE** Bill said most people who become addicted to alcohol or other drugs come from families where one or both parents were addicted. Was either of your parents addicted to alcohol or other drugs?

_____

_____

◆ **EXERCISE** Bill said he came to blame himself when his father abandoned him, and later blamed himself when his grandfather died. Bill said his father's leaving made him angry at both his father and himself, and also made him sad. Did your father or mother abandon you when you were young? If so, how did that make you feel?

_____

_____

_____

_____

◆ **EXERCISE** Bill said that as a child he could identify only two specific feelings: anger and sadness. He said he also felt an overriding sense of inner tension that became more and more intense as he grew older. What feelings could you identify when you were a child? Did you, like Bill, also feel an overriding sense of tension that became more intense as you grew older?

_____

_____

_____

_____

_____

_____

∾ Teen Years: Thirteen to Seventeen ∾

When I was thirteen years old we moved to Detroit, Michigan. Things went okay for a while. But then I started running around with a gang of kids from the neighborhood who were like me. Their fathers had abandoned them, too. They were being raised by their grandmothers while their mothers worked two jobs. Most had alcoholic grandfathers and alcoholic stepfathers who resented them. They felt abandoned and rejected, sad and angry, worthless and defective—just like me.

The kids I hung out with stayed out late on the corner, down by the liquor store. I started hanging out with them and staying out late too. I'd catch it when I got home, but I didn't care. To me, hanging out with my friends was worth the hassle I got from my mom and step-dad, or from my grandmother.

∾ First Alcohol Use ∾

I had my first drink of alcohol when I was thirteen, the same year I started hanging out with my new friends. One of the kids stole a case of beer from the bar where his mother worked as a waitress. We drank the beer in an abandoned house on a side street near the bar. I drank four beers fast and got drunk. After drinking the four beers, I felt relaxed and confident. I felt good about myself and good about the world—I felt high! Like magic, that almost overwhelming sense of inner tension disappeared. I got sick and threw up afterwards, but those four beers made me feel better than I'd ever felt before. I couldn't wait to do it again.

❧ First Blackout ❧

By the time I was fifteen, I was getting drunk as often as I could. When my friend couldn't steal beer from the bar where his mother worked, we'd all pitch in and pay a wino a dollar or two to buy some cheap whiskey for us from the liquor store. I built up a tolerance to alcohol fast. Later, I learned that increased tolerance is one of the signs that addiction is beginning to set in. The more I drank, the more I could drink. I stopped getting sick after a drinking binge.

I had my first blackout before I turned sixteen. A blackout occurs when you drink a lot of alcohol fast. It temporarily knocks out your memory. A blackout is another sign of addiction to alcohol. My friends and I were standing around in the shadows of an alley, drinking. We had a pint of cheap whiskey. The pint was half gone. We'd each had about three big gulps. One of my friends bet I couldn't chug the rest of the whiskey all at once without stopping. I said, "Give me that bottle." I tipped it up, gulped down the rest of the whiskey, and let the empty bottle fall and break on the concrete. My throat burned. My stomach rebelled, but somehow I held the whiskey down. My friends looked on in awe.

About ten minutes later I started staggering around like a fool. I was so drunk I could hardly stand on my feet. My friends said I cursed the air blue and wanted to fight everybody. They said I finally threw up in the alley. They walked home with me and I was able to sneak in the house without waking anybody. When I woke in the morning, I couldn't remember anything that had happened after the whiskey bottle fell and broke in the alley. I was also extremely hungover. It was Monday morning and I couldn't get up to go to school.

◆ **EXERCISE** Bill had his first taste of alcohol at age thirteen, and his first blackout at age fifteen. How old were you when you had your first taste of alcohol and your first blackout?

❧ First Major Consequence ❧

I experienced my first major drug-related consequence at age fifteen when I was expelled from school. I didn't like school because I felt as though I didn't fit in. In fact, I never felt I belonged and never felt accepted except when I was with the gang on the street, no matter where I was or who I was with. Also, by then I had developed an intense dislike for authority. I hated teachers, school crossing guards, policemen—in short, anyone with authority.

I got expelled toward the end of ninth grade. A lot of things led up to it. I skipped school about twenty days during the first semester. One of the gang members, Jeff, lived with his single mother near the school. Jeff's mother worked all day waiting tables at a restaurant. There was no one else in the house, so I could go there with Jeff and drink. His mom had a cupboard full of all kinds of alcohol. She never seemed to miss what we drank, and Jeff and I always made sure we left the apartment before his mother got home at 5:00 P.M. At other times I hid out from the truant officer at the public library. I'd sneak in past the desk, then sit in the back between the stacks and read to pass the time.

By this time, my behavior at school on days when I decided to show up had become unacceptable to the teachers and to the school administrators. I was sometimes hungover. I was moody and aggressive. I picked fights in the hallway and refused to cooperate with the teachers. I was angry all the time. My behavior got worse, more violent, more unmanageable. Looking back, I can see that alcohol was a big contributor.

Finally I was called into the principal's office. I remember it well. The principal said he'd never seen anyone's behavior go all to hell, as mine had, over such a short period of time. He pointed out that I had been a straight-A student throughout seventh grade and had even been elected president of my homeroom class. By the end of the eighth grade, I was barely passing my subjects, and on many occasions had been sent to detention for misbehavior or truancy.

By the end of the first half of the ninth grade, I was failing all subjects, had played hooky on twenty days, and had been in three hallway fights. The last straw, the principal said, was when I spoke disrespectfully to the music teacher during class and, when told to leave, left in a rage and broke a window when I slammed the door into the wall on my way out. The principal expelled me and told me not to come back to his school—ever.

The following September I got into serious trouble. I participated in a crime that involved robbery and assault with a weapon. Alcohol was a factor, and so was anger. I was arrested and placed in a detention center for teens. There were other people involved in the crime. When I refused to name them, I was placed in solitary confinement. I was in solitary for thirty-six days. I spent my sixteenth birthday there. Then I was sent to a Michigan reformatory. After my release a year later, I was placed on parole till I turned nineteen.

The reformatory had its own school on the premises. I was given the choice of working in one of the shops all day, pitching manure at the reformatory farm, or going to school. Of course, you can guess which option I chose. I went to school, which was set up to take students through ninth grade but no further. After I finished my ninth-grade classes with passing grades, the administrators put me to work in the reformatory library. Few inmates used the library, so I had a lot of time to read on the job. I could also take books to my building, and on Sundays I lay under a table in the dayroom and read all day. The reform-school English teacher said I had writing talent. He encouraged me to read widely and to write. I began to keep a journal. The art teacher said I had art talent and encouraged me to draw and paint.

◆ **EXERCISE** Bill had his first major consequence as a result of using alcohol or other drugs at age fifteen, when he was expelled from school. How old were you when you had your first major consequence from using alcohol or other drugs? What was the consequence?

_____

_____

_____

≈ Things Get Worse ≈

After I got out of the reformatory, my mother and stepfather insisted I get a job. Imagine that! My first job was busing dishes at a restaurant in downtown Detroit. I hated that job, and it didn't pay much. I quit after about a week and got a job unloading boxcars at the railroad yard. That was hard work too, harder than the restaurant job, but it paid better.

Of course, as soon as I got home I started drinking again. I felt as though I had a lot of catching up to do. Pretty soon, my drinking started to interfere with work the way it had interfered with school. I was often late for work, and sometimes I just couldn't show up on Mondays at all. I was seventeen by then, and I was drinking more and having more blackouts. My tolerance for alcohol was increasing fast. I couldn't believe how much I had to drink in order to get drunk, or even to cop a buzz. By then, I was a full-blown alcohol addict. I drank mostly beer or cheap wine.

I lost my railroad yard job when I showed up an hour late the day after my eighteenth birthday. I had a series of other low-paying jobs from then until I turned nineteen. I lost them all either directly or indirectly because of alcohol, although anger was also a factor. I was becoming more and more preoccupied with alcohol use. I was becoming more and more of a loner, too. I spent most of my time chasing the high. I associated only with other people like me. Our conversations went something like this: "I wonder where there's a party? Anybody know where there's a party tonight? Hey, man, got any money to put in on a bottle of vodka?"

I wasn't accomplishing anything worthwhile, but I had big plans. I wanted to go to art school, or to college. But there were certain things I needed in order to get into an art school or college and to succeed, and I didn't have them. I didn't have a high school diploma, I didn't have money for tuition, and I didn't have self-discipline. Even if I'd had those things, it wouldn't have mattered. I might have been able to enroll in art school or college, but I would have failed anyway. Why? Booze. Also, I had an attitude. I was full of anger and hated authority.

◆ **EXERCISE** When Bill turned seventeen, his tolerance for alcohol began to increase fast. He said he had to drink more and more in order to get drunk or even cop a buzz. When did you notice that your tolerance for alcohol or other drugs began to increase and that you had to use more and more?

_____

_____

≈ Early Adulthood: Age Eighteen to Twenty-Five ≈

Finally, I got fed up with Detroit. Not enough parties, not enough booze. My friends were addicted to alcohol too, or well on their way, but most of the ones who weren't behind bars by now had jobs. Some of them had even gotten married. My best friend, Floyd, worked at a GM plant in Pontiac. He made good money and encouraged me to go to work for GM too. But I was restless. And the old feelings I'd felt all my life of not belonging and not fitting in were now even more intense and more painful.

I'd developed a strong interest in literature and art while in reform school, but none of the old friends I'd grown up with on the streets in Detroit cared about books or art. The only thing I had in common with them anymore was getting drunk. I partied with them, but when the booze ran out and the party was over there wasn't anything to talk about. Once again I felt I didn't belong. Alcoholics always seem to feel as though they don't belong, no matter where they are or who they're with.

∾ On the Road (First Geographical Change) ∾

Like many people who get addicted to alcohol or other drugs I thought I'd feel better about myself, other people, and the world if I went someplace else and made new friends. I didn't have a car, so wherever I decided to go I would have to hitchhike. Since I didn't have a regular job I was always broke, so I would have to borrow road money. My addict's pride wouldn't let me admit it but part of the reason I left Detroit was because my friends were getting tired of supporting my alcohol habit and theirs too. Most of my friends worked hard for their money at factory jobs and were beginning to resent me for not paying my share of the tab, and I was starting to feel embarrassed about being so dependent on them.

Earlier that summer I'd read a *Life* magazine article about a place called Venice Beach, a seaside community near Los Angeles. The article said Venice Beach was "a slum by the sea" and the perfect locale for artists and writers who needed a place to develop their craft and where rent was cheap. While working in the reformatory library, I'd read some books by Ernest Hemingway. I enjoyed his stories and writing style and read everything he'd written up to that time. Then I read a biography of Hemingway. In the biography I learned that Hemingway was the kind of tough, hard-drinking adventurous old man of action I imagined my father to be. Hemingway became a role model for me. He became my hero and a sort of father figure. In fact it could be said that Ernest Hemingway had fathered an entire generation of young men who, like me, were aspiring writers and budding alcohol addicts.

In the biography I also learned that Hemingway had started out as a writer with only a high school diploma. He ended up in Paris, France, at around age twenty-one. In Paris, Hemingway met writers and artists who were college educated. He hung out with them and learned from them. Paris was Hemingway's college. So I figured I could learn what I needed about writing and painting if I went to Venice Beach and hung out with some of the college-educated artists and writers who lived there. Venice Beach would be my Paris, my college. In the magazine article about Venice Beach, there was a photo of a bearded scruffy-looking artist drinking from a half-gallon wine jug. Not every addicted person who thinks a change of environment will make things better decides to go all the way across the country, but I was one who did.

When I told my best friend, Floyd, that I was going to hitchhike to California, he tried to talk me out of it. When he saw it was no use, he gave me thirty dollars, drove me out of Detroit, and dropped me off where I would be likely to catch a ride.

Floyd drove me out of the old neighborhood in his hot new Chevy, through the city on Woodward Avenue, then through the suburbs to Interstate 94. Floyd stopped at a crossroads that looked like a good spot for hitchhiking. I got out of the car, hoisted my suitcase out of the backseat, and set it down on the shoulder of the road. Floyd put the gearshift in neutral, got out, and came around to the side of the car where I was standing next to the road. We kicked some gravel around with our feet. We shook hands. I promised to write, but we both knew I never would.

Floyd jumped back in the Chevy and drove off, leaving me standing there on the shoulder. He drove up the road, hooked a U-turn, and then barreled past in the opposite direction, grinning big and going about sixty in a blur of teeth and a rush of wind. I watched the Chevy shrink down to a black speck in the distance. Then I turned my back to the morning sun, turned my face away from my city, away from my family, my friends, and my home, and set my eyes on the long, long road that vanished to a point in the west.

My first objective was to hitchhike to Chicago where Route 66 began, then just stay on 66 all the way to L.A. Standing waiting for a ride, I thought of Jack Kerouac's book *On the Road,* which I'd read six times since it came out in 1957, and which lay in the bottom of my suitcase, along with my sketch pad and journal, under my socks and shorts. Standing at the side of the road, I also thought of Thomas Wolfe, whose books I'd read at the reformatory library, and inside my head I heard the famous words that Wolfe chose for the title of his first book, *You Can't Go Home Again.* I felt sad because I knew the words were true.

My first ride took me all the way across Michigan to South Chicago. I took a bus out of downtown Chicago to where Route 66 began. I started hitchhiking again. Three more rides took me to a crossroads outside Joliet, Illinois. It was midnight. I slept at the weed hotel in a field next to a gas station that was closed for the night, waking in the morning achy and stiff. I washed up at the gas station restroom, then hit the road again.

I hitched a ride with a traveling salesman who was going to St. Louis. The salesman was a booze hound like me. He took me to an Italian bar in East St. Louis where the bartender served the salesman and me the biggest draft beers I had ever seen—twenty-ounce monster schooners you had to use two hands to lift in order to keep from spilling. We each drank about ten of the monsters. The salesman paid the tab. When we left the bar, the salesman drove me to the St. Louis YMCA, in downtown. I'd told him my sad story, so he paid in advance for my room. The salesman left, and I hauled my suitcase to my room on the first floor. I staggered inside and shut the door. I dropped my suitcase on the floor and collapsed in an inebriated heap on the bed.

I slept the sleep of the dead. I woke early and ate a light breakfast at the YMCA cafeteria. Then I caught a series of streetcars and city buses that took me out of St. Louis, to Route 66 at the edge of the city. I stood at the side of the road all morning, sick to my stomach and sweating in the sun like a hog and thinking I'd pass out or even die from the heat before I ever got a ride. By noon I felt so hungover and dejected that I thought of giving up and heading back to Michigan. Just as I sat down on my suitcase to hold my burning face in my hands and to wallow deeper in self-pity, an old black four-door Dodge sedan with Arkansas plates pulled up next to me and stopped. The car was missing the right rear fender. There were big dents in the other fenders and there was rust everywhere you looked. The driver was a skinny little guy with unkempt hair that was brown flecked with gray. He looked about forty-five years old. He leaned across the seat and spoke to me through the passenger-side window.

"Where you going?" he asked.

"Los Angeles," I said.

"Got a driver's license?"

"Yes."

"Show me."

I showed him my valid Michigan license.

"My name's Hank, young fella," he said. "I'm going to Barstow, California. That's about ninety miles from L.A. Get in." He stretched his lips into a wide grin that showed empty places in his mouth where teeth used to be.

"Thanks for the lift," I said. "I go by Bill." I threw my suitcase in the back of the decrepit old Dodge and got in the passenger seat up front with Hank.

"It ain't exactly going to be a free ride, Billy boy." Hank grinned.

He put the car in gear and headed west on Route 66. About a mile down the road, Hank pulled in and parked in front of a beer store.

Hank came out of the store with two six-packs of beer. Wow, I thought and began to salivate. Instead of getting in the front seat, on the driver's side, Hank got in back.

"Okay, Billy boy," he said and tossed the ignition key over the back of the seat. The key landed next to me on the front seat, by the steering wheel. "Slide behind the wheel, Bill. From now on, you drive. I'll just relax here in the back seat and quench my thirst."

From then on, Hank stayed 75 percent drunk all the way to Barstow. I did all the driving. I drove eight or nine hours at a stretch. We stopped long enough to gas up, grab a burger to go and a couple more six-packs for Hank, then hit the road again. When I couldn't stay awake any longer, I pulled over to the side of the road and slept for two or three hours. The old Dodge's water pump blew near Santa Rosa, New Mexico, and we got stuck for several hours waiting for repair work. We waited at a beer joint next door to the garage. Hank allowed me to drink two beers while we waited. Two lousy beers. Hank wanted me sober so that I could drive straight and he could continue to sit drunk in the backseat and feel safe. I was disappointed, and very thirsty much of the time. It was a hot trip.

After the repairs we barreled the rest of the way across New Mexico that afternoon, flew across Arizona in the big starry night, and raced over the California border and into Barstow with the early morning sun glaring in the rearview mirror. Hank bought my breakfast at a diner, then dropped me off on Route 66 outside Barstow. Hank reached out his hungover, shaky hand and wished me luck. I thanked him for the long ride and the meals and he drove away. I stuck out my thumb.

Before long, a gray-haired lady driving a black Volkswagen stopped and picked me up. She was a retired grade-school teacher. She asked where I was headed. I said Venice Beach. She said get in, I can take you to downtown L.A. You can take the bus from there to Venice.

The retired grade-school teacher drove like a crazy woman. Coming down out of the mountains, from San Bernardino, I thought she would end up killing both of us. Downshifting on the curves to keep the Volkswagen from flying off the mountain, and talking a mile a minute, she told me her life story. I kept my eyes closed and watched an eyelid movie of my brief life flash before me.

The teacher dropped me off at Seventh and Spring in downtown L.A., across from a park called Pershing Square. She told me how to get to the bus station, wished me luck, and drove away. I carried my battered suitcase into the park. I sat on a bench near the center of the park and watched an old, thin wino with dirty, stringy, shoulder-length hair and scraggly beard walk past. He shuffled by, his head tilted back, empty pale-blue eyes gazing up at the yellowish hazy sky. Although the sign on the bank across from the park said eighty degrees, the wino wore an old Army overcoat that came down to his ankles. His dirt-encrusted swollen feet were bursting out of the sides of worn-out black tennis shoes. I could smell him walking by my bench. He didn't smell good.

I intended to go right from Pershing Square to the bus station. I picked up my suitcase and headed down Seventh toward Los Angeles Street, where the schoolteacher had said the bus station was located. Although I was only nineteen, I'd been drinking in bars and buying my own booze in liquor stores in Detroit since I turned seventeen. On my way to the bus station I stopped in a bar on Spring Street next door to a cheap hotel to see if I could get served. The legal drinking age in California was twenty-one.

The early-afternoon California sun was burning down through the smog, so outside on the street it was hazy-bright and hot. Inside the bar it was dark and cool in the air conditioning. It was so dark I had to pause inside the door and let my eyes adjust. It was my kind of daytime bar. I walked between rows of empty tables, across a small dance floor, over to the long wooden bar, set my suitcase down on the floor, and sat down on one of the tall stools. The bartender strolled over and asked me what I wanted. I ordered a beer.

The beer went down easy. It didn't taste any different to me than any other beer I'd ever had since I started drinking beer at age thirteen. But it really didn't matter to me then or at any other time, ever, what a beer tasted like. I drank strictly for the effect. Of course, after I drank the first beer I wanted another one. After the second one, I lost count of the number of beers I drank. The Chinese have a saying: The man takes a drink. The drink takes a drink. Then the drink takes the man. At some point I switched from beer to margaritas. I remember drinking a couple of margaritas, then switching to straight tequila by the shot.

I staggered out of the bar with my suitcase several hours later, lurched through the entrance of the cheap hotel that was next door, and paid for a room for the night. Once again, I slept the sleep of the dead and woke in the morning feeling and looking like hell. I took a shower and changed my underwear, grabbed my suitcase, and headed for the bus station.

I was tempted to stop at the bar where I'd gotten so drunk the day before, knowing I would feel much better if I bit off some hair of the dog, but I forced my legs to keep going down Spring Street toward the bus station. On the way, I stopped and stood in a doorway and reached in my hip pocket and pulled out my wallet and checked my funds. There was a ten-dollar bill in the wallet. I reached in my pants pocket and pulled out my change. I had two dollars in silver and three pennies. Twelve dollars and three cents. That was it. I wondered if it would be enough for a ticket to Venice Beach. I hoped so, because it was against the law to hitchhike in the city of Los Angeles. I didn't want to spend a night in the L.A. County Jail, not even one night, because I'd had enough of being locked up and because I'd heard the L.A. jail was worse than most. It was one hell of a long walk from downtown L.A. to Venice Beach.

I found the bus station on Los Angeles Street, down on skid row. The ticket to Venice was three dollars. I breathed a sigh of relief and got on the bus with my suitcase. The ride to Venice Beach seemed to take forever. The bus lurched and creaked and rocked and ground gears, and I stayed awake the whole time. There was a little guy inside my head who always showed up the morning after I got drunk He had on steel-toed shoes, and he was trying to kick out the walls of my skull. He was timing the kicks to coincide with the lurching and rocking of the bus and with the grinding of the gears. It hurt.

∾ Venice Beach ∾

The closer the bus got to the ocean, the better the air smelled blowing in the window. There was no Venice Beach bus station. The bus pulled up at a circle where Pacific Ocean Highway and Market Street intersected. It squealed its air brakes, belched smoke, gave one final lurch, and opened its doors. I hauled my suitcase down the aisle and got off.

I could see the ocean straight down Market Street just a couple of blocks away. Puffing under the weight of my suitcase, I hoofed it down Market straight toward the beach. I walked under the plaster arches that held up the facades of the buildings that faced the street and saw the genius of Abbot Kinney all around me. At the turn of the twentieth century Kinney spent millions of dollars designing and building Venice, California, to look as much as possible like Venice, Italy, complete with canals and imported Italian gondoliers. Kinney, who made his fortune on the legal drug tobacco and, ironically, died of lung cancer around 1920, wanted his Venice of the Americas to attract artists of all types and intellectuals from all over the world. He wanted Venice Beach to become the center of a New World Renaissance. It never happened. In the early 1930s, oil was discovered on the Venice peninsula. Runoff from the oil wells ruined the canals, and raw sewage piped from L.A. ruined the waters of Venice Beach. By the mid-1930s, nobody but the poor would live there.

When I got there it was 1959. The oil wells had run dry and L.A. was pumping its sewage somewhere else. The beach was clean and you could swim in the waters, but Venice was still a slum and rents were still rock-bottom low.

I hauled my suitcase all the way down Market to Ocean Front Walk, then out across the beach to the edge of the surf. I'd never been to the ocean before, not even to the Atlantic, which was not that far from Detroit. I dropped my suitcase on the sand and sank down on my knees in awe. There was a strong wind blowing in from the west and the roar of the surf was deafening. The wind caught the spray off the tops of the breakers and blew it in my face. It tasted salty/sweet and it felt cool on my hot face and arms. I stood up and gazed over the tops of the rollers and realized that I stood at the edge of the continent. The next chunk of land to the west was Hawaii, five thousand miles away in the middle of the Pacific Ocean. I couldn't hitchhike there. Who or what would give me a ride? A tramp steamer? A porpoise? Maybe a shark? No buses went there. I couldn't afford to fly, and I knew I couldn't swim that far. This was it—Venice Beach was the end of the road.

I walked back across the sand to Ocean Front Walk. I was thirsty. Maybe it was seeing all that water up close, tasting the salt spray, and feeling the hot sun reflecting off the sea and the sand.

My drinker's instinct told me there would be a watering hole nearby. There was, a joint called the West Winds bar. The entrance to the West Winds was on the boardwalk just a few blocks north of where I'd walked across the beach. I went inside through the open door and took a stool at the near end of the bar, next to the big front window that faced the ocean. A sign above the bar said, "Small Draft Beer 15 cents. Large 25." When the bartender came over, I ordered a large one. I knew I'd get more for my money.

I remembered reading about the Venice West Café in the *Life* magazine article before leaving Detroit. The Venice West Café was where all the Venice Beach poets and painters hung out. I asked the bartender for directions. Thanking him for his help, I picked up my suitcase and headed north on the Boardwalk. I didn't have any trouble finding the Venice West Café. It was just around the corner from the beach, on the left-hand side of Dudley Avenue and across from the Cadillac Hotel. I ended up getting a job there, washing dishes and flipping hamburgers. The guy who owned the place let me sleep on a couch in back till I could find somewhere else to sleep.

The Venice West Café catered mostly to down-and-out types said to be poets and artists and musicians and such. Some Venice West Café regulars actually were poets and artists and musicians, but many were full-time alcoholics or drug addicts who spent most of their time and creative energy partying and trying to score drugs. There were some very talented Venice West people, too, who were serious about their craft and produced excellent work. Few of them were addicted to alcohol or other drugs, and they rarely showed up at Venice Beach bars or parties. Then there were many who were talented and serious about their craft but who lost it all to addiction before they could produce anything worthwhile.

◆ **EXERCISE** Did you, like Bill, make geographical changes thinking that a new environment and new friends would make you feel better about yourself and the world?

_____

_____

◆ **EXERCISE** Because alcohol interfered so much with his employment, Bill was often without a regular job. He said he felt embarrassed because he was dependent on his friends and even had to borrow money to hitchhike to California. Were there times when your use of alcohol or other drugs interfered with your employment and you were dependent on friends? If so, how did that make you feel?

_____

_____

_____

_____

∽ First Use of a Drug Other than Alcohol ∽

My first use of a drug other than alcohol could have had a tragic ending. I was around nineteen years old. Sometimes there were parties down on the beach. If you went way down by the surf, about fifty yards from Ocean Front Walk where Dudley Avenue ran into the beach, the L.A.P.D. usually left you alone. They couldn't drive down there without getting stuck in the sand, and they couldn't catch you on foot. One night at a party down on the beach I drank two or three bottles of cheap California wine and popped a bunch of reds (Seconal). Then I passed out. I lay in an alcohol and barbiturate stupor right down at the edge of the surf. The tide had gone out with the moon during the night. The party broke up as I lay passed out. Everybody took off. They just left me there on the beach. That's how it goes when all your friends are drunks or addicts.

In the morning the tide came back in. I woke up in time to feel the surf pulling at my waist like a cold hand. The leading edge of the last roller washed over my face. A few minutes more and I would have been dragged out to sea. I would have been shark bait. So my first use of drugs other than alcohol turned out to be a near-death experience.

A few months later I started using Benzedrine, which is a form of speed. I liked to combine it with alcohol. The combination of alcohol and speed produced the kind of active, angry high I liked. Then I started smoking marijuana. Within a year after landing on Venice Beach, I was addicted to four drugs: alcohol, barbiturates, speed, and marijuana.

On a few occasions, I combined alcohol and barbiturates. Although I didn't know it at the time, that combination can cause unprovoked aggression, and even homicidal behavior. I found that out one night when I was twenty-one years old. I got drunk at a party on a combination of tequila and Seconal, went into an unprovoked rage at the end of the night, and attacked my best friend. My friend had gotten drunk and had left the party and passed out in the front seat of his car. I was drunk but still on my feet, and I was in a blackout. When I woke up the next morning and looked at myself in the mirror and saw I had a black eye and bruises all over my face, I knew something had happened the night before, but I couldn't remember a thing. I remembered arriving at the party and remembered drinking the tequila and popping some reds (Seconal capsules), but after that everything was blank. When my friend stopped over later and told me what I'd done, at first I didn't believe it. Then he showed me the bruises on his face, and the marks on his throat where I'd tried to choke him. He said he'd woken up in the front seat unable to breathe because I had my hands around his throat and was squeezing down hard on his windpipe. He said he managed to get my hands loose. We fought in the front seat of the car. At one point, I kicked out part of the windshield. He said he eventually slammed my face into the dashboard and knocked me unconscious. Then he drove me to the house where I had a sleeping room a couple of blocks from the ocean, and left me there passed out. I felt really stupid and ashamed and found it hard to face my friend for a long time afterward.

I combined alcohol with barbiturates on one other occasion. The results weren't as bad, but they could have been. I was at a party and had downed a lot of beer and popped some reds. Again I went into an unprovoked rage, but this time, before I could do any damage, three or four men at the party wrestled me to the floor and held me down till I passed out from exhaustion. Like the first episode, I had been in a blackout and couldn't remember anything that happened. But I began to wonder what kind of animal lived inside me. Whatever the animal was, I decided that alcohol combined with barbiturates was the key that unlocked the cage, and I vowed never to use the two drugs in combination ever again.

Although I never injected drugs, I did smoke marijuana that had been laced with opium whenever it was available. I was afraid of needles and wasn't self-destructive enough at the time to risk dying from an overdose. I used a sedative/hypnotic called Doriden, a big chalky pill known to junkies on the beach as a heroin substitute. Venice Beach heroin addicts crushed the pills, mixed in some water, and injected it. I never used Doriden in the injectable form, only popped the pills.

◆ **EXERCISE** Bill's first use of a drug other than alcohol was at age nineteen, when he lived in Venice, California. The drug he used was Seconal, a barbiturate. How old were you when you first used a drug other than alcohol? What drug did you first use?

_____

◆ **EXERCISE** A year after landing on Venice Beach, Bill became addicted to four different drugs: alcohol, barbiturates, speed, and marijuana. How many drugs have you been addicted to and what are they?

_____

_____

◆ **EXERCISE** Bill said he almost died as a result of combining alcohol with barbiturates. Did you ever have a brush with death as a result of combining alcohol with some other drug?

_____

_____

◆ **EXERCISE** Bill said that on two occasions when he combined alcohol with barbiturates he became extremely violent. Have you ever become violent when using alcohol or any other drug? If so, what happened?

_____

_____

_____

Not long after I arrived on Venice Beach, I dated and later married a girl I'd met at the Venice West Café. Her name was Susy. Susy was a high school dropout who liked to party almost as much as me. We were both drunk the night we met.

I still wanted to go to college. At that time, under California law, if you were over eighteen and could pass the entrance exam you could enroll at any two-year community college in the state, even without a high school diploma or GED. Not long after marrying Susy, I applied for admission at Los Angeles City College. I was twenty years old and was able to pass the entrance exam, and so was accepted. The tuition in those days was unbelievably affordable. In fact, my books cost more than my tuition. My new wife got a full-time job clerking in a dry cleaners and I worked part-time busing dishes in the college cafeteria. I had no idea what course of study to take but had to declare a major. I chose philosophy. When people asked me what majoring in philosophy would prepare me to do, I told them I was going to open a philosophy shop.

I slowed down my drinking and other drug use and managed to finish the first semester with better than average grades. Then I started using speed again. I had a B average going into my second semester but wasn't satisfied. I wanted all As. Using large amounts of speed, I could study more and get along on less sleep. My tolerance to speed increased to the point where the amount I had to use in order to get the same effect caused an irregular heart beat. In addition, I was staying awake twenty-four hours at a time, then grabbing three or four hours of sleep, then repeating the pattern over again. By the end of the second semester, I was a physical and emotional wreck and was failing all subjects. I had to drop out. Of course, I felt like a total failure. I reduced my intake of speed but started drinking heavily again.

Not long after I dropped out of college, my wife decided she'd had enough. She left and went to San Francisco to stay with her brother. The marriage had lasted for one drunken bout of back-to-back parties. It ended when neither of us could stand the other anymore.

◆ **EXERCISE** Bill's first marriage ended in separation as a result of his addictions. What effect has alcohol or other drugs had on your long-term relationships?

_____

_____

_____

_____

_____

_____

◆ **EXERCISE** Bill managed to acquire some college credits but had to drop out when his addiction to alcohol and other drugs began to interfere. Has alcohol or other drugs ever interfered with your educational goals?

____

____

Age Twenty-Five to Thirty-Five

After my first wife and I split up, I gave up my dream of becoming a famous artist or best-selling author and hitchhiked back to Detroit. I was twenty-three. I got a divorce and began dating the sister of one of my old drinking friends. We got engaged.

Just before my second marriage, I got a full-time job in a discount store. The pay was terrible. About a year later, when the manager transferred to a new store in Chicago, he said if I wanted to follow he'd make me his assistant. He said I'd probably take over his store when he got promoted again, maybe in about a year. By now my new wife and I had a son. We all moved to Chicago. After a few months in Chicago, I transferred to a store in Milwaukee, Wisconsin. I found out that when I became a manager my wages would still be substandard at best. So I quit and went to work in a tractor factory in Racine, Wisconsin. It was hard physical work and I hated it, but at least I could earn enough to support my family. One of the guys I worked with also owned a bar that he ran at night. I could drink there cheap!

Geographical Change

I thought the work I did at the factory was demeaning. It was production piecework, and the day I quit I told the foreman he should hire a chimp to take my place. So after two years at the tractor factory, it was back to Detroit. I got a job there in a machine shop where I could learn some skills.

I tried to become a good husband and good provider, and for a while I succeeded. But I was still drinking heavily, and had brought back from California two other addictions besides alcohol: my addictions to speed and barbiturates.

It was hard to find drug dealers in those days who could keep me supplied. Also, street prices for illegal speed and barbiturates were very high. So I started using doctors as drug pushers. It was easy to con them. All I had to say was that I was depressed and couldn't sleep, and that "my doctor" back in California had prescribed Dexedrine (speed) for the depression and Doriden for the insomnia. The doctors gave me what I wanted. It cost a little for the office call, but I could score prescriptions with five refills for speed and barbiturates for a fraction of what the drugs cost on the street. Before long, I was going through a month's supply of speed and barbiturates every five days, so I had to use a lot of doctors and still had to score for drugs on the street in order to take up the slack. One of the doctors got wise to my scam and refused to write more prescriptions. It was easy to find another doctor.

My addiction to alcohol, speed, and barbiturates grew worse. My anger got worse too. Over the next ten years I lost ten machine-shop jobs. Because I'd had so many jobs in so many different shops I could run almost any kind of machine known to man, so I could always get another job. Eventually, though, the word got around. I was a good worker but I drank too much and couldn't get along with people, especially people in authority and especially on Monday mornings when I'd show up hungover and irritable, if I showed up at all.

◆ **EXERCISE** Bill said he used physicians as well as drug dealers to obtain drugs. Have you ever used physicians as a way to obtain drugs?

_____

_____

∽ Another Geographical Change ∽

For awhile I stopped hunting for work in machine shops and took a job as a life-insurance salesman in a small western Michigan town. My wife's father owned some land there and gave us twenty-seven acres on which to build a house. We built our home and moved in. It was in a country setting with woods behind it. We both liked animals and acquired a dog and a cat.

The cat was pure black so I named it Schwatz, a variation on the German word for "black." Schwatz and I were pals right from the start. She was a lot like me. She didn't trust anyone. Her behavior was unpredictable. And sometimes she was meaner than a junkyard dog. Also, she liked beer. Toward the end of my drinking and drugging, that old black cat was the only creature I felt close to. By then I had no real friends left, only drinking buddies and people I used drugs with. I didn't even feel close to my family. In fact, I'd never really felt close to anyone. I always felt like a stranger, even in my own house. How could I feel close to anyone if I didn't trust anyone? How could I trust anyone if my own father wouldn't stick by me? That old black cat was my only friend. I can remember sitting on the couch, drunk, with the cat sleeping nearby, and saying only half jokingly, "Well, Schwatz, it's just you and me against the world."

◆ **EXERCISE** Bill said that towards the end of his drinking he didn't have any friends left, only drinking buddies and people he used drugs with. Have you ever felt that you didn't have any real friends left?

_____

_____

_____

◆ **EXERCISE** Bill said he ended up feeling close to no one. He said he always felt like a stranger, even in his own house. Have you ever felt like a stranger, even in your own house?

_____

_____

Our house sat right at the edge of a woods thick with old hardwood trees and conifers. Beyond the woods was a wide stream called Whiskey Run. It was aptly named, because during Prohibition days bootleggers stationed a few miles apart floated barrels of whiskey down the stream from local stills. Whiskey Run emptied into another stream, then into a small river that ran into Lake Michigan about twenty miles away. Powerboats sat at anchor where the river met the lake. The barrels of whiskey were loaded on board the powerboats and then quickly transported to Chicago to supply speakeasies there. Whiskey Run curved along the back of my property. The woods stretched from my house down to the edge of the near side of the stream. On the other side of the stream was a huge swamp.

I was a city boy, so even though I enjoyed walking in the woods and along the stream it also made me feel uneasy. As my addiction to alcohol, barbiturates, and speed grew worse, my fear and anxiety also increased. My fear and anxiety increased out of proportion to what was happening around me. In fact, my fear and anxiety levels were unreasonable.

One evening after popping a bunch of speed and drinking a few beers, I went for a walk in the woods. I lost track of time and started back home too late. It got dark before I was halfway home. I could no longer see the path, and I got lost. The uneasiness I felt turned into a full-blown panic attack, although I was never more than a few hundred feet from my house. I crashed around in the woods in circles for about an hour. When I finally broke out of the woods and saw the back light on my house, my shirt was drenched with sweat and my heart felt like it had exploded inside my chest. Walking in the woods and along the bank of Whiskey Run was no longer fun.

◆ **EXERCISE** As Bill's addiction to alcohol and other drugs grew worse, his fear and anxiety increased. As your addictions got worse, did your fear and anxiety get worse, too, as Bill's did? If so, describe one example.

_____

_____

_____

_____

_____

◆ **EXERCISE** Bill also said that his fear and anxiety increased out of proportion to what was happening around him. Looking back, did your fear and anxiety increase beyond what you would now say was reasonable? Give one example.

_____

_____

_____

_____

_____

_____

_____

∾ DWI ∾

I thought insurance sales was the perfect job. For the most part, I was my own boss. I had to come in to the office for a couple of hours in the morning but was free the rest of the day. Most of my sales calls were in the evening, so I went to the bar for lunch and usually stayed and drank the afternoon away. Then I'd go home for dinner and sober up a little bit and pop some speed before going to my first evening appointment. After my last sales appointment, I usually stopped for at least a few drinks on the way home. Sometimes I didn't have any appointments and just spent the entire day and evening drinking.

It was at the end of one of those days that I ended up arrested and in jail for DWI. I'd been stopped while driving under the influence at least a dozen times before but was always let go. On this occasion I'd been drinking all day and all evening. I staggered out the door of the last bar around midnight, drove out of the parking lot, and headed toward home. At one point I swerved over the center line. I saw the flashing red light in my rearview mirror and pulled over to the curb. The cops told me to get out of the car. They were going to see if I could walk a straight line. But I was so drunk I couldn't even stand on my feet without holding on to the car door. The cops arrested me and drove me to the station. I took the breath test and blew a 0.26, which meant I'd failed miserably. A 0.26 was more than twice the legal limit. Once again I was locked up, this time in the drunk tank. The police said they would have allowed someone to come and take me home if I hadn't been so verbally abusive. I felt humiliated and ashamed. When the jailer slammed the cell door shut and I heard the clanging of steel against steel, I went into a rage. There is nothing more heartbreaking, I think, than that awful sound. I'd lost my freedom again.

As a result of the DWI, I lost my license for ninety days and had to depend on my wife to drive me to the office and to my sales calls. My car insurance rates doubled. But when I got back on the road, I continued to drink and drive.

◆ **EXERCISE** Bill said he had been stopped while driving drunk at least a dozen times but was arrested only once for DWI. How many times have you been stopped when driving drunk and risked being arrested? Were you ever arrested for DWI?

_____

_____

◆ **EXERCISE** Bill went to jail for DWI. He said the sound made by the jailer shutting the cell door was "heartbreaking." Were you ever in jail as a result of DWI or for some other drug-related charge? If so, how did it make you feel?

_____

_____

∾ Car Accidents while Driving Drunk ∾

Prior to my DWI, I'd had two accidents while driving drunk. Neither of them involved another moving vehicle and I was never hurt badly enough to need medical attention, so the accidents were never reported. Following my DWI, I had another accident which could have been fatal and which was reported. I'd been to an afternoon Christmas party at the insurance office, drank up everything in sight, and was on my way home. It was snowing and the road was icy. I was driving way too fast for conditions and slid off the road onto the shoulder. I overcorrected and slid sideways onto the road surface. When the tires made contact with the shoulder on the other side of the road, the car rolled over. It rolled over several times, in fact, right in someone's front yard. Because I wasn't wearing my seat belt, I bounced around inside the car like a rubber ball. At some point my head made contact with the rearview mirror, knocking the mirror off the windshield and knocking me unconscious. The car came to rest on its passenger side. I ended up lying on my back against the seat with my feet on the passenger-side door. When I came too, I looked up and saw a man's face looking down at me through the driver's-side window. It was the owner of the house. He pulled the car door open. I climbed out, dazed but not seriously injured. I stood back and looked at the car. On the passenger side, the roof of the car was crushed almost level with the front seat. The car, which was a year old, was a total wreck. Although the cops came and made a report, for some reason they didn't question whether I'd been drinking. I got a ticket but no DWI. Not only was I drunk, I'd also been popping pills and was carrying twenty hits of illegal speed in my jacket pocket.

◆ **EXERCISE** Bill had two accidents while driving drunk before his arrest for DWI, and one after his DWI that could have been fatal. Luckily, none of the accidents involved other occupied vehicles. Have you ever had an accident while driving drunk or under the influence of a drug other than alcohol? If so, were you or someone else injured?

_____

_____

∽ Kicking Barbiturates ∽

I used very little alcohol during the last year of my barbiturate addiction. I was drunk all day and all night on the pills anyway. I knew if I drank on top of all those pills it would have killed me for sure. I stopped using speed as well.

After I'd been on Doriden for five years or so, practically nonstop, I'd built up an extremely high tolerance to the effects of the drug. Finally, the amount I had to take in order to cop a high was dangerously close to the lethal level. I was walking around like a zombie and not even copping a good buzz. I knew I had to kick. I decided to go through withdrawal cold turkey, that is, without medical attention. I didn't want to present at a hospital as an addict. Also, I didn't know how difficult the withdrawal syndrome would be, so I figured I wouldn't need medical attention. I decided to kick at home.

The first couple of hours weren't too bad. Then I started to sweat and tremble. After about six hours, the abdominal cramps set in. It felt like somebody was tying my intestines in knots. I knew it would probably get worse over the next twenty-four hours, so I told my wife to take our son and to go and stay at her father's house for a day or so. He lived nearby.

When my wife and son left, I locked myself in and waited to see what would happen next. I didn't have to wait long. Before midnight, the cramps got a lot worse and my whole body started to shake. Light from table lamps felt like needles in my eyes. My eyes wouldn't focus, and every once in awhile everything went black for a few seconds so that I wasn't able to see at all. That scared me a lot, because I thought I might end up permanently blind. My whole body shook so bad it rattled my teeth. I was having a seizure.

I lay on the couch and had to hold onto the arms to keep from falling off. My tongue felt three times bigger than it was and my mouth was dry. It felt like someone had packed my mouth and throat with cotton. I got up to go to the kitchen for a glass of water. When I stood up it felt like the floor was made of rubber. I couldn't get my balance. Standing there weaving back and forth, all of a sudden my whole body became very rigid. Then, just as suddenly, the tension let go. My body pitched upwards and backwards at the same time. I came down on my back on the arm of the couch. The convulsions continued as I lay on the floor next to the couch. I lost consciousness, then came to, then lost consciousness again. This pattern continued for an hour, maybe several hours—I have no idea how long. Sometime during the night I must have crawled back on the couch, because that's where I woke up in the morning.

I dragged myself from the living room to the bathroom, grimacing from the pain in my lower back. I stood in front of the mirror and looked at my face. It was pale and drawn, my eyes swollen and red. I held out my hands in front of me. They were still trembling. My whole body was trembling but the convulsions and seizures had stopped. The worst was over. I called my wife and told her she and my son could come back.

I had an intermittent tremor in my neck and shoulders that lasted two more weeks. I'd be standing talking to someone and all of a sudden my head would jerk rapidly three or four times to the left. I couldn't keep it from doing that. People looked at me funny.

A week after my withdrawal from Doriden, I started drinking again. Within a month, I was drinking as much as ever. I also started using speed again.

◆ **EXERCISE** Bill went through a very painful and potentially lethal withdrawal from barbiturates. Have you ever experienced a similar withdrawal, and if so, what was the drug that caused the withdrawal?

_____

_____

∿ Still Another Geographical Change ∿

Not long after my near-fatal accident, I got fired from my insurance sales job. I decided I needed a change in geography in order to change my luck. I moved my family to Indianapolis, Indiana, and went back to work in machine shops. I was thirty-three.

When I left Detroit, I was so out of shape that just dragging the garbage out to the street seemed like a major physical task. Machine-shop work was helping me to get into better shape, but about this time I also rediscovered the sport of weight lifting. I joined a health club and started working out. In spite of my drinking, I got strong fast. After about a year of training, I quit my machine-shop job and went to work as a health-club exercise instructor. I had a talent for helping out-of-shape people with low self-esteem get back in shape, and I was good at selling memberships. The new job helped increase my own self-esteem.

Of course, my alcohol addiction caused problems in my new job. One night I got angry with one of the other instructors who I thought had been cheating me out of some sales. I didn't say anything right away, but sitting at the bar the following evening, which was my night off, I thought about the situation and got angry all over again. I pounded down a lot of beers fast, then jumped in my car and drove to the health club. I knew that the instructor I was angry with would be closing up about the time I got there. I met him just as he was coming out the back door. We fought in the alley behind the club. The club owner fired me the next day. I went to work at another health club a week later. I lost that job, too, when I got drunk at the club Christmas party and got into a fight with the owner. I couldn't find another health-club job and had to go back to work in machine shops.

About the time I went back to work in machine shops, I joined the Central Indiana Weight Lifting Club (C.I.W.C.), a power-lifting club that competed as a team against other clubs throughout the country. I started training for competition. I never drank before going to the gym to train. I went to the bar and got drunk after I trained, or brought booze home with me. During the week I drank anywhere from six to twelve beers per night at the bar, or two or three bottles of cheap light wine at home. I didn't train on weekends, so I did my serious drinking on Friday and Saturday nights. My intake on weekend nights was approximately one case of beer (twenty to twenty-four bottles or cans), or the equivalent in liquor or wine.

Not long after I joined the C.I.W.C. my lifts were good enough for competition. I did okay at my first few power-lifting contests. In fact, I won a fourth-place trophy my first time out. I could have done better. I was always full of anxiety the night before a contest. I couldn't sleep unless I drank at least a six-pack or a bottle of wine before going to bed, so I was always hungover on the competition platform and ended up leaving my best lifts in the gym. My teammates knew how much I drank and encouraged me to stop. They said I had a good chance to establish a new Indiana state bench-press record if I did.

◆ **EXERCISE** Bill's use of alcohol interfered with his performance as a weight lifter. If you participated in a sport, did alcohol or other drugs ever interfere with your performance?

_____

_____

∾ Steroid Addiction ∾

In those days, the sport of power lifting was dominated by lifters who used anabolic steroids. Anabolic steroids are made of synthetic testosterone, the male hormone, and virtually every competition power lifter used them. All my teammates used steroids. I didn't want to use them because I'd heard bad stories about the side effects. It was thought that steroids could cause high blood pressure, strokes, and heart attacks even when the user was in good health. A former power lifter once told me he developed cancer of the testicles as a result of steroid use. He said an operation got rid of the cancer but left him sterile. He also told me that steroids could cause liver damage. But even without my using steroids my bench press was within thirty pounds of the existing state record, so my teammates pressured me to start taking them. They said if I used steroids I'd end up blowing the state record away and maybe even set a new world record in my body-weight class. I gave in and started using small amounts of steroids, which the team captain scored from a physician. Eight weeks later, my bench press was equal to the state record.

The problem was I was still drinking. I had some tenderness around my liver even before I started using steroids, and after being on a small amount of the drug for three months I started having side aches. The side aches were always worse the morning after a night of heavy drinking. Standing in front of the mirror one morning, I saw evidence of abdominal swelling in the area where my liver was located. A week or so later I was driving to work when all of a sudden I felt light-headed. A few minutes later I couldn't see the road. I couldn't see anything. It was as though someone had dropped a white sheet over the windshield of the car. I slowed down quickly, eased the car onto the shoulder and stopped. After a few minutes the dizziness passed and my vision cleared up. I drove on to work.

That night at the gym I told the team captain what had happened. He said the reason I was dizzy and my vision had blanked out was because I was using alcohol on top of the steroids. The captain and the rest of my teammates pressured me to stop drinking.

I didn't stop drinking then, but I tried to slow down a little. Steroids made me feel extremely confident and strong. In that way, steroids acted like speed or cocaine. There were times when I felt I could twist doorknobs off in my hand. Steroids increased my endurance and intensified my sex drive. They also intensified my anger and made me more aggressive. When I mixed alcohol with the steroids I became even more aggressive, and my anger got worse than it had ever been. I didn't become physically addicted to steroids, as I had to alcohol and barbiturates. I became addicted to steroids because they made me feel powerful. I didn't want to give them up, even when I finally saw that if I didn't, they would probably kill me.

◆ **EXERCISE** Bill used steroids to enhance his athletic performance as a weight lifter. Have you ever used steroids?

_____

◆ **EXERCISE** Bill said he became addicted to steroids because they made him feel powerful. If you used steroids, how did they make you feel?

_____

_____

_____

_____

◆ **EXERCISE** If you used steroids, did you become addicted to them? If so, why?

_____

_____

_____

_____

Other important things happened during this time period that helped me get ready to stop drinking. You will read about them when you get to the recovery part of my story, in the next chapter. For one thing, I saw the possibility of establishing a power-lifting record as a positive outcome that could help me make sense of interrupting my alcohol addiction.

3

Bill's Recovery

∾ Reaching Bottom ∾

I was getting ready to think about getting ready to quit, because I was suffering some painful consequences. I was reaching my "bottom." That's what had to happen to me before I was willing to seriously think about stopping my alcohol and drug use. Some people believe you don't have to "reach bottom." They say you can decide to stop drinking and drugging simply by making a mental decision to quit. You're supposed to be able to make a "reasoned" decision. That wouldn't have worked for me. You have to know you've had enough and want to stop. How do you know you've reached "bottom"? You measure it with pain. Pain was my yardstick.

Reaching bottom wasn't, for me, the result of a single event. It was the result of a series of events. Things happened over the course of a year or so that finally led to my decision to stop using alcohol and other drugs.

I hadn't used speed in about a year and hadn't used barbiturates in more than two years, but I was still using alcohol, marijuana, and anabolic steroids.

On a hot August Saturday afternoon I was sitting out in the front yard in the sun drinking beer. I'd been out the night before and was drinking to take the edge off a hangover. The little guy inside my head wearing the steel-toed shoes was thirsty. I knew if I didn't give him some beer he'd kick out one or two walls of my skull.

I was depressed. Sitting there in the yard in the glaring sun, I thought of my father. I remember thinking I didn't want to end up a sad old drunk like him. That was one of the things that led to my decision to stop using alcohol and other drugs. I looked at the half-quart plastic cup in my hand, shrugged my shoulders, and drank the rest of the beer. The little guy with the steel-toed shoes stopped kicking.

About a month later, when the leaves had turned and were falling in the yard, I watched a TV program about an alcoholic. It was about a guy who was around my age. The setting was Southern California. By the end of the program the guy had lost his family, his home, his job, his car—everything. He wound up a falling-down wino with sores on his face. Ironically, he ended up on Venice Beach. The last scene showed him lying there dead, face down on the sand, with the Santa Monica Pier in the background. He lay within a hundred yards of where

I nearly drowned the night I drank all that wine and popped all those Seconal capsules and passed out on the beach.

That TV program was another event that helped me reach bottom.

Not long after I watched that TV program, something else happened. My wife was diagnosed with a life-threatening immune-system disease. The disease attacked the connective tissue throughout her body. After a short hospital stay, she was sent home on medication. Her condition stabilized, but the large doses of medication needed to control the disease were also potentially life threatening. The dosage had to be decreased as soon as possible.

Although the cause or causes of my wife's disease were unknown, the medical experts thought stress was a factor. If stress wasn't the cause of the disorder, they believed that it certainly contributed to the condition. Therefore, part of my wife's treatment involved counseling sessions once a week with a therapist to help her deal more effectively with stress. I sat in on a couple of sessions with my wife, but most of the time she went to see the therapist without me. I thought the therapist was an okay guy and was glad he was helping my wife learn how to deal better with stress.

The therapist's name was Don. One evening Don called and asked me to come and see him alone, because he had something he needed to talk to me about. I agreed to meet with him the following afternoon. When I walked in, I noticed he'd rearranged his office. Instead of the client's chair sitting next to his desk, as had been the case other times I'd been in his office, it now stood next to the wall on the other side of the room. It was about ten feet away from his desk. Don pointed to the chair and asked me to sit down.

I'd closed the office door when I came in. Don got up and opened the door, saying it felt a little stuffy in there. We made small talk for a few minutes. Then Don said he had something to say that might make me feel bad, or even angry. Then I understood why he'd rearranged his office. Don cleared his throat, leaned forward, and folded his hands together on top of the desk. He told me that my wife's condition was not getting any better. He told me my wife's physician had said that the cause of my wife's condition was stress. Finally Don said, "Bill, you're the one causing the stress."

I heard what Don said, but my brain didn't want to understand what it meant. For several long minutes, I sat motionless and speechless and barely breathing. I saw Don look down at his folded hands. Slowly, the meaning of Don's words broke through. I had caused my wife's life-threatening illness. Her immune system had broken down under the stress caused by my addiction to alcohol and other drugs. I didn't know it at the time, but I was also using anger like a drug. My drinking always intensified my anger, and that added to the stress.

When I left Don's office, I felt numb. Walking slowly down the street to my car, numbness turned to guilt and shame. Before I pulled away from the curb, the guilt and shame turned to anger. I didn't go home. I went straight to the beer joint. I needed a drink. I needed a lot of drinks.

It was 3:00 in the afternoon when I walked into the cool darkness of the bar. Only one other person was sitting at the bar, someone I didn't know. I ordered a beer and drank it down fast. I switched to scotch and water and drank four or five of those, then I left and went to another joint. I made the rounds to all of my favorite spots. Then I went home at about 1:00 A.M. and crashed on the couch.

◆ **EXERCISE** Bill said he reached "bottom" not as a result of a single event but as a result of a series of events. Do you feel you have reached "bottom"? If you have, was it because of one event or was it because of a series of events?

_____

_____

∾ First Recovery Attempt ∾

My first attempt at recovery was only partial, but it was a start. I decided to stop using alcohol. I drove home one night from the bar, drunk, of course, at about 2:00 A.M. There wasn't anything unusual about that particular night. I wasn't in any worse shape than I'd been a thousand nights before. As usual, I was the last customer to leave the bar. As usual, when I got home I opened the door as quietly as possible so I wouldn't wake my wife and son. Closing the door behind me, I staggered into the living room, sat down on the couch, and reached over and turned on the lamp. Sitting there on the couch in the dim light from the lamp, I thought about my life up till then. Gazing bleary eyed at the wall opposite the couch, in my imagination I could see images of the future projected there. I could see how things would be in my life if I kept staggering down the path I was on. What I saw projected on the wall made me feel depressed. I recalled what I'd said to myself the preceding summer while sitting hungover out on the lawn. I'd said that I didn't want to end up a sad, old drunk like my father. Gazing at the wall, I saw an image of myself looking exactly like that—sad and old. Then I recalled what the team captain had said about my drinking. He'd said if I stopped I'd be able to set a new state record in the bench press, and the thought of that gave me a glimmer of hope. It made me feel that the pain of stopping would be worthwhile.

The next day I looked up the number for AA and called. Steve, a recovering drunk from AA, picked me up at the house that night in a broken-down old car and drove me to a meeting at a hospital in downtown Indianapolis. It was the eighth of February and the temperature was well below freezing. Cold air was blowing in on my feet through a big hole in the floorboard.

I'd been to an AA meeting before; in fact I'd been to two AA meetings. About eight years earlier, a friend back in Detroit talked me into going to one with him. I don't count that one because I got drunk on barbiturates before my friend came to pick me up and couldn't understand anything that was said at the meeting.

On another occasion, a doctor I was using as a legal pusher sent me to an AA meeting. He said he'd cut off my barbiturate supply if I didn't go to at least one meeting. Before my next appointment with the doctor, I showed up drunk at an AA speaker meeting. At an AA speaker meeting, a designated person gets up and talks about his or her drinking history, then about his or her recovery. About halfway through I stood up, caught the speaker's eye, flipped him the bird, then walked out. The speaker grinned, shook his head sympathetically, and continued his story.

As Steve pulled in and parked the car in the lot, he said the meeting he was taking me to was a speaker meeting. Steve led me to a side entrance, then down some stairs to a meeting room in the basement of the hospital. He said I didn't have to do anything but sit and listen. It was a big room full of people standing around smoking cigarettes and drinking coffee out of paper cups. Steve and I got some coffee and sat down. The chairperson brought the meeting to order.

The emphasis on prayer to open and close AA meetings made me uncomfortable. I was an atheist and resented what felt to me like a strong religious atmosphere. So when the chairperson opened the meeting with the Lord's Prayer, I cringed. I felt my face burn with resentment. Then the chairperson introduced the speaker, whose name was Bill L.

Bill L. was big, well over six feet, and weighed over two hundred pounds. He wore glasses and spoke in a deep voice. He told his story simply and straightforwardly. He told what his life was like when he was still drinking, why he decided to stop drinking, and how things were now that he'd been sober for three years. In some ways Bill L.'s story was remarkably similar to mine, so I found it easy to relate to. About a month later I asked Bill L. to be my sponsor. He accepted.

◆ **EXERCISE** Have you stopped using all addictive drugs, or is your recovery at this time only partial?

_____

_____

_____

∾ Benefits of Early Sobriety ∾

I stopped drinking the night I went to that AA speaker meeting, where I heard Bill L. tell his story. Within a week, I noticed that I felt better overall physically and I had more energy. I also noticed that I could see better while driving after dark. Prior to stopping the use of alcohol, I had a mild form of night blindness. The headlights of oncoming cars hurt my eyes and made my head ache. I'd been taking plenty of vitamin and mineral supplements, including vitamin A, but I might as well have been flushing them down the toilet. Large amounts of alcohol flush the vitamins and minerals out of the body about as fast as you can take them in.

At the end of my drinking days, I was essentially a beer drinker. I was drinking eight to twelve beers per day during the week and four times that on weekend nights. My body was used to a large intake of liquid every day, so when I stopped drinking beer I still had a terrible thirst. In addition to a lot of water, I drank two to three half-gallon jugs of unsweetened grapefruit juice every day. Only another recovering alcoholic could understand how anybody could take in that much liquid on a daily basis.

◆ **EXERCISE** Bill said he started feeling better overall a week after stopping the use of alcohol. In what ways did you feel better soon after you stopped using one or all of your drugs of choice?

_____

_____

_____

_____

_____

∽ Fall of the Wall of Denial ∽

About three months after I stopped drinking, my brain cleared enough so that I became aware of just how much I'd hurt other people over the years because of my addictions. All of a sudden my wall of denial collapsed, and the guilt and shame that had been hidden for so long behind that wall came suddenly into full view. Emotionally, I felt overwhelmed. Guilt and shame poured out of my subconscious like water from a burst dam. Sometimes I'd be at work at the gym and I'd find myself unable to control my feelings. I'd recall something I'd said or done while using alcohol or other drugs that had hurt my family, and I'd burst out crying. Sometimes the tears turned to rage—rage at myself for the pain I'd caused others. Sometimes I had to drop whatever I was doing and just run out of the place. I was attending meetings at the time at an AA clubhouse in downtown Indianapolis. I told my sponsor, Bill L., what was going on. He gave me his key to the clubhouse, which was near the gym, so I could go there during the day when the place was closed and I needed to be alone. At least that way I had a place to go when I couldn't stand to stay at work. I'd run down to the clubhouse and lock myself in, and pace and curse or pound on the walls with my fists until I could regain control of my emotional state.

Underneath the guilt, shame, and anger I was deeply depressed. I should have gone for counseling but I wanted to do it "right." According to most of my new AA friends, doing it right meant doing it without professional help and without medication. Many people in recovery don't need professional help or medication, but I did. I needed the fellowship and support I got from AA, but I needed more than that. I would finally get the help I needed, but not until I'd moved back to the Detroit area and relapsed into alcohol use.

A few months after I stopped drinking, I set a new Indiana state-record bench press in the 148-pound class. My original intention had been to stop drinking only until I'd established a new state record. But when the club statistician said that my state-record lift was only twenty-three pounds off the listed world record in my body-weight class, I decided to stay sober a little longer and go after the world record.

◆ **EXERCISE** About three months after Bill began his recovery, he became aware of how much he had hurt others and felt overwhelmed with guilt and shame. About how long after you began your recovery did you become aware of how much you had hurt others, and how did it make you feel?

_____

_____

_____

∿ Old Angry Behavior ∿

After becoming a bench-press champion, I opened a health club. The club stayed open for about three months. I wasn't drinking anymore but was still getting drunk on anger. When I opened the club I had no money for equipment, so some of my power-lifting friends lent me equipment in exchange for memberships. My angry outbursts at the gym soon drove them away. I would get angry and start throwing ten pound plates around the gym. My power-lifting friends took their equipment with them and I had to close up the gym.

◆ **EXERCISE** At any time during your recovery, did you get drunk on anger like Bill? Are you still using anger like a drug?

_____

_____

_____

∿ Return to Marijuana Use ∿

I started using marijuana again. I smoked a joint or sometimes two, but only at night before going to bed. To justify my use of marijuana, I convinced myself that all the years of abusing speed and barbiturates had caused permanent damage to the "sleep center" of my brain, and that I'd never be able to sleep without using some kind of sedative drug. I tried to make my sponsor, Bill L., see why I had to use marijuana. I said I couldn't live in the world completely drug free like most human beings, but he just couldn't seem to see it my way. Instead, he told me I wasn't really clean and sober if I was using marijuana. He also said my use of marijuana would keep me from growing emotionally: He said I needed to learn how to deal with emotional pain as much as possible without alcohol or other drugs. I didn't stop altogether, but I reduced my use of marijuana to about half a joint before bedtime. Much later, I found out that my sponsor had been right.

◆ **EXERCISE** Are you still trying to justify using a drug other than alcohol, such as marijuana?

_____

_____

∾ Kicking Steroids ∾

Knowing that my liver was already damaged from the effects of alcohol and other drugs, my sponsor managed to talk me out of continuing my use of steroids. Bill L. helped me see that I was using steroids as much for the high as to enhance my weight-lifting performance. He also pointed out that even if I did set a new world record in the bench press, I'd probably have to pay for it with my liver. In other words, the steroids would kill me. The intense feeling of confidence and personal power produced by steroids, along with the high I got out of competing, made it hard to give them up. It made me feel sad to know I would never again walk away with first place and would never set a new world record, which I knew was within my reach. Finally, though reluctantly, I stopped using steroids. I tried competing without them and was sometimes able to place within the top three—even with all the other lifters all pilled-up. But I was used to walking off the platform cradling the first-place trophy. Of course, with an ego as fragile as mine, second or third was never enough. I weighed all the pros and cons, throwing my liver on the scales along with the high I got from the drug, and decided to stop competing altogether. Without my being aware of it at the time, my sobriety had become more important to me than power-lifting trophies and state records.

◆ **EXERCISE** If you use steroids to improve athletic performance or simply to get high, why should you stop using them?

_____

_____

_____

_____

∾ Geographical Change (Again) ∾

Not long after I closed up my gym and stopped competing, I made yet another geographical change. I moved my family back to Detroit. It wasn't really a proactive move; rather, it was an attempt to try and run away from the feelings of loss around my decision to stop competing as a power lifter. My sponsor, Bill L., was against the move. "You need to grow where you're planted," he said. But I wouldn't listen.

I stayed off booze and other drugs, except marijuana, and returned to machine-shop work in Detroit. After working at the same shop with good attendance for about a year, I became second-shift shop foreman. Still unable to effectively manage my emotional state, I got into a shouting match with my boss one afternoon and got fired. I landed another job right away but lost that one too. Over the next couple of years, I had a series of machine-shop jobs in and around Detroit. I was rehired twice by one of the shops that fired me.

I continued going to AA meetings. I even started a new meeting at a hospital in Pontiac, Michigan. I was still using marijuana, and even though I hadn't used alcohol, speed, or barbiturates in about three years, I was still experiencing periods of deep depression and intermittent episodes of anger and rage. Depression had always been a problem for me and had now become worse than ever. In fact, depression had become a major trigger for my addiction. Looking back, I know my depression was related to my marijuana use, but I didn't know it at the time.

◆ **EXERCISE** Bill made a major geographical change soon after he began his recovery. Why did Bill's sponsor try to talk him out of making the change at that time?

_____

_____

_____

◈ Transcendental Experience ◈

I'd been sober only about six months when I moved back to Detroit. About three months later, at around nine months of sobriety, I had a sudden, highly unusual, and very powerful experience that is still hard to put into words. I call it a transcendental experience. The dictionary defines *transcendental* as something that is beyond the ordinary. It was certainly that—beyond the ordinary. I found out later that my experience was similar to the experience AA cofounder Bill Wilson had in 1934 when he was drying out in a detox ward at a hospital in New York City. He called his a spiritual experience and later referred to it euphemistically as his "hot flash." I had in no way been seeking to have such an experience. It just happened. Whatever it was, whether transcendental or spiritual, it shook my faith in atheism.

My extraordinary experience also resulted in a change in my thinking about the nature of cause and effect and about personal responsibility. When it occurred, I'd been sitting writing in my journal. It was after midnight. I'd just returned home from my second-shift job, and everyone else in the house was asleep. I was writing down my thoughts about how I had become addicted to alcohol and other drugs. I thought that the events of my childhood and my adolescence had shaped my behavior and personality, and that I had become an addict through a process of conditioning over which I had no control. My addiction to alcohol and other drugs, I reasoned, was not a choice I had made. Therefore,

I was not responsible for my addictions and could not be held accountable. What I choose to call my transcendental experience made me suddenly aware that my thinking about cause and effect had been faulty. I saw in a flash of insight that all along I had been one of the players, maybe even the most important player, in the process. I had made choices, and the choices I'd made had shaped my behavior more than any other factor. I just hadn't been aware of it. Now I had to change my thinking. Since in the past I'd been unaware of how much power I'd had in shaping my own life, logically I couldn't hold myself responsible for the poor choices I'd made. *But now I was aware.* I wasn't sure that I liked my new awareness. Because now that I had become aware that I played a major role in the shaping of my own life, it meant that now I was responsible. It meant that, more than anything else, the choices I made from now on would determine what I would become. The choices I made would determine whether I stayed clean and sober or whether I ended up relapsing back into active addiction. It meant that I could no longer in good conscience point the finger of blame at anyone else.

As another result of my transcendental experience, I began to believe that my life might have some special purpose. I also understood that what I had been doing with my life up to then was not it. That strange, exhilarating experience gave me hope, and some of the fear that had haunted me for so long went away. I was riding on a wonderful "pink cloud." I felt a pressing need to find out what I was supposed to do with my life. Whatever it was, I knew that alcohol and other drugs would not help me accomplish it. I also knew that continuing to use anger like a drug wouldn't help.

◆ **EXERCISE** About nine months after stopping the use of alcohol, Bill had what he calls a transcendental experience. Have you ever had a similar experience? If so, describe your experience and tell how it made you feel.

_____

_____

_____

_____

∽ Separation from Second Wife ∽

Even though I'd had this wonderful experience, my life was still a carnival—not like the Fun House either, more like the Chamber of Horrors. My marriage was collapsing. My relationship with my wife and son got worse instead of better. My anger was getting out of hand. My emotions were bouncing all over the place. The "pink cloud" had burst like a giant bubble. My old sponsor, Bill L., had warned me that it would happen and had urged me to stick around and grow where I was planted for at least another year in order to give myself a chance to stabilize.

My wife and I separated. My son, who was thirteen, went with her, and not long afterward began having trouble in school, then trouble with the police. Like most kids whose parents separate or divorce, he felt abandoned and rejected. Of course, he blamed himself for the separation. He felt that there must have been something wrong with him as a person, otherwise his mother and I would still have been together. One of my worst fears had come to pass. My son was now experiencing the pain of the loss that I felt as a child when I was abandoned by my father. The circumstances were different, but the outcome for my son was the same. I felt discouraged and at times hopeless. I felt the same kind of despair I'd felt when I was still drinking and using other drugs heavily. I clung to my sobriety with a desperation that sometimes brought me to tears.

Before the separation, my wife and I tried family counseling, but by then the situation was hopeless. My addiction to alcohol and other drugs had caused too much damage to our family system. My wife and I finally divorced.

◆ **EXERCISE** Bill said some things in his life seemed to get worse instead of better after he'd been in recovery awhile, and that he felt discouraged and hopeless. Have things sometimes felt worse instead of better for a period of time during your recovery?

_____

_____

_____

_____

_____

_____

∾ New Relationship ∾

After the separation, I started dating a woman I'd met in the AA program. We both had about two years of sobriety when we met. I was still using marijuana but stopped using it after awhile, to please her. I once told her that our personal histories were so much alike that we could have been born and raised in the same broken home. It was true. Psychologically, we could have been twins. I saw that as an asset. It wasn't. When things were good, they were truly very, very good. When they were bad, they were horrid. We didn't have arguments; we had wars. Although we didn't abuse each other physically, we had very intense verbal fights. I broke things. Being in a relationship with another recovering addict made everything crazier than ever.

◆ **EXERCISE** What reason did Bill give for things getting even "crazier" when he entered into a relationship with another recovering addict?

_____

_____

_____

∾ Anger Episode at AA Meeting ∾

I had been working a recovery program for nearly three years but still had occasional episodes of rage that were almost as bad as when I was still drinking and using other drugs. One night shortly after my AA girlfriend and I had moved in together, I went into a rage during a very intense war of words and broke some furniture. It was a particularly nasty episode, and it scared her badly. She ran out of the house and went to stay with her AA sponsor. Her sponsor was against the relationship from the start. She had said to my girlfriend, "Two sickies don't make a wellie." My girlfriend's father was a roaring alcohol addict and extremely abusive. He was physically abusive to her mother. My girlfriend said he sometimes literally "bloodied the walls" with her mother. She said she and her little brother would sometimes have to run out of the house when her father was having a drunken rage and hide in a field until he passed out or until the police came to arrest him. I had witnessed episodes of physical abuse as a child too, and it left traumatic scars on my psyche. But I didn't understand how much my anger triggered her posttraumatic stress issues. Sometimes, during my anger outbursts, she would be so stricken with anxiety she would simply collapse in a heap on the floor.

After my girlfriend ran out of the house on this particular occasion, I drove to one of our favorite AA meetings. I was still angry driving to the meeting. And for some reason I got it into my head that the AA group was somehow to blame for our problems. It wasn't true, of course, and it was irrational of me to think so. I arrived late to the meeting. Though I thought my girlfriend might be there, she wasn't. I raced up the stairs to the meeting room, burst through the door, and verbally attacked the entire group. There were about fifteen AA members sitting around the table. Yelling like a madman, I called them "a bunch of amateur psychologists." Everyone sat there, mouth agape. When I ran out, I slammed the door so hard I left it hanging by one hinge. Then I ran down the stairs to the fellowship room on the first floor to calm down.

One of the group members, Doug L., had a lot of years of sobriety and was also a counselor at a Detroit-area drug and alcohol agency. Doug followed me downstairs to the fellowship room. He came into the room and asked me if I wanted to talk. I was fairly calm by then, and said yes. He knew I wasn't going to hurt anybody, that I was just a very angry recovering addict, with inadequate emotional-state management tools, struggling to stay clean and sober. But one of the other members was scared enough to call the cops. Six of Detroit's finest showed up and asked Doug if he wanted them to take me away. Doug said no, that I'd just had a "little flare-up." Later the group voted on whether or not to allow me to come back to that particular meeting. The vote went narrowly in my favor. Feeling ashamed and embarrassed, I went back to the group a couple of weeks later and apologized. Doug L. became my new sponsor.

I was beginning to understand just how big my anger problem had been, and still was. But I had no idea what to do about it. Furthermore, there was a part of me that didn't want to let go of the anger. That part of me felt that if I let go of the anger, I would no longer have a way to change depression and other bad feelings. Anger made me feel powerful and strong. It gave my low self-esteem a temporary boost, although the dues I paid were dear. I should have sought help for my anger problem, but I didn't.

◆ **EXERCISE** Even after three years of recovery time, Bill had outbursts of anger that were almost as bad as when he was still using alcohol and other drugs. At any time since you began your recovery, have you had outbursts of anger like Bill had during his recovery?

_____

_____

_____

◆ **EXERCISE** If you think you have an anger problem like Bill had, why should you reach out for help for your anger problem now?

_____

_____

_____

∽ Third Marriage and Relapse ∽

Not long after my divorce became final, I married the woman I'd been dating from the program—my third marriage. My son wanted to be with me. He had been making things really difficult for his mother in my absence, so she was eager to let him go. I was awarded custody and my son came to live with me and my new wife. Now things got crazier than ever. My new wife and I were expecting a baby. My son had problems, and my wife resented him. The two of them fought. He and I both felt torn.

One night I had another one of my now infamous outbursts. I trashed the house, triggering another of my wife's PTSD flashbacks. She panicked and ran out the door and called the police from a neighbor's house. I hadn't hurt her, in fact I wasn't even angry with her, but I'd scared her. The cops came but didn't arrest me because my wife wouldn't press charges, but neither would she come home. She went to stay at her sponsor's house. There was no one to supervise my son, so I sent him to stay with his grandmother, who lived nearby.

I felt guilty and ashamed, and then I plunged into a deep depression. The depression got worse. I'd been depressed off and on all my life, but this was the worst case of depression I could remember. For about a week I fought hard against picking up a drink or a drug. Then I got drunk. It was a one-night relapse, and of course I woke up the next day feeling worse than ever.

◆ **EXERCISE** Bill said he had been depressed off and on all of his life. Have you suffered depression during much of your life?

_____

_____

◆ **EXERCISE** Have you often felt depressed, even now during your recovery?

_____

_____

◆ **EXERCISE** Has depression ever triggered a desire to drink or use other drugs, even during your recovery?

_____

_____

When I finally went for counseling, I felt suicidal. The counselor suggested a short stay in the hospital. I ended up staying in the hospital forty-five days. While I was there, the staff helped me sort things out. One of the things they suggested was that I change my field of work. They said all the psychological tests they'd given me indicated I would never be happy working in machine shops or factories, because I needed to work with people rather than machines. I agreed with their assessment. I had known for some time that if my life had a purpose beyond my body's taking in nourishment and giving off waste, that purpose probably had something to do with helping other people. While in the hospital, I found that I was sometimes more effective in dealing with fellow patients than the staff was. The staff and I both agreed that I should go back to school to become a drug and alcohol counselor. Because I was a recovering alcoholic and drug addict, state and federal funds would pay for my education and provide a minimum income while I was in school. Finally, I felt hope. I discovered my purpose and a way to fulfill it. My purpose—my mission—was to help other addicts learn how to live contented clean and sober lives. I'd found out what my mission was, and the depression began to lift. Now I had to find out how to get my own life in order. Otherwise, I would be unable to help anyone else.

◆ **EXERCISE** Have you ever felt suicidal? If so, write about the experience here.

_____

_____

_____

◆ **EXERCISE** Have you ever been hospitalized because of depression? If so, write about the experience.

_____

_____

_____

_____

While I was in the hospital, my pregnant wife left me and went to New York to stay with relatives. Later, she called and said she wanted to give our marriage one more try. My son and I joined her in New York state soon after our baby was born. Neither of us had jobs, so we moved into a small apartment that we could afford on our Social Service benefits. Living on "the dole" made me feel guilty and ashamed. But I was forty years old. I felt that if I didn't go back to school and retrain then for a new career, it would be too late and my chances of staying clean and sober would be greatly reduced.

One evening, the person in the apartment upstairs from us was playing his music too loud and keeping the baby awake. I called him on the phone and in an angry voice ordered him to turn down the music. Instead, he cranked up the volume even louder. I ran upstairs in a rage and kicked down his door. The landlord, who lived in one of the other apartments, called the police. They came but didn't arrest me, but my wife had had all that she could stand. She took my new son and ran away again. This time she meant it, and would never return to me or even call on the phone. She changed her name and went into hiding. I felt deeply sad and guilty and, of course, angry. I had no way of knowing at the time that after many, many years I would one day see my son again.

Once again, I plunged into depression. I didn't relapse but would have if help hadn't been available. A drug and alcohol agency nearby had a program for people who were in crisis and at risk for relapse. It was called a BUD program, which stood for Building Up to Drink. I sent my oldest son to stay with his grandmother in Michigan and entered the BUD program for a two-week stay. While there, I received intensive one-on-one counseling. At the end of two weeks, I was able to leave. I had been able to transfer my education benefits from Michigan to New York and had enrolled as a human-services major at the local community college. My first son returned from Michigan to live with me.

Having finally recognized that I had consistently made unhealthy choices in relationships, I decided not to get involved in another relationship for at least a year. I didn't even date. Instead, I devoted a lot of thought and journal pages to figuring out what I'd been doing wrong. One of the things I discovered was that I had chosen to have relationships with women who were too much like me. Two of my former wives were addicted to alcohol or other drugs; one had been abandoned by her parents. All of them brought a lot of the same issues into our relationships that I had brought, and it was not a good mix. In other words, I had consistently chosen to enter long-term relationships with women who were as emotionally unstable as I had been. For me, such relationships could not work.

◆ **EXERCISE** Have you made choices in relationships that led to the kinds of problems Bill had?

_____

◆ **EXERCISE** If you are not currently in a relationship, do you think it would help you make better choices in the future if you stayed out of relationships for a year?

_____

∼ Meeting Jan ∼

While in my second year of college, I met and started dating a woman whom I met in the school newspaper office. We both wrote for the paper. Jan also sold ads. I found Jan attractive from the start. She was intelligent and shared many of my interests. But all of the women whom I'd chosen to become involved with in the past also had these qualities. They, too, were attractive and intelligent. I wanted to know what Jan was like psychologically. I wanted to get to know her more deeply before I allowed myself to become emotionally involved with her, so I made a decision to put my feelings on hold until I knew more about her.

Like me, Jan was an adult college student. Like me, she was newly divorced. Like me, she was going back to school to train for a new career. Like me, she had chosen human services as her major. Unlike me, Jan had never been addicted to alcohol or other drugs. Also unlike me, she did not come from a family system where addiction to alcohol or other drugs was a problem. The man she had been married to for twenty years and who was the father of her children had never been addicted to alcohol or other drugs. After dating Jan for several months, I discovered that she was the most emotionally stable woman I had ever known— and just as exciting to be with!

Jan, whose children were grown up, got along well with my oldest son. Eventually, she and I married, and we all moved in together.

After two years of college, I became a counselor at a drug and alcohol clinic. Jan got a counseling job soon after that.

I loved my new career. I loved working with addicts and felt I had found the best possible way to accomplish my personal mission. Although I hadn't yet put my mission into exact words, I knew it had a lot to do with helping addicts recover.

For the first time in my life I had a job I liked. Working with addicts fulfilled most of my values and gave me an opportunity every day to use the skills I valued most. I was able to use my best skills as part of my job. My best skills were my verbal skills and writing skills, which I'd never had an opportunity to use as a factory worker or construction worker. I'd used my verbal skills when I worked as a salesman, but not in a way I found meaningful. I was able to put my verbal skills to good use during counseling sessions. I saw my job as an addiction counselor as "selling sobriety." And I had always enjoyed writing. Writing progress notes following an individual counseling session or writing a group note following a group therapy session or a lecture gave me an opportunity every day to use my writing skills. I had overcome my fear of public speaking and enjoyed giving lectures. I even wrote my own lectures. At the end of the day, I felt I'd accomplished something meaningful. It was easy to maintain my excitement and enthusiasm throughout the day, and I couldn't wait to get up and go to work in the morning.

◆ **EXERCISE** Bill made a major career change. He found that he was, in general, much happier working at a job in which he could use his most valued skills. Are you satisfied with your present employment situation? If not, have you thought of changing your career so that you might be happier in your work?

๛ Old Behaviors Continue to Interfere ๛

Even though I had the kind of job I'd always dreamed of, I still had problems in the workplace. Although I was often known as the best counselor wherever I worked, my reputation as an employee couldn't have been worse. I never had problems with clients. In fact, even though I was new and inexperienced and had less formal education than my colleagues, the agency director many times assigned the most problematic clients to me because I could often work with them when other counselors could not. But I couldn't seem to get along with my fellow counselors, and certainly not with my supervisor.

About a year after I was in the drug and alcohol counseling field, one of my clients who was on medication for depression got drunk and had a standoff with the police. His drug of choice for depression was 100-proof whiskey. The client was using a .22-caliber rifle to shoot at the police, as well as at passing cars, from a window of his girlfriend's house. His girlfriend had fled the scene. The police were using the house next door as a base, having sent the family who owned it to safety. The police were trying to negotiate with my client by phone, but he told them he would speak only to me. The police called me at my office and asked me to drive out to the scene and do a telephone intervention from their base. I got permission from the agency director to go. I drove to the scene and made telephone contact with my client. But by then, he was hopelessly drunk and in no mood to negotiate. The police stationed me outside, behind a squad car with a bullhorn. They told me to aim the horn at the house where the client was hiding and to tell him that if he came out without the rifle, he wouldn't be harmed. The police assured me they would do a mental-health arrest and take the client to a forensic hospital where he would get help. I did as they asked. After some time had passed, the client did come out of the house. He was carrying the rifle at his side but looked as though he was going to lay it on the ground. Confident that he would lay the rifle down, I stepped out from behind the car. As soon as I did, the client raised the rifle to his shoulder and quickly fired two shots at me. I heard one of the bullets whiz past my head and heard the other one strike the wall of the house behind me. I dove back behind the squad car. The client ran back in the house with the rifle. By then the SWAT team was there. About three hours later, the client emerged from the house again. He came out the front door and was walking slowly down the driveway toward the street. He was pointing the rifle at a squad car that was parked on the street across from the driveway. Three police officers were crouched behind the car. Continuing to walk slowly, the client started shooting into the side of the police car. Watching the scene unfold, I saw a marksman sneak up behind the client. The marksman squatted down, and from a distance of about one hundred feet shot the client in the back of the head, killing him instantly. My client was dead. I was traumatized.

Because I verbally attacked the police at the scene after they killed my client, my agency director told me I had to sign a statement that described my behavior as "unprofessional." My behavior was, in fact, inappropriate. However, still traumatized by the event and not having been offered professional counseling or debriefing through my agency, I refused to sign the statement. Instead, I resigned.

I took some time off for badly needed rest and recuperation, then went to work in another treatment agency. It was a large agency with several sites. I was soon put in charge of one of the satellite offices. That meant I was on my own most of the time. Still, I had to meet with a supervisor and attend staff meetings once a week at the main office. I kept tripping over my old issues with authority. But somehow my supervisor was able to put up with me and I was able to put up with him, so I was able to hold on to my new job—at least for a while.

◆ **EXERCISE** Have you changed careers, only to find that old behaviors continue to interfere with your work situation?

_____

_____

_____

᷸ In Business for Myself ᷸

Tension between me and my supervisor grew during the six months I was at the agency. Just before I decided to beat my supervisor to the punch by resigning before he fired me, I met a clinical psychologist who had recently opened his own drug and alcohol treatment agency. His name was Mike. Mike's business was booming. He had more referrals than he could handle alone, so he hired me as a consultant to help him with evaluations and to run groups. Mike knew my reputation as a counselor as well as my reputation as an employee. We came to an agreement right away. We agreed that I would work as a consultant. As a consultant, I'd be my own boss, pay my own taxes, etc. Mike agreed to give me supervision so that I could maintain my New York State Addiction Counselor credential. As a Ph.D., he could supervise an addiction counselor. I'd obtained my credential during my second year in the field. Mike agreed to give me the smallest amount of supervision, no more than absolutely necessary.

The professional relationship with Mike worked extremely well. Soon I had my own office space at the agency. Mike taught me how to administer, score, and interpret the MMPI (Minnesota Multi-Phasic Personality Inventory), which was a method he used to assess clients for alcoholism and drug addiction. As another perk, I had access to Mike's entire library of psychology textbooks. With Mike there to answer the questions raised by my reading of the textbooks, my understanding of human behavior increased exponentially during the time I worked with him.

About three years after I began working with Mike, new regulations required all drug and alcohol treatment agencies to be licensed, including small agencies owned by psychologists. Not wanting to jump through all the legal hoops and do all the paperwork, Mike closed his business and went to work for a large treatment agency that was already licensed. I could have gone on board with him but chose not to. I couldn't let go of my independence.

Unable to find enough consulting jobs to survive financially, I finally had to go back to work at another treatment agency. It was an outpatient agency. Soon after, I became the agency's program manager. I carried a caseload, ran groups, designed a family program, and supervised other counselors.

◆ **EXERCISE** Bill decided to go into business for himself, so that he could enjoy more freedom on the job. If you were to decide to go into business for yourself, what would it be?

_____

_____

_____

_____

⚘ Teaching at the Community College ⚘

The community college that Jan and I had attended wanted to start a drug and alcohol counseling curriculum as part of its human-services degree program. The college invited Mike, who had once been a professor, to design the program and teach the classes. Mike declined. Instead, he recommended me for the job. Since I didn't have a degree, the college couldn't hire me as a full-fledged professor. But they could bring me on as an adjunct instructor. By then I was a recognized expert in the addiction-treatment field, and Mike had given me a strong recommendation. Relying on my writing skills, I designed and taught addiction-counseling courses at the college for the next three years. At the time, I was the only one on staff there who knew more than the basics about addiction counseling, so most of the time I was my own boss. That was lucky for me and for the college because I was no better at dealing with authority figures than I'd ever been. The human-services department chairperson saw me for supervision once or twice each semester, and that was the extent of it.

I loved my teaching job. One of my unspoken goals had been to teach where I had gone to college, so it was a dream come true. The pay was not great, but the job gave me an opportunity to use my most valued skills and made me feel that I was doing what I needed to do in order to fulfill my personal mission. Of course, it also gave me lots of ego gratification.

I had reached many of my personal goals and had traveled a long way toward fulfilling my personal mission. But at times it felt like way too much, way too soon. Sometimes I felt as though I didn't deserve the success I was having. Other times I felt greedy for more. I often felt guilty instead of grateful and happy.

◆ **EXERCISE** Have you sometimes felt guilty about your successes instead of grateful and happy?

_____

_____

_____

⚘ Midlife Crisis at Age Forty-Five ⚘

I'd been alcohol free for about six years when at age forty-five I suddenly became aware that I had already lived more than half my life. I became aware that I would someday cease to be. I didn't have a belief system that would support me through this crisis, and I plunged into the worst depression I'd experienced in my life so far.

The depression came on slowly. In part, it was a result of working too hard and failing to get enough sleep. I was putting in forty hours at my program-manager job at the agency, plus another sixteen hours teaching and driving between home and the college. The long hours and the excitement of my success made me overtired and made my insomnia worse.

But the biggest contributor to my depression was my increased use of marijuana. Marijuana can cause depression, and it can also make a preexisting case of depression worse. I was still only smoking just before going to bed. But the effects of marijuana use are cumulative. The active ingredients get stored in the body's fatty tissue. Since the brain is largely composed of fat cells, a lot of marijuana had accumulated in my brain. In addition to the physical effects of the marijuana, the depression was also a result of the intense inner conflict I was going through. I was an addiction counselor who still used drugs. I told my clients and colleagues I was in recovery. I felt guilty and ashamed. I felt dishonest. I *was* dishonest. I felt like a phony. I *was* a phony.

The class I taught at the community college was on the fourth floor. Instead of taking the elevator, I used the stairs. I prided myself on being able to take them two at a time. One evening, when I parked the car and walked to the school's entrance, I noticed that I felt a little more tired than usual. I went inside and started climbing the stairs. There was no way I could take them two at a time that night. I could barely climb them one at a time. By the time I got to the fourth floor, I had to stop and lean against the wall. During my lecture that night, I stumbled over my words. I was impatient and irritable with my students.

The following day I made an appointment with a doctor. He referred me to a psychologist, who said I needed medication for depression. Of course, I didn't tell him about my marijuana use. About two weeks after starting on antidepressants the depression began to lift.

◆ **EXERCISE** Have you experienced the kind of "midlife crisis" Bill went through at age forty-five? If so, what did you do about it?

_____

_____

_____

_____

◆ **EXERCISE** Do you tell people you are in recovery but still use nonprescription drugs? If so, how does that make you feel?

_____

_____

_____

_____

⁓ Dalmane Addiction and Withdrawal ⁓

The depression medication worked, but I was still having trouble sleeping. I made another appointment with the doctor, still seeking a chemical solution to a problem with living. I told the doctor I couldn't use barbiturates, so he prescribed a supposedly nonaddicting sleeping pill called Dalmane. It worked for a while. There was a sedative effect with the drug but no euphoric high, so I didn't bother taking more than the prescribed dose. I even reduced my marijuana use. Within six months, the Dalmane wasn't working at all. I decided to stop using it. I was feeling increasingly guilty about my use of sleeping medication as well as my use of marijuana. I was starting to get brutally honest with myself. When I stopped the Dalmane, I immediately began to experience unpleasant withdrawal symptoms. I had sweats. I couldn't think straight. My joints ached.

I went to another doctor. The doctor I chose was a recovering addict himself. He confronted me not too nicely about my use of sleeping medication. You're a recovering addict, he said. You have no business using mood-altering drugs like Dalmane. Antidepressants maybe, but not sleeping medication. But Doc, I protested, it was prescribed! Bulls—t! he said. That's a copout. At first I was angry, but I knew he was right. He explained that withdrawal from Dalmane is like withdrawal from methadone. It would take several months. This good doctor arranged with a pharmacist to customize several bottles of Dalmane capsules for me, each of which contained increasingly smaller amounts of the active drug. I was able to wean myself off the Dalmane over the next three months. I was able to work at the agency and to teach my classes at the college while I went through Dalmane withdrawal.

⁓ One More Geographical Change ⁓

About a year after I kicked my Dalmane addiction, the community college decided to create a degree program from the addiction-counseling courses I had designed. They offered me full-time teaching status as well as the position of chairperson of the addiction-program department. All I had to do was finish my associate's degree, and all I lacked was a science credit and a math credit. By then, however, I was aware that my ongoing problem with authority was no better than it had ever been and that I would be unable to function effectively in the college's organizational structure, so I declined. The college went ahead with the program and hired somebody else to run it.

My job as program manager at the agency allowed me to make most of my own decisions without supervision. Still, I had someone I had to answer to—the executive director. Inevitably, conflict developed between us. We argued. Of course my responses were inappropriate. Before he had a chance to fire me, I resigned. I went to work as senior counselor at another agency, had conflict with supervision there too, and left to take a senior counselor position at a new inpatient treatment facility in Buffalo, New York. My wife Jan got a drug and alcohol counseling job at a Buffalo outpatient clinic.

✍ Kicking Marijuana ✍

Before leaving for Buffalo, I made a decision to stop using marijuana. The guilt and shame I felt about using marijuana finally forced me to quit. After all, I was a drug and alcohol counselor. I could no longer bear to maintain the deception. It was a long time afterward, though, before I could tell anybody that I'd used marijuana nearly every night during my first ten years in the alcohol and drug addiction–counseling field. My withdrawal from marijuana was surprisingly easy compared to any other withdrawal syndrome I'd gone through.

Still, old problems followed me to Buffalo—behavior problems. Even though I was now free of marijuana, I was still behaving in ways that made me feel stupid and ashamed. Right away, I started fighting with my coworkers and my supervisor. As usual, I had no problem with clients.

✍ Kicking Nicotine ✍

After taking a walk on a cold and snowy winter day about six months after starting my new job in Buffalo, I experienced severe chest pains. The pains were accompanied by a sensation of heaviness that felt as though someone were standing on my chest. When I called my doctor, he told me to meet him at the emergency room. I was diagnosed as having had a mild heart attack. I ended up in the intensive care unit for twenty-four hours, then on the cardiac unit for three days. Of course I couldn't smoke while in the ICU, so I was in severe nicotine withdrawal when I arrived on the cardiac ward. The first thing I did was to go into the bathroom and light up one of my unfiltered Lucky Strikes. I drew in about a yard of smoke and inhaled down to my toenails. As soon as I drew the smoke into my lungs, a chest pain struck that was even more intense than the one that had put me in the hospital. It sent me staggering back against the bathroom wall. It felt as though I'd been kicked in the chest by a mule. The chest pain passed as quickly as it had come. I made an immediate decision to stop smoking. Since that time, I have often wished I'd made a decision to quit much earlier. I smoked for thirty-five years, and some of the damage I did to my lungs would be permanent. Although in general I feel much better since I stopped smoking, I still suffer from lung congestion during winter, and also during summer when it gets really hot and humid.

Except for the withdrawal syndrome I suffered when I stopped using barbiturates, kicking nicotine was the hardest withdrawal syndrome I ever went through. As difficult as the withdrawal from barbiturates had been, the worst was over in forty-eight hours. Although I quivered and shook for two more weeks, I never had cravings for barbiturates after the first two days. Two weeks after I stopped smoking, I was still fighting off cravings almost 'round the clock. But I haven't smoked a cigarette since the day I made a decision to stop. That was fifteen years ago.

If you still smoke and decide to stop, I would suggest that you have a good plan in place to help yourself through the withdrawal syndrome. Get some help and some support. But don't put it off too long. People in recovery from addiction to alcohol or other drugs who continue smoking often end up with their lives cut short by smoking-related diseases such as cancer.

After another bout with chest pains and another trip to the emergency room, I found out that the chest pains were unrelated to a heart condition. Very thorough testing revealed nothing wrong with my heart. Instead, I had hairline cracks in my sternum (breastbone) that were the result of thirty years of training with heavy weights. My specialty was the bench press. I always used spotters to assist me when I was using very heavy weights, just in case I failed. But sometimes during a failed attempt, the weight would come down on my chest before the spotters could grab it. The weight never landed hard enough to break the sternum or one of the attached ribs, but sometimes it landed hard enough to cause a hairline crack. Over the years, some of the hairline cracks calcified. By the time I was around fifty, whenever I experienced a lot of emotional stress, it would cause the pectoral muscles to tense up and pull on the sternum. The resulting pain was easy to mistake for cardiac pain.

◆ **EXERCISE** If you smoke cigarettes and decide to stop, how will you deal with the withdrawal syndrome?

_____

_____

_____

_____

∾ More Job Changes ∾

When I got out of the hospital, I had an angry encounter with the agency director. I quit before he could fire me and got a senior counseling job at a new halfway house. I designed the lecture schedule and a crafts program. Somehow, I managed to stay out of trouble with authority figures long enough to get promoted to a site-director position at one of the other halfway houses run by the same umbrella agency. Soon after my promotion, I got into a conflict with the executive director. I resigned—again. I took another senior-counselor job at a Buffalo outpatient agency. That job lasted six months. I was fired before I had a chance to quit.

∾ Searching for Answers ∾

I couldn't figure out what the problem was. I hadn't used alcohol in more than ten years. I'd been off marijuana for more than two years. I'd even stopped smoking. I was no longer using antidepressant medication. I was completely drug free, yet an important part of my life was still unmanageable. I still couldn't hold a job. Although I didn't know what was wrong, I knew I needed to find out why I still couldn't get along with authority figures and keep a job.

Back in Business for Myself

In order to find the answers to my inability to deal with authority and hold on to a job, even jobs I loved, I decided to go back into business for myself. I thought it would help me figure things out. And if I still couldn't figure things out, at least I'd be my own boss again. I became a freelancer, like before, and worked as a consultant for a master's-level social worker whose private practice had become too big for her to handle alone. She specialized in DWI clients. I did assessments for her and ran alcohol-education groups. I received little or no supervision, which was exactly the kind of supervision I liked.

Becoming a Trainer for Other Counselors

When I went to work again as a consultant, I'd been in the substance-abuse treatment field for ten years. I'd given hundreds of lectures, most of which were based on original material that I'd written down on yellow legal pads and saved. I reviewed it all one day and discovered I had enough for a small book. I also discovered that I could easily modify what I'd written and use it as material for training other counselors. Most states, including New York, require counselors to be credentialed. I polished some of the material and used it to design courses for counselors, and I sent the courses to the credentialing boards of several states in the region. Most of the material was approved, and I immediately started presenting workshops to drug and alcohol counselors. I gave workshops in New York, Ohio, Michigan, Indiana, and Illinois.

Discovering My Addiction to Anger

The first few courses I designed and presented to counselors were around anger management. It proved the old saw that you end up teaching to others what you yourself need to learn. I ultimately discovered that I was addicted to anger in the same way I'd been addicted to alcohol and other drugs. I used anger and rage like a drug to change feelings such as anxiety, depression, and fear into a feeling of power.

Development of Pathways to Peace

After discovering that, for me, anger was just another drug, I applied what I knew about addiction to the problem of chronic anger. I found out soon enough that I wasn't the only person who used anger like a drug to change feelings. I found that many, if not most, people in recovery from addiction to alcohol and other drugs were like me. They also used anger like a drug and were hooked on it. I also knew that anger was often referred to as the number-one killer of recovering addicts, because it was the number-one trigger for relapse. My thinking around the subject led to my writing a book on anger. The book led to the development of the Pathways to Peace self-help program for people who, like me, used anger like a drug to change how they feel. The book I wrote is used by Pathways to Peace groups; it is titled *The Pathways to Peace Anger Management Workbook* (Hunter House Publishers, 2003).

◆ **EXERCISE** Bill finally discovered that his biggest roadblock to recovery was anger. Has anger been a problem for you since you began your recovery?

_____

_____

∾ What My Life Is Like Now ∾

When I look back over the years of my recovery, I am amazed. I have come far along that hard and rocky road. Yet I know I have much more to learn. My life is no longer the carnival it once was during my early recovery. I am in a stable relationship with a woman for whom I feel the deepest love and respect, and whom I hold in the highest possible unconditional positive regard. I am no longer merely clean and sober. I enjoy the happy and contented clean and sober life that I once thought would always be beyond my reach. For me, the impossible dream has come true.

∾ Reunion with My Youngest Son ∾

Of all the gifts that I have received as a result of my recovery, one gift stands out above all others. My third wife took my youngest son away when I went back to college. Nineteen years passed. I tried to find him but was unsuccessful. My wife had changed her name and gone into hiding. But over the years that followed, she kept track of me. It was easy for her to do so because I always had a listed telephone number and I remained in western New York. In addition, she and I had mutual acquaintances who helped her keep track of me. Finally my ex-wife gave my son, who was twenty by then, my most recent published phone number.

He called very early one morning. Neither my wife, Jan, nor I was awake when the call came in, so the message machine picked it up. Jan was up first and went downstairs and checked the machine. She came back upstairs and said there was a message on the machine and that I'd better go and listen to it. She didn't say what the message was or who had called. I went down and retrieved the message. The voice said, "Hi. My name is Will Fleeman. I'm looking for Bill Fleeman." The first thing that struck me was his voice. It sounded so much like my voice, it was like listening to a message from myself. Could it be? I thought, and my heart skipped a couple of beats. The caller had left a number to call back. I wrote down the number on a message pad by the phone and put the receiver back in the cradle. Taking a deep breath, I picked up the receiver again and dialed the number. The same voice that had left the message answered the phone. My mouth went dry. My heart rate shot up above the graph. For a minute, I was speechless—struck dumb. It was him! Soon after that phone call, my son and I were reunited at my home in western New York. It was wonderful!

If I hadn't stayed clean and sober, and if I hadn't overcome my addiction to anger, my son and I may never have met. My son's mother and I met not long afterward and made amends to each other.

◆ **EXERCISE** Bill says his reunion with his son was the most remarkable gift given to him as a result of his recovery. What is the greatest gift you have received, so far, as a result of your recovery from addiction to alcohol or other drugs?

_____

_____

_____

_____

∾ Developing Pathways to Sobriety ∾

After I'd worked a recovery program for ten years that used the twelve-step program as a guide, I looked at my life and saw that I needed extra help. I couldn't have stayed alive without the fellowship of AA and NA. Yet even after ten years I felt on the brink of relapse most of the time—if not relapse back into active use of alcohol and other drugs, then relapse back into old self-destructive behaviors.

I read literally hundreds of books searching for that elusive state called "contented sobriety." I read all of the twelve-step program literature. I read books on psychology, including ones written by Jung, Freud, Adler, even B. F. Skinner. I read pop psychology and New-Age self-help books. I read books on philosophy by Bertrand Russell, Jean Paul Sartre, Albert Camus, and others. I read the _Koran_, the _Bible_, and esoteric spiritual texts including the _Tibetan Book of the Dead_. I read everything in sight. I talked to hundreds of people who, like me, were recovering from an addiction to alcohol or other drugs. Out of all of that printed matter and out of all of those conversations came the self-help program Pathways to Sobriety, as well as the book you're reading right now. Appendixes B and C explain in detail how Pathways to Sobriety self-help groups work.

◆ ◆ ◆

I've included my story here in such detail in order to help more people relate more personally, and to help people relate more deeply. Now we get into the part of the workbook where you will be asked to take a close and courageous look at your own life. Take your time with each exercise, but I recommend spending at least an hour or two once or twice a week working on the exercises. The next chapter starts by helping you conduct a self-assessment, because the first step in the recovery process involves understanding and taking responsibility for your own addiction.

4

The Self-Assessment Process

To assess means to take an honest look at and to determine the importance or value of something. To *self-assess* means to take an honest look at and to evaluate yourself. To achieve a lasting, contented sobriety, you must take an honest look at yourself as a person with an alcohol or drug problem.

✎ The Importance of Self-Honesty ✎

A wise man named Socrates lived in Greece twenty-five hundred years ago. He said, "Know thyself." He meant know who you are, what you are, and what you believe. And above all, Socrates meant be honest with yourself. If you are honest with yourself you will be honest with others.

When you used alcohol and other drugs you often lied to yourself and to others. You lied to yourself and others to protect your drug use. Lying was a part of your denial, a part of your addiction. What if you had told yourself the truth and had told others the truth? You know what would have happened. When things got really bad in your life, if you hadn't lied to yourself, you would have had to stop drinking or using other drugs. You had to lie to yourself and others in order to justify continued use of your drug of choice.

Lying to yourself and others fed your denial. You couldn't even think right. How could you think intelligently when all you had to think about was lies? But now you want to be honest with yourself and with others because you want to change, and you know you can't change unless you get honest.

Start by getting honest with yourself. That's the first step. Then you can get honest with others. Start by admitting the lies you told yourself in the past, then make a commitment to self-honesty. What lies did you tell yourself in the past? Did you tell yourself you could stop drinking or using other drugs anytime you wanted? That's a lie addicts often tell themselves. What other lies did you tell yourself?

What lies did you tell others? Did you lie to others about how much you drank or how much you used? What other lies did you tell others?

Being dishonest with yourself and others creates a huge stumbling block that stands in the way of your recovery. After awhile people stop believing you, and then they just stop wanting to communicate with you. If your family stopped wanting you around, did you ever wonder why? Did you ever wonder why people sort of rolled their eyes when you said something, even when you were telling the truth?

Message from Dianne

Hi. I'm Dianne. My life was a mess till I started my recovery. I was addicted to speed and to alcohol. Once I got clean and sober, it took two years to convince my family that it was true. I'd been clean two whole years and my family didn't believe it! I didn't blame them. I'd lied to them for so long. Now my family trusts me. I'm going to do whatever it takes to stay clean and sober. I don't ever want to lose my family's trust again. It hurts too much.

Honest communication is hard to get back. But there was a time when you didn't lie to yourself, a time when you didn't lie to others. At one time, people trusted you. You can rebuild that trust, but it will take time. Don't give up.

◆ **EXERCISE** What will happen to your recovery if you keep lying to yourself and others? Write it down.

_____

_____

_____

_____

_____

◆ **EXERCISE** List three times when lying wrecked your relationship with someone you cared about.

_____

_____

_____

As you can see, self-honesty is crucial to recovery. It is the one requirement in the self-assessment process. You must not lie to yourself.

Watch for three pitfalls. They will trip you up and make self-honesty impossible. Watch for:

1. **Rationalization:** To rationalize means to make a plausible but untrue excuse for something you have done. You are rationalizing when you say things like, "Things went bad between me and my significant other. I felt upset and there wasn't anything else I could do but pick up a drink (or a drug)."

◆ **EXERCISE** Think of the last time you picked up a drink or a drug. What excuses did you make? Write them down.

_____

_____

_____

2. **Minimizing:** Minimizing means lying to yourself about how much or how often you drink or drug. "I never get too drunk." "I only use alcohol or drugs once in a while." These are examples of minimizing.

◆ **EXERCISE** How have you used minimizing to defend your using behavior? Write down three examples.

_____

_____

_____

3. **Blaming:** Blaming means lying to yourself about responsibility. It means telling yourself and others that your behavior is their fault. "My father used to beat me up when I was a kid for no reason. It is his fault I abuse chemicals now." That is an example of blaming.

◆ **EXERCISE** How have you used blaming to defend your using behavior? Write down three examples.

_____

_____

_____

Now you are ready to do your self-test. It will complete your self-assessment.

Read the questions and check the "yes" or "no" box following each question. Be as honest as you can.

		Yes	No
1.	Have you ever harmed yourself or anyone else, physically, mentally, or emotionally, while using alcohol or other drugs?	☐	☐
2.	Have you ever sought medical care due to alcohol or other drug use?*	☐	☐
3.	Have you ever lost a job because of alcohol or other drug use?*	☐	☐
4.	Have you often felt guilt or remorse after using alcohol or other drugs?	☐	☐
5.	Has a significant other ever left or threatened to leave because of your use of alcohol or other drugs?*	☐	☐
6.	Were you ever arrested when alcohol or other drugs were a factor?*	☐	☐
7.	Have you often felt unable to control your alcohol or other drug use?	☐	☐
8.	Has a friend or loved one said you have a problem with alcohol or other drugs?	☐	☐
9.	Has a counselor or therapist ever said you have a problem with alcohol or other drugs?*	☐	☐
10.	Have you ever "blacked out" or been unable to remember what you said or did while using alcohol or other drugs?	☐	☐

How to Score the Test

A "yes" answer to just one of the ten questions shows a problem with alcohol or other drugs. It shows that you abuse alcohol or other drugs. A "yes" answer to any of the questions marked with an asterisk (*) shows a serious problem with, or addiction to, alcohol or other drugs.

Have you been honest with yourself? Did the test show that you abuse or are addicted to alcohol or other drugs? If so, please study the agreement on page 69 carefully. You are urged to sign the agreement before going on.

∽ Conclusion ∽

Congratulations. You have just completed a major task. Your self-assessment represents a giant leap forward in your recovery. Refer to this agreement often, especially if you begin to have doubts about whether or not you are addicted to alcohol or other drugs. Make a copy of your self-agreement to carry with you. If you ever have an urge to drink or drug, read your self-agreement—and don't pick up a drink or a drug!

Self-Agreement

If you did an honest self-assessment, you know whether or not you have a problem with alcohol or other drugs. If your assessment revealed a problem, then you know that you must stop using alcohol or other drugs. Are you serious about stopping? If you are, consider the self-agreement below. Look it over closely. Think about it. Then decide. It is an agreement you make with yourself. If you violate the agreement, you violate yourself.

   If you decide to sign this agreement, have it witnessed. Sign it in the presence of someone you like and admire. And have that person sign as witness.

I,_____, enter into the following agreement with myself:

   1. I agree that I have a serious problem with, or am addicted to, alcohol or
      other drugs.

   2. I agree that my drinking or other drug use has harmed others and/or myself.

   3. I agree that I have used alcohol or other drugs to change how I feel about myself,
      others, and the world.

   4. I agree that in the past I have used rationalizing, blaming, and minimizing to jus-
      tify my alcohol or other drug use, and that I must get honest with myself in order
      to change.

   5. I agree to stop using alcohol or other drugs.

   6. I agree to complete this workbook and continue to work a recovery program.

   7. I agree that my alcohol or other drug use has never been justified and can never
      be justified. However, if I relapse back into alcohol or other drug use, I will
      accept responsibility for the consequences and will resume my recovery program.

Date: _____

Signature: _____ Witness: _____

The agreement you signed and had witnessed is not just words on paper. It is a binding docu-ment. It is a pact with yourself. Signing it means you have made a sincere commitment. You agree to fulfill all of the terms. If you break this agreement, who will know? You will know. The witness you like and admire will know.

5

Understanding the Nature of Addiction

In the last chapter, you learned about the importance of self-honesty. You learned about rationalization, minimizing, and blaming, the three pitfalls that could trip you up and make self-honesty impossible. You completed a self-assessment. Finally, you signed a self-agreement.

In this chapter, you will learn more about the nature of addiction. You will learn how the social use of alcohol and other drugs differs from abuse and addiction. You will find out how you learned your patterns of using alcohol or other drugs. You will also learn how issues of grief and trauma can play a part in patterns of abuse of or addiction to alcohol or other drugs.

∾ Social Use vs. Abuse and Addiction ∾

Social Use of Alcohol or Other Drugs

Not everybody who uses alcohol or other drugs becomes addicted. For example, some people who use the drug alcohol do not experience negative consequences as a result of their use. Sometimes they are called "social drinkers." Usually, social drinkers use alcohol only occasionally. Almost always, social drinkers consume only small amounts of alcohol at a sitting. They rarely drink enough to become intoxicated. If a typical social drinker were stopped at a DWI checkpoint, he or she would likely pass the sobriety test. Social drinkers rarely suffer negative consequences as a result of alcohol use. They don't get arrested for DWI, they don't lose their family, their job, their freedom, or their self-respect. Some people use other drugs such as marijuana or even cocaine and do not become addicted. They usually use small amounts of these drugs once in a while in social situations, and for some reason do not become addicted. Sometimes this pattern of drug use is called "recreational use." However, people who use these drugs, even in small amounts and only occasionally in social situations, are always at risk of becoming addicted. Almost all cases of addiction to alcohol and other drugs begin with occasional use in social situations. Also, people who use illegal drugs under any circumstances always run the risk of being arrested for possession of illegal drugs.

If you have a problem with alcohol or other drugs, then you cannot safely use any amount of alcohol or other drugs.

Abuse and Addiction

Some people have a serious problem with alcohol or other drugs. They have developed an alcohol or drug *habit*. In some cases, the habit becomes an addiction. Abusers and addicts end up with life problems because of the use of drugs. Sometimes they harm themselves or other people. They develop a pattern that leads to frequent use of their drug or drugs of choice, and they experience serious personal consequences.

Message from Louis

Hi. My name is Louis. I'm addicted to alcohol and cocaine. I started out on alcohol. I was sixteen the first time I drank. At first, I didn't abuse alcohol. But when I started college, my drinking got out of control. All my friends at college drank heavily. There was a lot of pressure to go to the bars and drink to intoxication. By the end of my first semester, my drinking began to interfere with my education. My grades went down. Sometimes I was too hungover to go to class, too hungover to study effectively. During spring break, one of my dorm mates introduced me to cocaine. I used cocaine off and on for a couple of months, then more often. Finally, I got hooked on cocaine too.

◆ **EXERCISE** Do you know someone you consider to be a social drinker? How is that person's use of alcohol or other drugs different from yours?

_____

_____

⮑ What Is Addiction? ⮐

Most people don't start out abusing alcohol or other drugs. They start out experimenting with limited use, then they use more and more until they begin to experience consequences that are directly or indirectly associated with their use of alcohol or other drugs. Usually the onset of addiction is a gradual process.

Look at the illustration on the next page. It represents a continuum of addiction. Think of the continuum as a line stretching from wall to wall across a room. The left-hand wall represents limited use of alcohol or other drugs. Usually, the user manages to avoid negative consequences.

The next point on the continuum is problem use. It means you have had one or more perhaps relatively minor problems as a result of alcohol or other drug use. For example, your spouse or significant other may have threatened to leave, or your employer may have threatened to fire you. You may have suffered a severe hangover, or even a blackout.

Abuse of alcohol or other drugs is the next point on the continuum. It is located more than halfway out from the left-hand wall. At this point your use of alcohol or other drugs has led to more serious consequences. Instead of threatening to leave, your spouse or significant other may have followed through and actually walked out. Your employer may have actually fired you. You may have been arrested for the first time for driving under the influence of alcohol or other drugs.

The right-hand wall represents full-blown addiction to alcohol or other drugs. Your spouse may have sued for divorce. You may have lost more than one job due to your use of alcohol or other drugs. If you are a student, you may have been expelled from school, and alcohol or other drug use may have been involved either directly or indirectly. You drink or use other drugs to the point of intoxication almost every time. It now takes large amounts of alcohol or other drugs in order to feel drunk or high. In fact, you may no longer be able to experience the kind of high you felt when you first started using alcohol or other drugs, no matter how much you use. Your health may have begun to deteriorate. Your doctor may have told you that your blood pressure is too high and may have suggested that you stop drinking or using other drugs. You may now be suffering from the early stages of liver disease.

Alcohol/Other Drug Addiction Continuum

Left-Hand Wall ← → **Right-Hand Wall**

Limited Use	*Problem Use*	*Abuse*	*Addiction*
Experimental or occasional use.	Frequent use.	May drink/drug daily, or go on lengthy binges.	Daily heavy alcohol/other drug use.
Low tolerance.	Increased tolerance.	Very high tolerance.	Extremely high tolerance or reverse tolerance.
Experiences euphoric high (cops a buzz).	Euphoric high.	Euphoric high.	No euphoric high.
Feels normal the next day.	Suffers painful hangovers the next day (doesn't feel normal).	Severe hangovers.	**Major problems develop**—life-threatening withdrawal syndrome, loss of family and friends, multiple job losses, multiple DWI arrests.
No significant problems.	Significant other, friends, parents complain.	**Significant problems develop**—significant other leaves or threatens to leave, job loss, DWI.	
	Some binge drinking.	**Maybe some medical problems**—high blood pressure, irregular pulse, swollen liver, depression, insomnia, anxiety.	**Major medical problems**—stroke, heart attack, significant damage in all organ systems, maybe irreversible brain damage.
	Minor problems develop—misses work/school, maybe first DWI.	Increased number of blackouts.	Very frequent blackouts.
	Occasional blackouts.		

◆ **EXERCISE** Look at the continuum again. Mark an "X" where you would place yourself on the line.

◆ **EXERCISE** Have you ever experienced a problem of any kind because of your use of alcohol or other drugs? In other words, have you ever lost something as a result of using your drug or drugs of choice? Write about it here.

_____

_____

_____

_____

✍ Developing Tolerance to Alcohol and Other Drugs ✍

You develop an addiction to alcohol or other drugs as a result of using them over and over again and experiencing a "high" each time. Your brain enjoys the high and wants to repeat it.

As a person becoming addicted to alcohol or other drugs, you develop a high tolerance to your drug of choice. You need more and more of the drug to feel high. High tolerance is a hallmark of addiction. You also suffer a rebound effect from the drug after it wears off. You suffer a hangover.

◆ **EXERCISE** Are you becoming addicted to alcohol or other drugs?

_____

◆ **EXERCISE** What does high tolerance to a drug mean?

_____

_____

◆ **EXERCISE** What is the rebound effect?

_____

_____

◆ **EXERCISE** If you have ever suffered a hangover, how did it make you feel?

_____

_____

❧ Addiction as Learned Behavior ❧

You had to learn how to use and abuse alcohol or other drugs. You didn't start out with the intention of becoming addicted. But somewhere along the way, your use of alcohol or other drugs got out of control. Your alcohol or drug use became a habit. You used your drug or drugs of choice more and more often and in larger and larger amounts. The more you used, the more you wanted to use. The more you used, the more you forgot how to use other ways to change how you feel. Your drinking or drugging got out of control. You developed a pattern of abuse.

❧ How Did You Learn Your Addiction? ❧

You learned your addiction, in part, from other people. You may have learned it from one or both of your parents, or from your brothers or sisters. You probably learned some of the pattern of your addiction from kids you grew up with. You learned it from what you saw and heard that others did.

You learned a major part of your pattern of addiction from the results you got when you used alcohol or other drugs. You felt pleasure when you got drunk or used some other drug, such as marijuana or cocaine. You copped a high. Your brain recorded the high in your memory, in the brain's pleasure center. The memory of the high was etched deeper in memory each time you got high.

In the beginning, when you first started using alcohol or other drugs, you probably didn't have strong negative results. Otherwise, you probably wouldn't have developed an addiction. You used alcohol or other drugs to experience the pleasure of the high and to change negative feelings like fear or depression into positive feelings like confidence or courage, and you succeeded. You didn't suffer negative consequences. You didn't lose anything. You didn't go to jail and lose your freedom. You didn't get hurt. You used alcohol or other drugs and received only pleasure, rarely pain. You were consistently rewarded with pleasure. That's how you learned your addiction. That's how you learned to use alcohol or other drugs to feel high and to change painful feelings into pleasurable feelings.

> ### *Message from Raymond*
>
> **My name is Raymond. I'm from Arizona. I always thought I drank "normally."** But I grew up in a house where there was daily use of alcohol. Both of my parents drank, and my father drank a lot—eight or ten beers a day, a lot more on weekends. Sometimes my father got drunk and started arguments with my mother. Then they'd fight. I mean, they'd hit each other. All my friend's parents drank heavily too. So, to me, heavy drinking was normal.

◆ **EXERCISE** How did you learn your addiction? Who and what taught you?

_____

_____

❧ Patterns of Alcohol and Drug Use and Abuse ❧

There are two basic patterns of alcohol and drug use and abuse: daily and episodic.

1. **Daily use and abuse:** Many, if not most, people who are addicted use and abuse alcohol or other drugs every day or nearly every day. They may drink or use other drugs more on certain days—such as weekends—than on other days, but they use alcohol or drugs more or less daily. They have a *daily pattern* of use and abuse.

2. **Episodic use and abuse:** Some addicts do not use or abuse alcohol or other drugs every day. Instead, they maintain abstinence for several weeks or even several months at a time and then start drinking or using. They may drink or use very large amounts of alcohol or other drugs every day for several days in a row, or for several weeks in a row, then maintain a period of abstinence again. They go on binges. They have an *episodic pattern* of use and abuse.

◈ **EXERCISE** What is your alcohol/drug use and abuse pattern?

_____

_____

_____

◈ **EXERCISE** If your pattern of use and abuse is the daily pattern, how many times per week do you drink or use?

_____

◈ **EXERCISE** If your pattern of use and abuse is the episodic pattern, about how many times per year do you drink or use?

_____

❧ Addiction and Grief ❧

Grief is a feeling of great loss. People suffer grief when they lose something that means a great deal to them, or when they lose someone they like or love very much. Addicted people develop a sort of deep friendship or love affair with alcohol or other drugs. So when addicted people stop using alcohol or other drugs, they suffer grief. Whether they decide on their own to stop or whether they are forced to stop, they grieve the loss of their drug or drugs of choice. To the recovering addict, sometimes it feels as though an old friend has died or a loved one has suddenly walked out of his or her life. The addict goes through a period of time when he or she mourns the loss of his or her drug or drugs of choice.

◆ **EXERCISE** The feelings listed below are feelings associated with grief. Check the ones you have experienced during your recovery.

☐ sadness ☐ anger ☐ depression ☐ guilt/remorse

☐ loneliness ☐ anxiety ☐ confusion

∽ The Five Stages of the Grief Process ∽

There are five stages in the grief process:

1. Denial

2. Anger

3. Bargaining

4. Depression

5. Acceptance

The first stage in the grief process is called *denial*. When you lose something you greatly value, at first you can't believe it happened. You want to deny the loss. The denial stage of the grief process usually passes quickly. The second stage of the grief process is *anger*. During this stage, you see that the loss is real. You see that it really happened, and that makes you angry. You may even rage at the loss. The anger stage of the grief process can last for days or even months. The third stage is *bargaining,* and it also usually passes fairly quickly. The fourth stage of the grief process is *depression*. Like the anger stage, it may last a long time. The final stage of the anger process is *acceptance*. It can take one to three years—or more—to reach the acceptance stage of the grief process.

◆ **EXERCISE** When do people suffer grief?

_____

_____

_____

_____

◆ **EXERCISE** Name the five stages of the grief process.

1._____   4._____

2._____   5._____

3._____

◆ **EXERCISE** As a person recovering from addiction to alcohol or other drugs, you are grieving the loss of your drug of choice. Write down the feelings you have experienced or are now experiencing due to the loss of your drug.

_____

_____

_____

_____

Message from Al

Hi. I'm Al. I'm addicted to amphetamines, which on the street are called speed. When I stopped using speed I went through all the stages of the grief process one stage at a time. Sometimes it seemed I experienced all of them at once. I went through the denial stage of the grief process within a few days. Then the anger set in, and I got stuck there for awhile. I even made a bargain with myself, telling myself I could probably use a little speed maybe just once in awhile. When the depression started, I jumped back into anger. It went on that way for quite awhile. Finally, I accepted that I was an addict. I knew I could never use speed or any other drug, not even alcohol, ever again. I'm glad that part of my recovery is over— the grief part.

∽ Traumatic Events and Addiction ∽

Some people who develop problems with alcohol or other drugs were abused as children. They were beaten or raped, or they suffered trauma because of things they saw happen to others. Some people who are addicted to alcohol or other drugs were abandoned by one or both parents. They felt rejected and afraid and could not predict what was going to happen to them. Often they blamed themselves for what happened. The trauma they suffered led to feelings of low self-esteem. They lived with depression, anxiety, anger, and other painful feelings every day of their lives. Later these feelings became major triggers for alcohol or drug

Message from Rhonda

My name is Rhonda. I'm from San Diego. I'm addicted to alcohol and some other drugs too.

Neither of my parents abused alcohol or other drugs. And I never suffered trauma, not during childhood or at any other time in my life. There was never a lot of tension in my home. I was never abused. I never witnessed violence in my home, or in my neighborhood. Yet I got addicted to alcohol and some other drugs. How come?

My mentor explained it to me this way. She said two types of people get addicted to alcohol or other drugs. My mentor says one type is set up almost from the start to develop an addiction, because of things that happened to them or because of things they saw. Their inner tension level is very high. My mentor said addicts who grew up in violent surroundings fit into this group. They feel depressed all the time, and full of anxiety and fear. They use alcohol or other drugs in order to get some relief from these painful feelings and to try and reduce their inner tension level. My mentor says they get addicted very quickly, almost from the first time they use.

The second type of addict is different. My mentor told me they never experienced trauma in their lives, not during childhood or as adults. Their inner tension level is not remarkably high. They don't have as much fear and tension as those who come from traumatic backgrounds. Usually they don't get addicted to alcohol or other drugs as fast as the first group. But this type does find out that alcohol or other drugs produce extremely pleasurable feelings. They learn that any painful feelings they might have, such as anxiety or shyness, seem to go away when they use alcohol or other drugs and that any good feelings they might experience, such as confidence or excitement, get more intense. They keep using alcohol or other drugs over and over until, finally, they get hooked on the high. My sponsor says I'm that type of addict.

use. The homes they lived in were almost like a war zone, and there was constant tension around them. The constant tension around them led to a more or less permanent increase in their level of inner tension. Studies show that the inner tension level of many people who are addicted to alcohol or other drugs is often higher than normal—sometimes much higher. *Some people learn to use alcohol or other drugs to relieve their inner tension, and then they become addicted.*

You may have suffered trauma during childhood or at some other time in your life. If so, the traumatic events you experienced may have contributed to your use of alcohol or other drugs as a way to alleviate the increased tension level caused by the trauma. You do not have to resolve your issues of trauma *now* in order to stop using alcohol or other drugs. Even without resolving those issues completely, you can stop and stay stopped if you are fully committed to recovery. If you continue to work a recovery program and complete this workbook, you will learn how to cope with the inner tension. *You must avoid using traumatic experiences from the past as an excuse for continuing to use alcohol or other drugs in the present.* In order to heal completely from addiction and live a *happy* clean and sober life, however, someday you must forgive those who harmed you, and you must forgive yourself.

Many people who become addicted to alcohol or other drugs have never experienced trauma. Bear in mind the main reason people use alcohol or other drugs: *to change painful feelings into pleasurable feelings or to intensify pleasurable feelings.* This category of addicted people use the drug often enough and in large enough quantities to become addicted.

PART TWO

Understanding the Process of Recovery

6

The Eight Parts of the Whole Self

This chapter begins Part II of the workbook, which focuses on helping you understand the process of recovery from addiction to alcohol and other drugs. In this chapter you will be introduced to an important concept that will form the foundation upon which the other chapters in Part II are built.

It is useful to think of the whole self as made up of eight interactive, interdependent parts. I call these the "eight parts of the whole self." Each part depends on the other seven parts, and each part affects the other seven parts. Addiction to alcohol or other drugs affects all eight parts of the self. In order to fully recover from your addiction, you will find that you will need to change and grow in a balanced way in all eight of parts of your whole self.

The eight parts of your whole self include the following:

1. The biological/emotional part—your body and your emotions

2. The environmental part—your surroundings

3. The behavioral part—your actions and words; everything you do

4. The skills part—what you are good at; what you have learned

5. The values/goals part—what is important to you; what you want to be

6. The beliefs part—your attitudes about yourself and your world; what you believe is true

7. The mission part—your purpose in life; why you are here

8. The transcendental/metaphysical part—your feelings of connectedness to others and to the great mystery of the rest of the cosmos

You will learn more about each of the eight parts of the whole self in later chapters.

∾ The Eight Parts of the Whole Self
Compared to an Eight-Cylinder Engine ∾

One way to understand the eight parts of the whole self is by comparing it to an eight-cylinder engine. Imagine that you are like a car with an eight-cylinder engine. To function fully and well, all eight cylinders must be in good shape. Each cylinder must cooperate and do its job. If all the cylinders cooperate, the car will take you where you want to go.

But what if one cylinder develops a problem? What if it becomes damaged? It will function poorly and will be unable to cooperate well with the rest of the cylinders. It will throw everything out of balance and cause the whole engine to miss and lurch and lose power. Left unattended, the condition of the damaged cylinder will get worse and worse. Finally, the car will stop working altogether.

The damaged cylinder will have a negative effect on the rest of the cylinders, causing the other cylinders to work too hard. Soon another cylinder will develop problems, then another and another until, finally, the whole car will break down. The same is true of the recovery process. Full recovery from addiction to alcohol or other drugs means recovery of the whole self—recovery of all eight parts.

∾ The Biological (Physical/Emotional) Part of the Self ∾

Effects of Alcohol and Other Drugs on the Body

Addiction to alcohol or other drugs has a damaging effect on biology. In fact, overuse of alcohol and other drugs has a damaging effect on every organ system of the body.

All the most widely used drugs, including alcohol, can cause death by overdose. A combination of alcohol and barbiturates (sleeping pills), both very powerful central-nervous-system depressant drugs, is more dangerous than either drug by itself and can lead to death in relatively small doses. Each of these drugs potentiates the other. That means that when they are used together, the depressant effect of each drug multiplies. When combinations of alcohol and sleeping pills don't end in death, the user is sometimes left in a permanent vegetative state because so many brain cells die from the combined effects of the drugs.

Your health is determined by what you eat and by what you do with your body. Nutrition is an extremely important part of the process of recovery from addiction. A well-balanced diet of nutritious food will help to create a healthy body. A poorly balanced diet of junk food will create an unhealthy body. Overeating will cause you to gain weight, which may lead to feelings of low self-esteem. For many people who are addicted to alcohol or other drugs, a feeling of low self-esteem is a major relapse trigger. All of the other vital parts of the whole self influence the condition of the body.

Your body also needs rest and sleep. Most authorities say that you need six to nine hours of sleep each night in order to feel rested and alert. Just a day or two without adequate sleep will have a negative effect on how you feel and how you function. It will cause your tension level to rise. That will increase your sensitivity to frustration and anxiety, which are also relapse triggers.

Obviously, your body is important. If you are in good physical health, you feel good. When you feel good, you are more likely not to want to use alcohol or other drugs.

Effects of Alcohol and Other Drugs on the Emotions

Alcohol and other drugs have a damaging effect on the emotions as well as on the body. This is because they affect brain chemistry, and brain chemistry affects the emotions. Alcohol and other depressant drugs, such as opiates (heroin, morphine, etc.), barbiturates (Seconal, Nembutal, etc.), and marijuana, slow down central-nervous-system activity. Depressant drugs may cause you to feel depressed instead of high. Stimulant drugs such as cocaine and speed cause depression on the rebound, that is, when the drugs wear off. Stimulant drugs increase brain activity well above normal. When stimulant drugs wear off, they cause brain activity to crash well below normal, potentially causing you to feel severely depressed. Both classes of drugs can cause you to think suicidal thoughts, and may lead to suicide. In fact, most authorities agree that alcohol or other drugs are involved in more than half of all suicides.

Stimulant drugs, such as cocaine or speed, and sometimes depressant drugs, such as marijuana or hashish, can also cause an increase in feelings of anxiety and fear. Sometimes the increased fear and anxiety turn into paranoia, which can cause you to irrationally think that some other person or people are plotting to harm or even kill you. The heightened state of fear and anxiety may cause you to harm or even kill the person or people whom you imagine to be plotting against you.

Sometimes alcohol and drug use causes you to experience a condition called *amotivational syndrome.* In this condition, you lose interest in almost everything except seeking and using the drug.

Sometimes alcohol or other drug use causes a *blunting* of emotion, so that you cannot experience strong emotion of any kind. In this state, you feel neither joy nor sorrow and instead experience a flatness of emotion.

Alcohol, Other Drugs, and Mental Disorders

In some cases alcohol and other drugs have been known to cause major mental disorders. Recent studies show a strong relationship between schizophrenia and heavy marijuana use, especially when use has been heavy and more or less continuous since the early teens or before. Schizophrenia is a major mental disorder involving loss of contact with reality, delusions of grandeur and persecution, and blunted emotions. Long-term heavy use of alcohol can also lead to schizophrenia.

Alcohol also has a direct effect on the brain, and long-term heavy use can cause severe damage to important areas of the brain. In addition, a single episode of binge drinking over the course of two or three days can cause loss of short-term memory recall. Called Wernicke's syndrome, this condition is not the same as loss of memory due to a blackout. In the case of a blackout, you will still be able to make use of your memory. The mechanism will be okay. With Wernicke's syndrome, by contrast, the condition often results in permanent damage to short-term memory.

Message from Don

I'm Don. I'm addicted to alcohol and speed (amphetamines). I did a lot of damage to my body over the years. In fact, it's a miracle that I'm still alive. I smoked a couple of packs of cigarettes a day, too. I didn't exercise or eat right. I had a beer gut and high blood pressure. I had black circles under my eyes because I didn't sleep well, maybe three or fours hours a night, and it was restless, fitful sleep. I avoided looking at myself in the mirror, because every time I looked my self-esteem went down a couple more points.

Low self-esteem was one of my major triggers. Finally, I went to an inpatient treatment agency and got clean and sober. In treatment, I learned about the importance of exercise and good nutrition and adequate sleep. I started getting my body back in shape, and my self-esteem improved. After getting out of treatment, I continued with an exercise program. I continued practicing good nutrition and getting healthful sleep. Low self-esteem is no longer one of my triggers.

◆ **EXERCISE** What happens to an eight-cylinder engine when one of the cylinders develops a problem? What happens when the problem goes untreated?

_____

_____

_____

_____

◆ **EXERCISE** What does comparing the whole self to an eight-cylinder engine have to do with understanding the recovery process?

_____

_____

_____

_____

◆ **EXERCISE** What will happen if you don't pay attention to your body?

_____

_____

_____

◆ **EXERCISE** Name some things you could do that would improve the way you take care of your body.

_____

_____

_____

✑ The Environmental Part of the Self ✑

Your addiction to alcohol or other drugs may have caused a great amount of damage to the environmental part of your self. Certainly at least some damage has occurred.

You live in relationship to people, places, and things. The sum total of these people, places, and things is your outer environment. You could not survive without having certain people, places, and things in your life. If you have been addicted to your drug of choice for one or more years, chances are you have experienced some environmental losses or have been threatened with some losses. Maybe your wife or husband or significant other has walked out of your life. You may have lost one or more jobs, or had your car repossessed. These losses often happen to people addicted to alcohol or other drugs.

The people, places, and things you choose to have in your environment influence the health of your body, either directly or indirectly. They influence how you behave and what skills you develop. They influence your values, your goals, and your beliefs. They influence your sense of mission and your sense of connectedness. People, places, and things affect all of your parts in one of two ways: in a positive way or in a negative way.

Your mind is another kind of environment, your mental environment. Your addiction to alcohol or other drugs has also affected your mental environment. No doubt the effect has been negative. Your mental environment includes your thoughts, your transcendental sense, your beliefs, and your attitudes. It encompasses your values and goals. Your mental environment also includes your automatic behaviors. Your mental environment affects your outer environment, and your outer environment in turn affects your mental environment.

Message from Bill

All of my friends were like me—addicted to chemicals. We all came from the same kind of outer environment. We grew up in homes where there was alcohol or some other kind of drug abuse, and where there was anger and violence. My friends and I hung out in the same places. We had the same interests, more or less, and did the same things. We all developed essentially the same mental environment, too. Even our thoughts about the world were similar. When I started my recovery, I began to see the negative influence my old friends had on my mental environment—on my thoughts, my beliefs, my attitudes, and my values. I also saw the negative influence certain places and things had on me. I stopped hanging out with my old friends. And I stopped hanging out in the old places and holding on to the old things. If I hadn't made changes in my outer environment, my mental environment would have stayed the same as well. In order to recover from addiction, I had to make these changes.

◆ **EXERCISE** Name the two ways people, places, and things influence you.

_____

_____

◆ **EXERCISE** List three people in your life who could have a negative influence on your recovery.

_____

_____

_____

◆ **EXERCISE** List three people in your life who could have a positive influence on your recovery.

_____

_____

_____

◆ **EXERCISE** List three places and three things in your life that could have a negative influence on your recovery.

_____

_____

_____

◆ **EXERCISE** List three places and three things in your life that could have a positive influence on your recovery.

_____

_____

_____

If your addiction to alcohol or other drugs had not had a negative effect on your behavior, you may not have decided to stop drinking or using other drugs. But your addiction did have a negative effect on your behavior. It led to actions that caused you to lose things or people.

Behavior is action. If a certain action gives you pleasure, you will naturally want to repeat that action. If the action gives you very intense pleasure, you may end up repeating that action over and over no matter what.

Some actions become habits. You create habits by repeating certain actions over and over. You created your alcohol or drug habit by repeatedly using alcohol or other drugs. Fortunately, you can change your habits.

Message from Martin

My name is Martin. I wanted to start my recovery using the intellectual approach, by analyzing the causes of my addiction. Once I found out the causes, I thought, then I could easily stop. Meanwhile, my behavior stayed the same. I kept using cocaine. Finally, it dawned on me: I had to change my behavior first. Finding out why I became addicted to cocaine in the first place had to come later.

Recovery must start with behavior. You must stop using alcohol and other drugs. That is the first step you must take along the road to recovery. You can't wait; you must stop now. If you do not change your behavior now, you will experience additional painful consequences. You will lose more things. You will lose more relationships, more jobs, more opportunities, more of your self-respect. Your physical and mental health will get worse.

You must change in all parts of your whole self, but you must change your alcohol- or drug-using behavior before you can change anything else.

◆ **EXERCISE** How did you use behavior to create your addiction?

_____

_____

_____

◆ **EXERCISE** What will happen if you don't change your alcohol or drug-using behavior now?

_____

_____

_____

∽ The Skills (Learning) Part of the Self ∽

Alcohol and other drugs impair brain function, usually temporarily, but sometimes permanently. Learning any task, especially a new task, is much harder if your brain is impaired. You have probably found it impossible to learn some tasks when impaired by alcohol or other drugs. Now you are faced with learning a very difficult new task: recovery.

As a human being, you have developed many useful skills to help you survive in the world. Although you were not born with skills, you were born with the ability to learn skills. Your ability to learn new skills makes it possible to change your behavior and to recover from your addiction. Now that you have made a sincere commitment to recovery, you must learn new skills, techniques that will help you deal with the things that trigger your addiction.

Message from Bill

I was a skilled weight lifter and a skilled machine operator. I had some art skills. But I didn't know how to manage my feelings. I didn't have those kinds of skills. I didn't know how to deal with depression and anxiety or other negative feelings, except to get high. In fact, getting high, either on drugs or rage, was the only "skill" I had when it came to managing my feelings. And, in a way, addiction is a skill. It is something you learn by practicing alcohol- or drug-using behavior over and over. The problem is, it's a negative skill. When you use alcohol or drugs to deal with negative feelings, you have to pay dues. I paid a lot of dues.

◆ **EXERCISE** Why do you need skills and techniques to recover from your addiction?

_____

_____

_____

_____

◆ **EXERCISE** List five important skills you have learned that help you in your life.

1. _____

2. _____

3. _____

4. _____

5. _____

❧ The Values/Goals Part of the Self ❧

Values

Your addiction to alcohol or other drugs affected your values. Your addiction caused you to focus on values that supported your denial and kept you stuck in the addiction process. Therefore, full recovery from your addiction requires you to look closely at your values and to change some of your values.

Values and goals are closely connected. Values are the things and feelings that are important to you. They give you guidance about what things will give you pleasure and what things will bring you pain. Values tell you what to pursue, what to avoid, and what to think about. Values have a strong effect on your behavior, influence the skills you develop, and directly determine your goals. In other words, your values have a significant effect on every other recovery level. You will learn more about values later in the workbook.

Goals

Your addiction has probably had a negative effect on your ability to set goals and to achieve them. When you were using alcohol or other drugs, how many times did you set a goal and then fail to reach it? Chances are, you failed many times.

Goals are the things you want to have and the things you want to do. They are plans for the future. You set goals in order to obtain things that will cause you to feel the pleasure of your valued feelings. Your goals can even affect your body. Goals reinforce your skills and help you make sense of your behavior. Full recovery from your addiction to alcohol or other drugs depends on your goals.

Your goals and values can give you strong reasons to stay focused on your recovery and give you the energy to keep growing and changing. They give you something to look forward to; they give you hope. You will learn more about goals later in the workbook.

Message from Eduardo

My name is Eduardo. I live in New Mexico, and I'm a recovering heroin addict.

I didn't know what values were, and I didn't care. I had no goals and didn't see why I should set any. I had no idea what was really important in my life, and I felt I had nothing to look forward to. I didn't know what to do or where to go. I felt lost and powerless. Then I started my recovery. I learned about how my values were connected to whether I recovered from my addiction. I found out I felt good about myself when I was learning something, so learning became one of my top values. Then I found out about the importance of goals, and started to set some goals that would make me feel good. My main goal right now is to keep working on my recovery from heroin addiction. But I also want to go to college. I'm studying to take the GED so that I can get my high school diploma. That's an important goal to me since I want to go to college. Going to college is another goal I've set. Finding out about my values and learning about goals has helped make my recovery from heroin addiction seem worthwhile.

◆ **EXERCISE** What are values and what are they for?

_____

_____

_____

◆ **EXERCISE** Name at least three of your valued feelings.

_____

_____

_____

◆ **EXERCISE** Name at least three things you value.

_____

_____

_____

◆ **EXERCISE** What do goals do for you?

_____

_____

_____

◆ **EXERCISE** Do you have some goals? If so, name them.

_____

_____

_____

_____

Your addiction to alcohol or other drugs influenced your beliefs. Your addiction encouraged you to acquire a set of beliefs that supported your addiction and helped you to rationalize continued use of alcohol or other drugs. In fact, you could not have continued using and abusing alcohol and other drugs, especially when you began having painful consequences, if you hadn't acquired a set of beliefs that would support your addiction.

Your beliefs are one of the most powerful driving forces in your life. Beliefs are strong feelings about what you think is true or false or right or wrong.

You acquired your beliefs through a learning process. You learned your beliefs from other people. You learned them from your parents, from friends, and from teachers. You learned some of your beliefs from the books you read and from the movies you watched. You learned some of your beliefs from things that happened to you.

You have learned certain beliefs about yourself and about other people, and certain beliefs about the world. You have learned beliefs that are positive, and you have learned beliefs that are negative.

Your beliefs will have a powerful influence on whether you recover from your addiction. Your beliefs give you the energy and the will to change. They deeply influence every other part of your whole self, and all other parts influence your beliefs.

In another part of the workbook, you will learn more about beliefs. You will learn the difference between beliefs that support your recovery and beliefs that keep you stuck in the addiction process. You will learn to become aware of your beliefs, you will learn to tell the difference between positive and negative beliefs, and you will learn how to change negative beliefs into positive beliefs that support your recovery by affecting you in a positive way.

◆ **EXERCISE** Name a belief you have about yourself.

_____

_____

_____

_____

◆ **EXERCISE** Name a belief you have about other people.

_____

_____

_____

_____

◆ **EXERCISE** Name a belief you have about the world.

_____

_____

_____

_____

∾ The Mission Part of the Self ∾

During your active addiction to alcohol or other drugs, you probably felt as though your life had no purpose. Most addicted people feel that way. If you thought about the meaning of your life at all, you probably concluded that your life mission was to suffer.

A complete personal identity usually includes a sense of a personal mission. Your mission statement is a description of your life purpose. Your personal mission is your reason for living, occupying space, doing, learning, feeling, acquiring things, believing, and being. Awareness of your personal mission will help you make sense out of everything else and will help you stay focused on your main goal: to maintain your recovery.

In a special part of the workbook, you will learn more about your mission. You will learn how to write your mission down, so that you can use it to help you recover from your addiction.

◆ **EXERCISE** What is a mission?

_____

_____

_____

◆ **EXERCISE** Why is a sense of mission important to your recovery program?

_____

_____

_____

_____

_____

∽ The Transcendental Part of the Self ∽

The Pathways to Sobriety Workbook does not use a religious approach to recovery from addiction to alcohol or other drugs. *The Pathways to Sobriety Workbook* and the Pathways to Sobriety self-help recovery program use an essentially cognitive and behavioral approach to recovery. Pathways to Sobriety focuses not only on helping people change their behavior but also on helping people change their thinking. This makes sense, because thinking determines behavior. People cannot stop using alcohol or other drugs unless they change how and what they think about their drug of choice. But people who want to stop using alcohol or other drugs once and for all, and who want to be happy, cannot succeed without also changing how they think about themselves and other people and how they think about how they relate to the rest of the cosmos.

Most people who are addicted to alcohol or other drugs lose interest in the transcendental or metaphysical part of their whole self, that part of the self that is concerned with the bigger questions, such as "Why are we here in the first place?" or "What is the meaning of life?" Some addicted people were never aware of that part of the self in the first place. Others have developed strong resentments around this important part of the whole self. Some have become atheists and end up making a religion out of their atheism.

All people have a transcendental part. It is the part that helps you feel connected in a positive way to other people, to the natural world, and to the rest of the cosmos. If you feel connected in this way, you may discover a purpose that is even more powerful than your personal mission. To fully recover and heal from your addiction to alcohol or other drugs, you must pay attention to the transcendental part.

Many people believe that the transcendental part of the self has the most power. When you develop this part of yourself, it can generate revolutionary change in all other parts of the self. Revolutionary change is big change, which can lead to an overall transformation of all other recovery parts. *In fact, when change takes place in the transcendental part of the self, it forces the rest of the self to change, too!* Sudden, dramatic personal change is almost always triggered by major change at the transcendental level.

◆ **EXERCISE** Why is the transcendental or metaphysical part considered the most powerful of all the parts of the self?

_____

_____

_____

_____

_____

Message from John

My name is John. I live in Los Angeles. I'm a recovering cocaine addict. I was raised in a strict religious home. I was forced to go to church and Sunday school three or four times a week. My mother tested my knowledge of Bible verses. If I answered wrong, my mother beat me with a strap. After I got older, I angrily rejected any ideas about religion. Later, I got hooked on cocaine. Then cocaine became my god. I finally stopped using cocaine, but I wasn't happy. My Pathways to Sobriety mentor told me just being clean and sober wasn't enough. He said I had to be clean and sober and happy. My mentor said I had to find a way to feel connected. He said if I didn't, I wouldn't be happy and would likely relapse back into active addiction. So I started to open up my transcendental part. I did a lot of reading. I studied different spiritual ideas. I was surprised to learn that spiritual doesn't have to mean religious. Right now, I attend a Unitarian church. To be a Unitarian you don't have to believe in God. But most Unitarians believe in the worth of all human beings and believe in helping each other out. I feel connected to my new Unitarian friends. Because of the things I'm learning, I'm beginning to feel connected to the rest of the world. But my search is far from over. I'm still exploring other ideas.

The Eight Principles of the Pathways to Sobriety Recovery Program

The Pathways to Sobriety recovery program is based on eight principles. The eight principles follow a logical order, and they are closely related to the eight parts of the whole self. In order to completely recover from your addiction to alcohol or other drugs, you must change and grow in a balanced way in all eight parts of your whole self.

FIRST PRINCIPLE | *Admitting to the Problem*

We admit we have abused or have been addicted to alcohol or other drugs. We have stopped using all nonprescribed drugs, including alcohol, and now accept responsibility for our addiction.

The first principle, admission of the problem, is closely related to the biological part of the whole self. If you have been addicted to alcohol or other drugs, that means your body was addicted as well as your mind.

Tens of thousands of people have stopped using alcohol or other drugs once and for all. You have now stopped using all nonprescribed drugs, including alcohol, and are working a recovery program. You know that you must remain abstinent in order to stay on the road to recovery.

In addition, you know that you must accept responsibility for your addiction as well as for your recovery. You did not take responsibility for your addiction in the past. Instead, you blamed others. Now you accept responsibility for your addiction and you accept responsibility for the consequences you suffered as a result of your alcohol or other drug use and abuse. You must also accept responsibility for the harm you caused others during your active addiction. In order to fully recover and heal from your alcohol or drug addiction, you must stop blaming. You have completed and signed the Abstinence Self-Agreement at the end of Chapter 4.

Now you are responsible for following through. What if you break your agreement? You are now accountable for your behavior. That's what the agreement means—that you are accountable. And if you break the agreement you signed, it means you must get back on track.

◆ **EXERCISE** Have you completed your self-assessment? Have you admitted you have abused or are addicted to alcohol or other drugs?

_____

◆ **EXERCISE** Have you stopped using alcohol and all other nonprescribed drugs?

_____

◆ **EXERCISE** Have you now accepted responsibility for your addiction?

_____

SECOND PRINCIPLE | *Making Recovery Choices*

We understand that our environment can either support our recovery or work against it. Whenever possible, we choose people, places, and things that support our recovery.

As you have already learned, people, places, and things make up your environment. We would all like to think that the behavior we engage in and the choices we make are not influenced by other people, by places, and by things. But the truth is, the people we associate with, the places where we hang out, and the things we surround ourselves with all have a very powerful influence on our choices and on our behavior. Whenever possible, you will need to make changes in your environment in order to increase your chances of recovering from addiction and to decrease your chances of relapsing back into active use of alcohol or other drugs.

◆ **EXERCISE** Name three things in your environment that support your recovery.

_____

_____

_____

◆ **EXERCISE** Name three things in your environment that work against your recovery.

_____

_____

_____

◆ **EXERCISE** What harmful behaviors do you need to stop in order to increase your chances of avoiding a relapse back into use of alcohol or other drugs?

_____

_____

_____

_____

◆ **EXERCISE** Describe something you have done that you feel guilt or shame about.

_____

_____

_____

_____

◆ **EXERCISE** Make a list of people who hurt you. Do you have a resentment toward them?

_____

_____

_____

_____

◆ **EXERCISE** How could forgiving the people named above help your recovery?

_____

_____

_____

_____

◆ **EXERCISE** Make a list of some of the things you need to forgive yourself for.

_____

_____

_____

_____

◆ **EXERCISE** Make a list of at least five people you have harmed as a result of your abuse or addiction to alcohol or other drugs.

_____

_____

_____

_____

◆ **EXERCISE** Who will you apologize to first? What will you say?

_____

_____

_____

_____

◆ **EXERCISE** How will apologizing help you in your recovery?

_____

_____

_____

_____

_____

THIRD PRINCIPLE | *Recognizing That the Use of Alcohol or Other Drugs Is Never Justified*

As people recovering from addiction, we now know we can never justify using alcohol or other drugs, or other addictive behaviors, to change how we feel.

In the past you used alcohol or other drugs to change painful feelings into pleasurable feelings or to intensify certain pleasurable feelings. You made excuses and even lied to yourself to justify your addictive behavior. There were times when people said things or did things that hurt your feelings, and you ended up feeling sad or depressed. You responded by using alcohol or other drugs to reduce the emotional pain. Then you ended up paying dues. But as someone who is addicted to alcohol or other drugs, you now must find other ways to respond when people hurt you.

Sometimes things just happened. Maybe the company you worked for went broke and you were laid off; or maybe a close friend moved to another state, and you ended up feeling rejected and abandoned. If things like this happened to you, you very likely responded by getting drunk or high. Then you ended up paying dues. You lost something you valued and ended up feeling worse instead of better. Now you must ask yourself the following:

As someone with a serious addiction problem, can I ever justify picking up a drink or a drug?

You must put all arguments aside. You must commit yourself to the belief that using alcohol or drugs is never justified.

◆ **EXERCISE** List two times you picked up a drink or a drug and felt justified.

_____

_____

◆ **EXERCISE** As a person with an addiction problem, why is picking up a drink or a drug never justifiable?

_____

_____

_____

_____

FOURTH PRINCIPLE | _Learning New Techniques_

_We are now learning new clean and sober techniques
that help us to manage our emotions._

Like Bill, you learned that drinking or using drugs changed your feelings. You probably learned that the very first time you picked up a drink or a drug. At first, it seemed to work like magic. Then as your addiction began to take hold, using alcohol or other drugs to change how you feel didn't work as well as at first, and you started having painful consequences. Finally, the good feelings produced by alcohol or drugs no longer outweighed the pain of the consequences. In the past, you used your addiction almost like a skill. Now you have decided to stop using chemicals to change how you feel, and you are working a recovery program. But in order to succeed, you must learn new skills—new nonaddictive ways to change how you feel.

◆ **EXERCISE** How old were you when you learned that using alcohol or other drugs changed painful feelings into pleasurable feelings or made good feelings feel even more pleasurable?

_____

◆ **EXERCISE** How would learning new ways—new skills—to feel good help you in your struggle to overcome your addiction?

_____

_____

_____

_____

FIFTH PRINCIPLE | *Choosing New Beliefs*

We discovered that the negative beliefs and values that helped support our addiction were counterproductive. Now we discard those negative beliefs and values and are discovering new, positive beliefs and values that support our recovery.

In order to continue any harmful behavior, you must have a set of beliefs and values that supports the harmful behavior. Like Bill, you acquired a set of negative beliefs about yourself, other people, and the world that supported your addiction. If you hold on to these old, negative beliefs and negative values, they will continue to keep you stuck. Now it is time to identify and discard those negative beliefs and values, and time to replace them with a new set of positive beliefs and values that will support your recovery from your addiction.

◆ **EXERCISE** Why must you identify, discard, and then change old negative beliefs about yourself, other people, and the world, and why must you change your negative values?

_____

_____

_____

_____

SIXTH PRINCIPLE | *Setting Meaningful Goals*

When we were addicted, we lacked meaningful goals. Now we set and move toward meaningful goals that reflect our new, positive values and beliefs.

In the past, you were so busy with the business of addiction that you probably were unable to set reachable, meaningful goals. If you did set goals, chances are you failed to reach them. Or even if you were able to set some goals and reach them, you may have felt disappointed instead of good because the goals you set did not reflect positive values.

◆ **EXERCISE** Did you set reachable, meaningful goals when you were using alcohol and other drugs?

_____

_____

◆ **EXERCISE** If you managed to set and reach some goals when you were using alcohol and other drugs, how did reaching them make you feel?

_____

_____

_____

_____

_____

_____

SEVENTH PRINCIPLE | _Finding Our Purpose_

We have discovered, or have chosen to believe,
that our lives have a special purpose that can be fulfilled
only if we remain clean and sober.

The belief that your life has a purpose is the master key to personal change and growth. If you believe you have a special reason for being alive, then you will have a special reason to stop using alcohol or other drugs—a *big* reason. You have a big change to make, and you must have a big reason to make the change.

Recovery from addiction is difficult. At times, things will be *very* difficult. Without a strong, overriding sense of purpose, you may be unable to continue with the struggle.

◆ **EXERCISE** You may still believe your life has no meaning, no purpose. How will that belief keep you stuck in your addiction?

_____

_____

_____

_____

_____

_____

EIGHTH PRINCIPLE | *Being Fully Committed to Recovery*

Being fully committed to remaining abstinent from alcohol and all nonprescribed drugs, we now choose to live according to a set of beliefs, values, and goals that supports our recovery, and to help others find their pathways to sobriety.

Recovery from addiction is an ongoing process. In order to stay happily clean and sober, you must continue to work hard at making positive changes in all eight parts of your whole self. Your behavior, your attitude, and your outlook will change. Finally, your entire character will change in a major way. Having found your pathway to sobriety, you will then experience the satisfaction and joy of passing on what you have learned and of helping others to recover from their addiction. You will be transformed.

This principle—sometimes called the transformation principle—is perhaps the hardest principle of all to embrace.

Other people have hurt you. Holding on to these hurts is called *resentment.* If you hold on to these hurts, you will be unable to heal completely from your addiction. Your resentment will keep you stuck in the addiction process. You have also done things that have hurt others, and you probably feel some guilt and shame. You must get past the resentment, guilt, and shame; you must let go of it. The way to let go is to forgive.

In order to *heal* from addiction, which means to live a *happy* clean and sober lifestyle, you must forgive those who harmed you, and you must forgive yourself for the harm you have done to others. Forgiving others and yourself will release the guilt, shame, and resentment that have kept you stuck in your addiction. This is not a simple task; it is an ongoing process. In Chapter 20 you will learn more about forgiveness.

In order to maintain a happy clean and sober lifestyle, you will need to live by a new set of beliefs, values, and goals. Ultimately, you may feel a strong need to share what you have learned with other addicts so that they, too, may recover from addiction. In fact, it is hoped that you will feel *compelled* to pass on to others what you have learned in this workbook. If you should reach this highest plateau, that of sharing your success with others, you will have reached the highest possible transcendental level.

◆ **EXERCISE** Why must you keep working hard at your recovery?

_____

_____

_____

_____

_____

◆ **EXERCISE** What rewards will you enjoy if you continue to work hard on your recovery?

_____

_____

_____

_____

_____

_____

◆ **EXERCISE** What does passing on what you are learning have to do with your personal growth?

_____

_____

_____

_____

_____

_____

_____

Message from Bill

At first, as I began to heal from my addiction to alcohol and other drugs, I was unaware of the specific principles I was following. I wasn't even aware I was following certain principles. But I noticed that my behavior was changing. I noticed that I was feeling better about myself, other people, and the world. I knew, vaguely, that I was following some kind of plan. But I wanted to know exactly what I was doing so that I could help others. I spent a lot of time thinking about the principles involved in my recovery, and then I wrote them down.

8

Motivating Yourself
to Change

You have now begun to follow the principles involved in the Pathways to Sobriety program. Before we explore the principles in more detail and learn some additional techniques you can use to help you live contentedly clean and sober, the next three chapters will offer you some basic tools for motivating you to get sober and for relapse prevention.

In this chapter you will learn a method that will increase your desire to stop using alcohol or other drugs and increase your desire to recover from your addiction. The motivational method presented here is based on the story *A Christmas Carol*, by Charles Dickens. You may have seen the movie or video, or you may have read the book. The main character in the story is Ebenezer Scrooge.

You may recall that Scrooge is visited by several spirits. One of the spirits takes Scrooge back into the past and shows him things he said and did that harmed others. The spirit also shows Scrooge what he has lost because of his behavior. Another spirit takes Scrooge into the future and shows him that he will continue to lose more things if he doesn't change.

The spirits make it clear to Scrooge that he has to completely change not only his behavior but his entire character. They show him that he has to undergo a complete transformation. Otherwise, he will continue to lose things and will never be happy. The lesson Scrooge learns from the spirits is a painful one, but it also holds a ray of hope.

The technique presented here is written in the form of a script. You could simply read the script to yourself, but it would be better to have a friend read it to you while you sit back and listen. If you wish, you could have a counselor read it to you. Another option is to tape-record yourself reading the script, then play the tape back while you listen.

Find a quiet, comfortable place to do this exercise. Choose a place where you will be undisturbed for at least twenty minutes. The script should be read slowly. The reader should pause after each sentence. Pausing will allow you time to process and personalize the information. The script should be followed as it is written and should be read with feeling. The reading should take at least fifteen minutes. Anything less than fifteen minutes will not allow you to thoroughly process your feelings.

Message from Bill

Dickens' story *A Christmas Carol* has always been one of my favorites. I have read the book and watched the video many times over the years. Of course I haven't quoted from the story exactly as Dickens wrote it. That would be plagiarism. I simply used it as a guide. When I wrote down the motivation script, you could say that I tried to enter into the spirit of Dickens' story. Then I used the script to increase my desire to stop using my drugs of choice and to stay stopped. I got good results. I wasn't exactly happy with how it made me feel at first. But it increased my motivation, and that's the result I wanted. I read the script again whenever I feel a decrease in my motivation to maintain a clean and sober life.

⁓ Motivation Script ⁓

Part One

Close your eyes and relax. Think about your drugs of choice. Let your mind drift back to the very beginning of your addiction. Think about the things you have lost because of your addiction to alcohol or other drugs. You know by now that addictive use of alcohol or other drugs has a negative effect on every part of your whole self, from the physical to the mental. Since the very beginning of your addiction, what have you lost because you chose to use chemicals to change how you feel?

Think about the effect alcohol or other drugs have had on your physical and mental health. If you drank or used other drugs even for just a few years, your health may have suffered ill effects. If you used addictive chemicals for a much longer period of time, chances are your health has suffered a great deal. You may have developed high blood pressure or heart trouble, depression or anxiety. Since alcohol and other drugs have a negative impact on every part of the body and brain, chances are you have experienced at least some medical problems due to your addiction.

Think about how much money your addiction has cost you. Have you ever tried to estimate how much you spent across the bar, if alcohol was one of your drugs of choice? If you were a bar drinker and you abused alcohol for five or ten years, how much did you spend? Ten thousand dollars? More than ten thousand dollars? It could have been a hundred thousand dollars, or even more, if you drank in bars for fifteen or twenty years. Take a guess, if you dare. What could you have done with all that money, whatever the amount, if you hadn't spent it on alcohol?

How has your addiction affected your outer environment, the people and places that are important to you? Did you lose a relationship that was important to you, or a friendship? Did you lose more than one relationship or more than one friendship because of your alcohol or other drug use? Did you lose your spouse? Your children? Did you lose one or more jobs? If you have lost one of these valuable things as a result of your addiction to alcohol or other drugs, how did that make you feel? How does it make you feel now as you recall those losses?

You know that the abusive use of alcohol and other drugs has a negative effect on people's behavior, and the effect is never good. How has your addiction affected your behavior in the past? Has your addiction caused you to behave in ways that made you feel ashamed or guilty or stupid? Have you hurt other people's feelings with things you said while under the influence? Have you done physical harm to others or to their property as a result of an alcohol- or drug-induced rage? If alcohol or other drugs have caused you to behave in these ways, what was the effect on your self-respect? Is that one of the things you have lost—your self-respect? If you lost your self-respect in the past as a result of your addiction, how did it make you feel then? How does thinking about it make you feel now?

Education is one of the ways people acquire skills. How did your addiction affect your education? Were you ever suspended or kicked out of high school or college when alcohol or other drugs were a contributing cause? Did you ever fail courses as a result of alcohol or other drugs? If you lost educational opportunities because of alcohol or other drugs, how did that make you feel at the time, and how does it make you feel now?

Goals and values help give meaning to people's lives. Think about how your addiction has affected your ability to set and reach goals. Have you ever set an important goal and then failed to reach it because of alcohol or drug use? If so, how did that make you feel? How does it make you feel now, thinking back on the loss of that goal?

Your system of values is a very important part of your whole self. How has alcohol or other drugs affected your values? Were you ever sent to jail as a result of DWI, or for some other alcohol- or drug-related charge? If you were ever locked up, even for just a few hours, as a result of alcohol or drug abuse, then one of the things all human beings value most was taken away from you—namely, your freedom. You may have lost your freedom for longer than a few hours. You may have lost it for a few days, a few months, a few years, or even longer. As a result of your addiction you may have lost your freedom for many years. In fact, you may be in prison as you read this. How did losing your freedom make you feel when you lost it? How does thinking about the loss of your freedom make you feel now?

Your beliefs have a powerful impact on every other part of your whole self. Over time, addictive use of alcohol or other drugs has a negative effect on beliefs. Alcohol and other drugs can cause people to lose beliefs that once served them well, and can cause people to form new beliefs that reinforce addiction and block recovery. Did you once have a strong, positive belief that helped you deal with the world in a healthy way, only to have it dissolved over time by alcohol or other drugs? Maybe you once believed that at least some people could be trusted. Then certain painful experiences occurred in your life that were caused either directly or indirectly by your use of alcohol or other drugs, and you ended up believing that absolutely no one could be trusted. Your alcohol or drug use may have dissolved the original positive belief that made you feel safe in most situations, and a strong negative belief may have taken its place that prevented you from feeling safe in any situation. If because of your addiction you lost a positive belief that helped you deal more effectively with the world, how did that make you feel then? How does it make you feel now?

In order to be emotionally healthy and happy, people need to feel as though their life has special meaning. They need to feel that their life has a purpose that goes beyond their body's taking in nourishment and giving off waste. They need to feel a sense of mission. Before you became addicted to alcohol or other drugs, you may have felt that your life had a special meaning, even if you couldn't put it into words. You may have felt a sense of mission, that your life had purpose. If you did, chances are your addiction took that away from you. Or maybe you never had the feeling that your life had meaning and purpose. In fact, that might have been one of the reasons you developed your addiction in the first place. Every day of your life, you may have been filled with what psychologists call *existential angst.* In other words, you may have always felt that your life lacked meaning. To be filled with existential angst is to be filled with emptiness. You may have become addicted to alcohol or other drugs in an attempt to find a meaning for your life. But your addiction only increased the emptiness you felt at your core. It only made your life seem more meaningless. Whether you once felt your life had meaning and then you lost it to alcohol or other drugs, or whether you never felt your life had meaning and you drank or used drugs in an attempt to find meaning, alcohol or other drugs left you feeling empty. Other than leaving you with that awful feeling of emptiness, how else did losing your sense of purpose or having it elude you make your feel? How does it make you feel now?

The transcendental part of your whole self, which some people call the spiritual part, is closely related to your sense of purpose. Without some form of sustenance, the transcendental part shrivels up and makes you feel that a part of you has died. Very likely, your addiction had the same kind of effect on your transcendental part as it had on your sense of purpose. If you once felt connected to other people, to the universe, and to the rest of the cosmos in a positive way, alcohol or other drugs probably took that feeling of connectedness away from you. If you lacked a sense of connectedness, then your addiction made sure you would never enjoy that feeling as long as you continued to use your drug(s) of choice. If your addiction took away your feeling of connectedness or made it impossible to develop a feeling of connectedness, so that you ended up feeling totally alone and abandoned, what effect did that have on you? Besides feeling alone and abandoned on a cosmic scale, how else did it make you feel?

Now think of all the other things you lost because of your addiction. Think about all of the losses, one by one. Take your time. Get in touch with how those losses made you feel; get in touch with the pain.

In *A Christmas Carol*, people talk about Scrooge behind his back. They say negative things about him. When you were using alcohol or other drugs, what do you think people were saying about you behind your back?

(Pause.)

Now, like Scrooge, travel into the future. Go five years into the future, and imagine you are still using alcohol or other drugs to change how you feel. Carry all the pain of your past losses with you into the future. The pain of those losses is heavy, isn't it? It weighs you down like a ball and chain, and every new loss adds weight to the load. Five more years have passed; you are still using alcohol or other drugs to change how you feel. What is the status of your physical and mental health now, after five more years of active addiction? How much money has your addiction cost you after five more years? How many relationships have you lost now? How many friends? How many jobs? How many career opportunities have you lost? What is your behavior like after five more years? How about your self-respect? How do you feel about yourself now, after five more years of active addiction? Is your feeling of self-respect better or worse than it was? Have you lost any educational opportunities? And your goals—how many more goals have you failed to reach because you have spent five more years abusing alcohol or other drugs? What has been the effect of five more years of addiction on your freedom? How many months have you spent in jail? Or how many years? Think about your belief system now. How many more positive beliefs have you lost to your addiction after five more years? Now consider your sense of purpose. Has it improved over the past five years? And your sense of transcendental connectedness? What is it like now? Finally, what are people saying about you behind your back after you have spent five more years abusing alcohol or other drugs? Get in touch with how much worse things are in your life after five more years of active addiction. Get in touch with all of the feelings.

Now jump ahead another five years. Ten years have gone by, and you are still using alcohol or other drugs to change how you feel. What is your life like now? What has your addiction cost you after ten more years? What is the condition of your physical and mental health? How much money have you spent across the bar or at the crack house? How many more relationships have you lost? How many friends? Maybe you don't even have a relationship anymore, nor any friends. Maybe you're living under a bridge somewhere, alone, in a cardboard box! How many jobs have you been fired from? What is your behavior like now? Maybe your behavior is so bad by now that nobody can stand to be around you. How many goals have you failed to reach? Or are you no longer even capable of setting goals? How much freedom have you lost after ten more years of drinking or drugging? Are you in prison now (or again)? Have you killed somebody during a drug deal gone bad? Are you doing prison time for DWI homicide? Is your self-respect totally gone? How about your belief system, now that you've spent ten more years drinking or drugging? Do you have any positive beliefs left, or has alcohol or other drugs torn them all to shreds? And your sense of purpose—do you wake up in the morning feeling so empty that you can barely generate enough energy to get out of bed? After ten more years of active addiction, do you feel so disconnected from other people that you begin to think you don't even belong to the human race? Count up your losses. Get in touch with the pain. Who knows, maybe you're not even alive anymore. Maybe someone has killed you in self-defense! Or maybe the cops have found your body behind some garbage cans in an alley, dead from an overdose! Finally, what kinds of things do you think people are saying about you behind your back now?

(Pause for at least sixty seconds.)

Part Two

Now use your imagination to come back to the present. You can open your eyes while you rest for a few moments; like Scrooge does in *A Christmas Carol*, take a breather.

Now close your eyes again and prepare for another visit to the future. In your imagination, see yourself five years in the future. But this time there is a big difference. It's five years from now, and you have stopped using alcohol or other drugs to change how you feel. You haven't used chemicals for five whole years! You have learned how to manage your feelings without using alcohol or other drugs. You have stopped using and have learned new ways to respond to old triggers. You have been working a recovery program for five years.

You have been alcohol- and drug-free for five years. Get in touch with the benefits! What is your life like now? What is the condition of your physical and emotional health now that you've been clean and sober for five years in a row? What about your finances? How much money have you been able to save now that you've stopped spending it on alcohol or other drugs? How about your relationships? Do you now have a loving and supportive relationship in your life? More true friends? Has your employment situation changed for the better after five years of clean and sober living? Chances are it has. Maybe you've landed the job of your dreams. How is your behavior different, and how has it impacted your self-respect? Are you feeling good about yourself now, maybe for the first time in your life? Consider how your educational pursuits have benefited from five years of ongoing sobriety. Maybe you've obtained your GED and have enrolled in college. Maybe you've gone back and finished your degree. Because you have been drug-free for five years, what goals have you set and reached? What have you been able to accomplish? What effect has five years of sobriety had on your values, for example, your freedom? By now you have let go of the negative beliefs that kept you stuck in addiction for so long, and you have replaced them with positive beliefs that continue to support your recovery. Your worldview has changed, and now you feel better about things. Because you've been working a recovery program for five years, now you have a sense of purpose and a transcendental orientation that supports you when nothing else can. Now you greet each day with a positive attitude, and you know that you are moving toward a future that holds good things for you. After five years of clean and sober living, what do you think people are saying about you behind your back?

(Pause for thirty seconds or so.)

Now go five more years into the future. You've been clean and sober for a total of ten years. Get in touch with the benefits you know you will receive after ten whole years of sobriety! After ten more years, imagine how good your physical and emotional health could be. How much better off will you be financially? How much improvement will you see in your relationships and friendships? Your employment situation could be almost too good to be true! Your behavior may have changed so much for the better that people look at you with astonishment and with a degree of respect that sends your feelings of self-respect to their highest level ever. Because you've been clean and sober for ten years, you have been able to accomplish most of the goals you've set and are working happily toward more goals. You no longer fear for your freedom; your sense of mission and purpose has grown even stronger and more meaningful; and you start and end each day feeling connected in a positive way, at peace with the world.

(Pause for sixty seconds.)

Now allow yourself to drift back slowly to the present and become aware of your surroundings. You have considered all the possibilities. You have seen two different futures. Like Ebenezer Scrooge, you have seen what your life will be like in the future if you fail to completely change in the present. You have seen how much worse your life will be, inevitably, if you continue to use alcohol or other drugs to change how you feel. You have also seen how things *could* be. You have seen how much better your life will be, inevitably, if you stop using alcohol or other drugs once and for all and diligently work a recovery program that will lead to a healing from your addiction.

And now, like Scrooge, you must make a choice. You must choose your future, and you must choose now because time has run out. You don't have any more time! Which future will you choose?

Now sit quietly and allow your mind and body to thoroughly process what you have just done. Allow your mind to process the thoughts and memories; allow your body to process the feelings attached to the thoughts and memories. Spend at least five minutes processing.

You may want to read the above script more than once. Read it any time you notice a decrease in your motivation to continue working your recovery program.

◆ **EXERCISE** How did you feel after you finished reading or listening to Part One of the motivation script?

_____

_____

_____

_____

◆ **EXERCISE** How did you feel after finishing Part Two of the motivation script?

_____

_____

_____

_____

◆ **EXERCISE** What was the choice you made at the end of Part Two?

_____

_____

◆ **EXERCISE** What do you think about that choice now?

_____

_____

◆ **EXERCISE** Go back and read the script again. You can just read it to yourself this time. The script asks you to remember some of the thing you lost because of your addiction. Write down the first thing that you lost.

_____

_____

◆ **EXERCISE** Write down some of the other things you lost.

_____

_____

_____

_____

◆ **EXERCISE** People in *A Christmas Carol* say negative things about Scrooge behind his back. Write down what you think people were saying about you behind your back.

_____

_____

_____

_____

◆ **EXERCISE** Write down what you think you will lose in the future if you do not recover from your addiction.

_____

_____

_____

_____

◆ **EXERCISE** You are now working a recovery program. You are learning how to manage your emotions without the use of alcohol or other drugs. Write down how you think you will benefit if you continue your recovery.

_____

_____

_____

_____

_____

◆ **EXERCISE** Write down some of the things you would like people to say about you.

_____

_____

_____

_____

_____

9

Relapse Prevention

Way back in Chapter 1 I stated, "Once you start on the road to recovery, from then on the name of the game is relapse prevention." That means all the skills and techniques presented in this book—not just the ones in this chapter—are designed to help you prevent a relapse. However, this chapter is titled "Relapse Prevention" to help you focus on and understand a very important relapse-prevention concept.

∾ Understanding the Relapse Process Using the Niagara Falls Metaphor ∾

What Is a Metaphor?

A metaphor is a comparison that involves figurative language. This workbook compares the relapse process to being in a boat on the Niagara River, just above the Niagara Falls. *The Pathways to Peace Anger Management Workbook* uses the same metaphor to help people understand the anger process.

The whole world knows about the Niagara River and the Niagara Falls. People from all over the world have visited the falls. If you haven't visited the falls, you have probably seen movies about it or seen it on television. One of the Seven Wonders of the World, the mighty Niagara River and Niagara Falls are among the earth's most powerful natural phenomena.

The volume of water that pours over the falls stretches the imagination. It pours over the falls at the rate of 203,000 gallons per second! But just a few miles upstream from the falls the river moves slowly, almost lazily, along. People fish from boats in that part of the river. You can't see or hear the falls from there. If you were fishing from a boat in that part of the Niagara River, you would feel safe. Your boat would be equipped with an engine and a pair of oars, so you would have some control over your boat.

But if your engine failed and you lost your oars overboard, you would no longer have control over your boat. You would find yourself at the mercy of the current, and the current would carry you rapidly toward the falls at an ever-increasing rate of speed. Naturally, the Niagara River moves faster and faster the closer it gets to the falls, and the power and energy of the river increases.

If you yelled for help at that point, someone might hear you and respond; you could be saved from going over the falls. Another boat could reach you and tow you and your boat to shore, or a helicopter could drop a line and pluck you out of the river.

But a hundred yards or so from the brink of the falls, the river becomes a rushing torrent. If you weren't saved before you got to that point, all would be lost. No one could overcome the power of the river to rescue you. In order to avoid injury or death you would have to find a way to get out of the river before reaching that point. It's no wonder that part of the Niagara River is called the "point of no return."

People who fish in the Niagara River come prepared. Few people lose control and plunge to their death. Accidents happen sometimes, but they are rare. Of course, a few people have actually chosen to take the plunge over the falls on purpose for glory and fame. They've used all kinds of methods for going over the falls, including wrapping themselves in rubber tires. But it is a 160-foot plunge to the bottom of the gorge. Hitting water from that height is like diving from the top of an eight-story building onto concrete. In addition, the bottom of the gorge is littered with boulders, so you can count on the fingers of one hand the number of people who have survived a plunge over the falls. A few people have even used the falls to commit suicide.

◆ **EXERCISE** What is a metaphor?

_____

_____

_____

◆ **EXERCISE** What other interesting things do you know about the Niagara River and Niagara Falls?

_____

_____

_____

_____

_____

_____

_____

THE NIAGARA FALLS METAPHOR

The Relapse Process

3 SECONDS   EUPHORIC RECALL   CRAVING   3 MONTHS

FINAL WARNING

COMPULSION

CONSEQUENCES

10% Conscious

90% Subconscious

CUES

Whatever
you see, hear,
smell, taste,
or feel

TRIGGERS

- Anxiety/Fear
- Depression
- Rejection
- Embarrassment
- Craving

CHOICES (ANCHORS)

- Exercise
- Call Someone
- Change Physiology
- Change Mental Focus
- Pray/Meditate
- Fire Aversion Stimulus

NORMAL BASELINE TENSION

The Relapse Process and the Niagara Falls Metaphor

According to the Niagara Falls metaphor, the relapse process is like finding yourself in a small boat in the Niagara River, somewhere upstream from the falls, except that your boat is without engine and oars. That means you and your boat are at the mercy of the current. In this comparison of the relapse process to being in a boat on the Niagara River, picking up a drink or a drug equals plunging over the falls. If you plunge over the falls by picking up a drink or a drug, there will be consequences. You will lose something you value. You will lose your job or your relationship or your freedom, or you will lose another chunk of your self-respect.

Because of the unconscious nature of the relapse process, you are not at first aware that you are in the river. It's scary to think that might be the case, but it is true. You have used alcohol or other drugs over and over for long enough to have developed an addiction. When you have an addiction, you are often unaware of the behavior connected with your addiction. You are unaware when you are in the part of the addiction process called *relapse*. In this chapter you will learn how to be aware when you are in the relapse process. In the next chapter you will learn how to stop the process and get out of the river.

◆ **EXERCISE** How is the relapse process like being in the Niagara River?

_____

_____

_____

◆ **EXERCISE** Part of the metaphor talks about "going over the falls." What does it mean to "go over the falls"?

_____

_____

_____

∾ The Five Stages of the Relapse Process ∾

STAGE 1 | *Cues and Triggers (Feelings)—Plunging into the River*

Cues can be people, places, and things. Cues are things you can see or hear. Seeing someone you have used drugs with could be a cue. The sound of someone opening a beer could be a cue. Some cues are things you remember. The memory of the dope dealer's face could be a cue. The memory of the voice of someone you talked with at the bar could be a cue, and so could a memory of the words they said. Sometimes you can avoid cues, but most of the time you have little control over when, where, and how cues happen. Cues are the stuff of life; they just happen, and they are often beyond your control. The good news is that you can learn how to control memory cues and you can learn how to deal with the cues you cannot avoid. The key word is learn.

Cues connect to and evoke feelings that are either painful or pleasurable. Painful feelings are negative; pleasurable feelings are positive. Whether a cue leads to a painful feeling or a pleasurable one depends on how you think about the cue. If you think of the cue as painful, it will cause a painful feeling. If you think of the cue as pleasurable, it will cause a pleasurable feeling. *Any feeling, whether painful or pleasurable, that causes you to want to use your drug of choice is a relapse trigger.*

Relapse triggers are not always painful feelings, but painful feelings like fear or frustration are typical relapse triggers, because they increase your tension level. (You have tension in your body all the time because you are alive. It is called *baseline tension*. Baseline tension is normal tension.) But pleasurable feelings like excitement or joy might also be relapse triggers, if you use alcohol or other drugs to increase the pleasure these feelings bring. Cues are happening in the environment all the time. When a cue leads to a feeling that you associate with your drug of choice, then it is a relapse trigger. The relapse trigger increases your tension level, causing it to shoot up above normal. The increased tension is what plunges you into the relapse process. To use the metaphor, it is what causes you to end up in the Niagara River in a small boat without engine or oars.

As soon as you become aware of a trigger, stop and think: "I have only three seconds to get out of the river before my boat reaches the falls!" If you assume you have only three seconds to get out of the relapse process, you may have a chance to interrupt the process before it's too late—before you reach the point of no return and plunge over the falls.

One of the keys to recovery from an addiction is to learn how to manage the feelings that trigger the relapse process. Another key is to learn how to deal with the cues that cause the feelings. In the next chapter, you will learn some techniques and skills that will help you deal with cues that cause relapse feelings.

◆ **EXERCISE** Name three people, places, and things that you think are cues that lead to your relapse triggers.

_____

_____

_____

_____

_____

_____

◆ **EXERCISE** Name the trigger (feeling) that each cue connects to or evokes.

_____

_____

_____

_____

_____

◆ **EXERCISE** What is the difference between a cue and a trigger? Give two examples of each.

_____

_____

_____

_____

STAGE 2 | *Euphoric Recall (First Red Flag)*

Euphoric means pleasurable; *recall* means to remember. Euphoric recall is a memory of a time when you used alcohol or other drugs and it made you feel good; it made you feel high and you didn't suffer negative consequences. You didn't go to jail; you didn't get hurt or hurt someone you loved. You didn't end up suffering some kind of punishment. Instead, you felt rewarded. You experienced euphoria (you got high). Euphoric recall is a natural part of the typical relapse process.

You were already in the Niagara River before euphoric recall happened. Your tension level had increased to a high level. *Your increased tension causes euphoric recall.* Your tension level automatically increases when you don't do something right away to interrupt a relapse trigger.

You have no control over euphoric recall; it happens automatically. Euphoric recall causes you to move faster toward the falls. When you experience euphoric recall, you begin to anticipate the pleasure you would feel if you were to pick up a drink or some other drug. The relapse process acts much like the Niagara River. The closer the Niagara River gets to the falls, the more the power and speed of the river increases. During euphoric recall, your brain remembers a time when you used alcohol or other drugs and experienced pleasurable results; you felt drunk or high and avoided negative results. The anticipation of pleasure, along with the increased tension, increases your desire to drink or use other drugs. It pushes you faster and faster toward the point of no return.

You must learn to see euphoric recall as a big red warning flag. As a warning flag, euphoric recall pops up out of the river and loudly says, "You fool! You are in the Niagara River, heading for the falls!"

◆ **EXERCISE** What does *euphoric recall* mean?

_____

_____

◆ **EXERCISE** Why is euphoric recall called a "red flag"?

_____

_____

STAGE 3 | *Craving (Final Warning Flag)*

A craving is an intense, urgent desire or longing. In this case, a craving is a strong urge to use your drug of choice.

Like the flow of the Niagara River, relapse is a process that never stops and never slows down. What happens to the Niagara River the closer it gets to the falls? You have already learned the answer to this question. The power and speed of the river increases. The relapse process doesn't stop or slow down either. Once you're in the relapse process, unless you take steps to get out of it, your tension keeps increasing, just like the river's speed. You move faster and closer to the act of using your drug of choice. You must do something to interrupt the process.

When you have a craving to use your drug of choice, you are close—very close—to the falls. Just as the river has picked up speed, your tension level has increased. *The increase in your tension level causes the craving.*

It is much harder to fight off the craving than it is to interrupt the process before the craving kicks in; that is why it is so important to get out of the river as soon as possible. The closer you get to the falls, the harder it is to get out.

A craving is a bigger, brighter red flag than one caused by euphoric recall. It says, "You fool! Not only are you in the Niagara River heading for the falls, you are right at the brink! You are in white water!" This is the final warning flag!

During the craving stage, it is as though two different people are inside your head yelling at each other. You may not be aware of them, but they are there. One voice urges you to go to the liquor store or bar and slam down some alcohol, or to the dope man's house to score and use crack or heroin or Ecstasy. It says, "Do it!" That voice takes you into deep denial; it wants you to justify and rationalize. That voice doesn't want you to remember the consequences you experienced when you used alcohol or other drugs in the past. It wants you to forget about that and think only of the pleasure you might experience if you drink or use. The other voice urges you *not* to drink or use some other drug. It says, "No. Don't!" That voice wants you to avoid relapse. It wants you to stop and think. It wants you to remember the consequences you suffered in the past. That voice wants you to remember the guilt and remorse you felt because of the pain you caused others. You struggle, trying to decide which voice to listen to. But when you experience a craving to use alcohol or other drugs, it means your tension level has risen extremely high. You will have to make a decision very quickly, because you are close to the point of no return. You must not give in to the first voice; if you listen to the first voice, you lose.

◆ **EXERCISE** Stage Three of the relapse process involves what is called a *craving*. What does the word *craving* mean?

_____

_____

◆ **EXERCISE** How is a "craving" different from "euphoric recall"?

_____

_____

_____

_____

◆ **EXERCISE** Why is a craving called the "final warning flag"? Where are you in the river when a craving happens?

_____

_____

_____

_____

STAGE 4 | *Compulsion*

Up to this point you have had a choice, although you may not have been aware of it. You have had opportunities to stop yourself from going over the falls. You had opportunities to interrupt the process because although you may not have paid too much attention, you were aware you were in the river and you had two strong warnings that danger lay ahead.

But there is a big difference between a *craving* and a *compulsion*. When you felt a craving, had you been aware of the relapse process, you would have known you were in the river and could have chosen to take some actions to help yourself get out of it.

> *When you feel a compulsion to do anything,*
> *whatever it may be, you no longer have a choice.*

When you have a compulsion to use alcohol or other drugs, you no longer have a choice. You have no choice because you are no longer aware you are in the river. When you feel a compulsion, it means you can't stop. That's the definition of *compulsion*. A compulsion is an irresistible impulse to do something, in this case, something irrational. It means you are already over the falls. It means your tension has increased beyond the point of no return and you have lost control. When you feel a compulsion to use chemicals to change how you feel—either to change a painful feeling to a pleasurable feeling or to increase the intensity of a pleasurable feeling—you no longer have control. The relapse process has taken control of you.

Here is another way to understand a compulsion. The mind is like an iceberg. Only about 10 percent of the iceberg—just the tip—shows above the water line. The other 90 percent floats underwater, hidden from view. The 10 percent that rides above the water line can be compared to the conscious mind. The part underwater can likewise be compared to the subconscious mind.

Your addiction is a habit. You have many other habits besides your drug habit, and all of them are stored in your subconscious mind. Habits are automatic behaviors. Your habits stay down in the subconscious mind until something triggers them into action. It is as though they are asleep there. Certain things will wake up habits. Things that wake up habits are called triggers (feelings). Every habit has its own trigger or triggers.

Your subconscious mind watches for triggers. When a trigger connected to a certain habit occurs, the subconscious mind notices it. Then it wakes up the habit that was asleep, and it causes you to go into action—automatically.

That is how it works with your alcohol or drug habit. That is what happens when you feel a compulsion to use your drug of choice. Your tension level increases because you haven't done anything to stop the process. Your tension level continues to increase until finally it reaches the point of no return. That's when you feel a compulsion.

When you feel a compulsion, your conscious mind stops functioning and your subconscious mind takes over. That's when you lose control. You end up going over the falls, unable to stop yourself. Then you crash at the bottom of the gorge and suffer negative consequences.

◆ **EXERCISE** What does it mean to have a compulsion?

_____

_____

◆ **EXERCISE** Why do you no longer have a choice once you reach the compulsion stage?

_____

_____

◆ **EXERCISE** When you reach the compulsion stage, who or what is in control of the addiction process?

_____

_____

STAGE 5 | *Consequences (Negative Results)*

Message from Tommy

I'm Tommy, a recovering heroin addict from Texas.

I've never been to the Niagara Falls, but my uncle went there a few years ago. He brought back some pictures and a videotape. Comparing the relapse process to the Niagara Falls has really helped me understand it. It helps me know when I'm in the relapse process. And it helps me know where I am in the process and what I need to do to get out. I use the Niagara Falls metaphor to help me stay aware of the process.

You suffer consequences when you use alcohol or other drugs to change how your feel. Although consequences are not always negative, in this discussion we consider consequences to be the negative results of your actions. Losing something you value is a negative result. When you go over the falls, you cannot avoid losing something you value. You may get arrested for DWI or for possession of a controlled substance and as a consequence lose your freedom. You may lose a job opportunity, you may lose your spouse, or you may lose your self-respect. You end up feeling bad instead of good. You end up feeling guilty and ashamed, or you end up feeling embarrassed. The point is, you have to suffer the consequences.

The guilt, shame, and embarrassment become triggers, too. These painful feelings keep you stuck in the addiction process; they send you right back into the river. The process becomes a circulating pump. A cue happens. That is, you see or hear or remember something that leads to a relapse feeling. The feeling triggers your addiction; you plunge into the river; you do or say something that hurts someone, or something happens; you go over the falls and crash down into the rocky gorge; you lose something you value; you feel guilty and ashamed; then the guilt and shame circulate you back through the process. Pretty soon you think you must be crazy!

But there is a way out. You can learn how to stop the madness once and for all and get out of the circulating pump. You can change. You can arrest the addiction process. The next chapter will help you learn how.

◆ **EXERCISE** What are consequences?

_____

_____

◆ **EXERCISE** Write down three negative consequences you have had because of your alcohol or other drug use.

_____

_____

_____

◆ **EXERCISE** Describe the "circulating pump" effect of guilt and shame.

_____

_____

_____

◆ **EXERCISE** List the five stages of the relapse process.

_____

_____

_____

10

Interrupting the
Relapse Process

Let's review some things from the last chapter. You learned your addiction by repeating alcohol- or drug-using behavior over and over in response to certain feelings (triggers). You developed a drug habit—an automatic behavior that is now permanently stored in your subconscious mind. Your subconscious mind includes all the habits you have learned, but it also includes your instincts. The instinct to breathe is stored in your subconscious mind. You do not have to learn instincts; you are born with them.

Now that your use of alcohol or other drugs has become an addiction, you have learned to respond automatically by using alcohol or drugs whenever your brain notices one of your triggers. Your subconscious mind has taken over the operation of your addiction, and you have lost control of the process. Now you may find yourself using, or strongly craving to use, alcohol or other drugs even when you have made a conscious decision not to.

But you can learn new ways to respond to the same old triggers. You can decide to make different choices. Then you can learn to repeat the new choices over and over in response to old triggers. Learning new choices and then learning how to repeat the new choices instead of picking up a drink or a drug when triggers occur is the beginning of recovery from your addiction. It is the beginning of the healing process. The new behaviors will eventually grow into a new habit and become automatic. You will acquire a new habit called "recovery from alcohol or other drug addiction"; then your subconscious mind will take over the operation of the healing process.

∾ Will You Ever Forget Your Alcohol or Drug Habit? ∾

Once a behavior becomes a habit, it is impossible for your brain to forget it. Habits are stored in brain cells—permanently. Therefore, you will never forget your alcohol or drug habit. You will never forget how to use alcohol or other drugs to change how you feel.

Consider the skills necessary for driving a car. Your driving skills are a habit that is stored in your subconscious mind. Will you ever forget how to drive a car? No. You will never forget how to drive a car, and you will never forget how to use alcohol or other drugs to change how you feel.

(**Note:** There is one method that would cause you to forget your alcohol or drug habit, but using it would be a very drastic measure. Here's the method: go to a brain surgeon and ask him or her to use a scalpel to remove the tissue in the part of your brain where your alcohol or drug habit is stored. That is the only way you can forget any habit.)

You are a human being. You will probably find yourself in the addiction process or the relapse process from time to time, no matter how hard you try to avoid it. But you can learn how to get out of the process; you can learn how to get out of the river before you go over the falls. If you choose to stay in the process, even though you now know how it works, then your tension will continue to increase. Finally, your old alcohol or drug habit will take control again. You will feel a compulsion, and your alcohol or drug habit will escape from your subconscious mind like a raging beast from its cage. You will plunge over the falls again, because you will no longer have a choice.

> ## Message from David
>
> **My name is David. I'm from New York.**
>
> I was working a good recovery program. I learned some new skills, and I was handling triggers better than ever. I hadn't drunk or used any other drug in three months. Then I stopped focusing on my program so much. I stopped doing some of the things that I had learned. I wish I hadn't gotten so complacent. I started to think I had it made, that I didn't have to think about my recovery anymore. I forgot that I had an addiction. About two weeks later I suffered a disappointment. I lost out on a job I was sure I'd get. Man, I needed that job! Disappointment is one of my major triggers. I plunged into the river, and before I knew it I was too far downstream. I went to one of the gin joints where I used to hang out. You can guess the rest. I found out I hadn't forgotten how to use alcohol to change how I feel.

◆ **EXERCISE** Why will you never be able to "forget" your alcohol or drug habit?

_____

_____

_____

_____

ᘒ Three Steps to Interrupt the Relapse Process ᘒ

STEP 1 | *Check Your Body*

You are not aware when your alcohol or drug habit gets triggered during the first stage of the relapse process. A trigger occurs, and you don't notice it. That is because your subconscious mind operates your addiction. Your subconscious mind notices the trigger, but it doesn't let your conscious mind know. So *you* remain unaware of the trigger.

Remember: The relapse process is like the Niagara River and Niagara Falls. If you are unaware you are in the river, you will be unable to get out in time. You will go over the falls. You must learn to be aware when you are in the river as soon as a trigger occurs. The trigger is the first step of your alcohol or drug habit; the trigger is what plunges you into the river. So the first step to getting out of the river is to have a way of knowing you are in it.

As mentioned earlier, at this point you already have a certain level of tension in your body. This normal level of tension is called *baseline tension*. When a trigger to use alcohol or other drugs occurs, your tension level suddenly increases. It shoots up above normal; it spikes. You have no control over the increased tension. It is like what happens when you sit down and cross your legs and tap that certain spot just below your kneecap. When you tap that spot, your lower leg automatically jumps. It is sometimes called the "knee-jerk" response. It is a reflex. When a trigger to use your drug of choice occurs, your tension level responds in a similar way. It jumps higher.

Your body will know immediately when a trigger occurs. It will immediately send you the message that your tension level has increased. You must learn to get in touch with how your body sends you the message. Your tension will increase more in a certain body area than in another, but that is an individual thing. That is, different people feel the increased tension in different body areas. First, you must find out *where* you feel the increased tension in your body; next you must learn to notice *when* the tension level in that body area increases. Then you will have a handy way of knowing when you are in the relapse process. The trigger causing the increased tension could be fear or frustration; it could be anxiety or disappointment. The trigger could be any one of a thousand feelings, but you don't have to know exactly *what* the trigger is. You don't have to name the feeling. All you have to know is that your tension level has increased.

Step one to interrupting the relapse process, then, is to check your body. Check to find out where your body feels increased tension; then you will know when you are in the relapse process. The exercise below will help you find out where you feel increased tension in your body.

◆ **EXERCISE**

A. Think of a time when you felt a strong desire to use alcohol or other drugs.

B. As you recall the strong desire, pay attention to your body tension.

C. Notice exactly where your body feels the most tension. Now complete the following sentence:

When a trigger happens, I feel a sudden increase in tension in my (circle the body area that applies to you): stomach, lower back, back of the neck, jaws, behind my eyes, other (write down the area) _____.

Now you know what body area you feel increased tension in when a trigger happens. Now you have a way of knowing when you are in the river. Practice paying attention to that area of your body. You must learn to notice your triggers as soon as possible, so you will have the best possible chance of getting out of the river. If you fail to notice the triggers right away, your risk increases. If you fail to notice the triggers until you feel a compulsion, it will be too late; by then you will already be over the falls.

STEP 2 | *List Your Triggers, Choices, and Consequences; and List the Benefits of Staying Clean and Sober*

Step one to interrupting the relapse process is to find a way to know you are in the process. You've learned to get in touch with how your body tells you when your tension increases. Now you must learn how to be aware of the entire addiction process. You must learn how to be aware of what your triggers are, how to be aware of your choices, and how to be aware of the potential consequences of your actions (what you will lose if you go over Niagara Falls again). You must also learn to be aware of the benefits of recovering from your addiction. Until you have learned how to maintain awareness of the process, your addiction will continue to control you and run your life. You must take back control.

In step two, you will identify and list your triggers, choices, and consequences as well as the benefits of finding other ways to respond to your triggers. A blank chart has been provided on page 130 so you can complete this task. As you read the rest of this section, write down your lists on that page.

Important: After you have made your lists, make three copies of the full chart. Carry one copy in your wallet or purse. Tape a copy to the wall next to the bathroom mirror. Keep a copy where you read or watch television. Look at the lists every day. Looking at them will help you stay conscious of how your addiction works and of how you will profit by stopping the use of alcohol and other drugs and by finding new ways to respond to triggers. What will happen if you simply make the list and never refer to it again? The answer is obvious: Once again you will forget how your alcohol or drug habit works. Your addiction will drop back down into the murky bottom layers of your subconscious mind; it will take charge of your life again. You will continue to lose things you value.

◆ Triggers

You have learned that triggers are always feelings, like those listed below. You know that it is your triggers that put the addiction process in motion. Ask yourself: "What are the feelings that act as triggers for my alcohol or drug habit?"

Examples of triggers:

- embarrassment
- anxiety
- frustration
- excitement
- disappointment

Each of these feelings is a common trigger to use alcohol or other drugs. Very likely one or more of them apply to you. But there are probably many others that apply to you and that are not listed among the examples above. Make sure you list all of your major triggers. Use the blank chart on page 130.

◆ Choices

"Choices" here means things you could do instead of responding to triggers in the same old way, by picking up a drink or a drug. Below is a brief list of possible choices. Whatever choices you choose to put on your list must be your choices, not someone else's choices. The choices you list must be things you would actually do. In addition, you need a lot of choices. You need choices that will work anytime, anywhere. You need choices that will work at 2:00 in the afternoon when you are at work. You need choices that will work at 2:00 in the morning when you are at home and can't sleep. You need choices that will work no matter when you are in the river and no matter where you are in the river. You may be way upstream, where the river runs slowly, or way downstream, where the river runs faster, closer to the point of no return.

When you list your choices, ask yourself: "What could I do instead of going over the falls when a trigger occurs?"

Examples of choices:

- call someone on the phone
- pray
- exercise
- meditate

Later in the workbook you will learn other new choices. Be sure to add them to your list.

◆ Consequences

"Going over the falls" here means picking up a drink or a drug. When you go over the falls, you suffer consequences. You lose something you value. No one goes over Niagara Falls without suffering consequences. The list below is just to get you started. When you make your list, get in touch with how you will feel if you suffer the losses on your list.

What do you think you might lose if you relapse back into active alcohol or drug use and go over Niagara Falls again? Will you end up in prison this time, because you killed someone in a fit of alcoholic rage? Or because you got busted for selling drugs? Will you lose that one human being who cares anything about you? What will you lose? To get started, ask yourself this question: "What will I lose if I go over the Niagara Falls again?" Pay attention to how the losses make you feel.

Examples of consequences:

- loss of spouse
- loss of freedom
- loss of job
- loss of self-respect

◆ Benefits of Staying Clean and Sober

It is hard to change any behavior that has become a habit. You have learned you have an alcohol or drug habit. Knowing what you will lose if you don't stop using your drug of choice, and if you don't stay stopped, is important. But knowing how you will benefit if you stay clean and sober is also important. If you cannot see a benefit, it will be harder to stop using alcohol or other drugs and harder to stay stopped. To "benefit" means good things will happen for you. Ask yourself: "How will I benefit by stopping my use of alcohol or other drugs?"

Examples of benefits:

- more trust in relationships
- greater peace of mind
- maybe get a better job
- increased personal freedom
- able to keep a job
- better health
- longer life

Making this list is an important part of your recovery from your addiction. It is an important part of the healing process. Take your time when making your list.

STEP 3 | *Exercise Your New Choices*

Here's another important part of the metaphor. Each new choice is like an anchor in the bottom of your boat. Each anchor has a different length of rope attached. When a trigger occurs, you must throw an anchor toward shore and hold on to the end of the rope. The anchor must sink into the earth on the other side of the river; then *you* must pull yourself out of the river. Notice the key word: *YOU.*

Your new program will seem strange and uncomfortable to you at first. You may find that some of your new choices do not work as well as you thought they would. If so, it is okay to change them or add new ones. The same is true of triggers, consequences, and benefits. Change and add to your list when you need to. Your recovery program, like you, is a work in progress! The secret to your success is to keep working on it.

Any program of recovery from alcohol or drug addiction must be self-initiated and self-maintained. That means you have to be the one in charge. It means you have to be the one who decides and the one who acts. That is how recovery works.

Although you must not rely on someone else to save you, at the same time it is extremely important to reach out for help. In fact, you should ask for help wherever and whenever possible. Attending Pathways to Sobriety meetings can provide the kind of help you need (you will learn more about meetings later in the workbook). Attending twelve-step meetings such as AA or NA can help. Talking with a counselor can help. Yet you must be in charge of your own recovery; you must take charge of the process. You are the one who is responsible for your healing; you run the show.

> ### *Message from Bill*
>
> **I was not good at organizing. But I knew I needed a way to understand my addiction to alcohol and other drugs.** So I had to find a way to organize my thinking about it. Also, I had to have a way to maintain awareness of how my addiction worked. I had to get things down in writing so I could look at them. Then I had to go into action. That's why I developed the Niagara Falls metaphor.

◆ **EXERCISE** Step three to interrupting the addiction process is the action step. What does it tell you to do?

_____

How Your Addiction Works, and How You Will Benefit
from Staying Clean and Sober

TRIGGERS	CHOICES	CONSEQUENCES	BENEFITS

PART THREE

Changing Your Behavior

11

Basic Considerations

In this chapter you will learn how important it is to pay attention to the basics. You will learn about how nutrition, exercise, and sleep habits affect recovery from addiction to alcohol and other drugs. You will learn how maintaining a schedule can help you stay on the road to recovery. You will learn about the importance of relaxation, and you will be given an opportunity to learn a method of relaxation to help you deal with stress.

◈ Nutrition ◈

How you take care of your body has a great deal to do with how you feel. Nutrition has a direct effect on the biological (physical) part of recovery from addiction to alcohol or other drugs.

Poor nutrition has a negative effect on your ability to manage feelings that could lead to relapse back into active alcohol or drug use. A diet high in sugar, for example, can lead to mood swings that may intensify triggers. You need a well-balanced diet that is low in sugar. You need plenty of protein. Ideally, you should eat a variety of foods, including plenty of fresh fruits and vegetables. Try new fruits and vegetables; they add texture, color, taste, and interest. They also add vitamins and make eating and preparing food more fun.

Use of caffeine increases your body's tension level and makes it harder to control your emotions and avoid relapse. Caffeine can also increase anxiety. Increased anxiety leads to an increase in tension level. If anxiety is one of your relapse triggers, use of caffeine could lead to a craving to use alcohol or some other drug in order to bring your tension level down.

You need to have regular meals. Going long periods without eating a regular meal (more than five to six hours) makes you more sensitive to your addiction triggers.

◆ **EXERCISE** Pay attention to your diet over a week. Is your diet well balanced, with plenty of protein, vegetables, and fruit?

_____

_____

◆ **EXERCISE** Are you limiting your intake of sugar and caffeine?

ᵔᵔᵔ Sleep and Rest ᵔᵔᵔ

It is normal to have sleep problems when you first stop using alcohol or other drugs. You may find yourself waking up after only a couple of hours and being unable to get back to sleep. You may also find yourself having vivid dreams, even scary dreams. This is a sign that your body and brain may be trying to make up for loss of R.E.M. sleep. R.E.M. stands for *rapid eye movement*. R.E.M. sleep occurs about every ninety minutes throughout the night, when you are dreaming. Experts believe that the brain needs a certain amount of R.E.M. sleep. Certain drugs, including alcohol, act to repress R.E.M. sleep, so you may have gone long periods without the benefit of this important part of the sleep cycle. Give your body and brain up to three months to adjust to being drug free and to return to a normal pattern of sleep.

Anything that increases your tension level could threaten your sobriety. Inadequate sleep or rest leads to increased tension. You would need adequate sleep and rest even if you didn't have an addiction to alcohol or other drugs. As a person with an addiction problem, however, you need to pay close attention to how much sleep and rest you get. Inadequate sleep and rest will intensify all your triggers.

Establish regular bedtimes and regular wake-up times. Avoid sleeping during the day as a way to deal with boredom; doing so will make it harder to get the solid nighttime sleep your body needs. Once you have established good sleep patterns, you will feel more rested, and you will be less likely to feel triggered to use alcohol or other drugs.

◆ **EXERCISE** Do you get adequate sleep and rest? How do you feel when you get up in the morning? Do you feel rested? Or do you feel you need more sleep?

ᵔᵔᵔ Physical Exercise ᵔᵔᵔ

Any activity that helps you feel better about yourself helps you to maintain a clean and sober lifestyle. Exercise is an activity that serves this purpose. Regular exercise releases "feel-good" chemicals from your brain that are called *endorphins*. These feel-good chemicals have a positive effect on your self-esteem. Regular exercise also gives you a sense of accomplishment.

You should exercise regularly, but you should avoid overexercising. There are many kinds of exercise. You can pump iron, you can walk or jog, or you can enroll in an aerobic-dance or yoga class. If you are in early recovery and have a sleep problem, moderate exercise early in the evening will help you sleep.

Note: Check with your doctor before starting any exercise program.

◆ **EXERCISE** List three kinds of exercise you would enjoy.

_____

_____

_____

◆ **EXERCISE** How will you get one of these exercise programs going? When will you start?

_____

_____

∾ Relaxation ∾

Relaxation is another important basic consideration. You need to know how to relax in order to deal effectively with stress. For most recovering alcoholics or drug addicts stress is a major trigger. In the past you probably used alcohol or other drugs to deal with stress. Alcohol and certain other drugs tend to have a relaxing effect. Now you must learn how to relax without using alcohol or other drugs. The relaxation method described below will help you manage stress. It is an easy technique. You can learn it quickly, and you can benefit from it immediately. If you have trouble sleeping, try this relaxation method before going to bed.

Message from Ron

My name is Ron. I'm an alcoholic from Minneapolis.

I never paid attention to what I ate. Sometimes I ate right, most of the time I didn't. It seemed like I never got enough sleep, maybe three or four hours a night. I rarely exercised, and when I did I usually overdid it. The only way I knew how to relax was to get drunk or stoned. At first the alcohol and pot helped me to relax. But later, as my addiction got worse, alcohol and pot stopped helping me relax. Sometimes, in fact, booze and pot hyped me up more than they helped me relax. It drove me crazy!

Then I stopped using alcohol and pot. I had to. But then I didn't have a way to relax anymore. I almost relapsed a couple of times. Finally, I learned how important it was to pay attention to my body. I became aware of how my eating habits and lack of exercise affected my mood. I read a book on nutrition and got started on a sensible exercise program. I stopped drinking coffee before going to bed. I exercised moderately. My mood improved and I slept better.

I saw how stress (frustration, anxiety, etc.) triggered my addiction, so I knew I had to learn how to relax. Also, I learned a relaxation method. After a couple of weeks I was able to relax more than I had ever been able to relax in the past. That also helped me sleep better. Making these changes made it easier to deal with relapse triggers.

A Relaxation Method to Help You Manage Stress

You will need a quiet place where you can sit alone and undisturbed for ten to twenty minutes. Sitting in a comfortable chair with your feet on the floor will probably work best.

The best time of the day to relax is whatever time of day or night suits you. Most people find early morning or late evening to be the best time to use this method.

You are encouraged to record on an audiotape the steps outlined below. Then you can sit back, relax, and listen to the instructions without worrying about leaving something out.

Relaxation is a learned process, a step-by-step procedure like driving a car or brushing your teeth. Go to your place of relaxation, and assume the position you've decided to use when you relax. Turn the lights down. You may want to light a candle. Here are the steps.

1. Start by breathing slowly and deeply, and continue to breathe that way.

2. Relax your posture.

3. With your eyes open, and continuing to breathe deeply and slowly, make three statements (silently, not aloud) about what you see. For example, "I see the room bathed in candlelight; I see a chair over in the corner; I see shadows dancing on the wall in the candlelight." Say the words on the out breath.

   At the end of the third statement, add, "And now I'm beginning to feel relaxed and calm." Now close your eyes and go to step four.

4. With your eyes closed, and continuing to breathe deeply and slowly, make three statements about what you hear, saying the words on the out breath as before. For example, say, "I hear the sound of a dog barking in the distance; I hear the sound of water running in the kitchen; I hear the rhythmic sound of my own heartbeat; and now I'm beginning to feel more relaxed and calm."

   Switching from what you see to what you hear allows your conscious mind to let go of visual images so that it can concentrate on sounds.

5. Continuing the same breathing pattern, and with your eyes shut, make three statements about what you feel externally, saying the words as you breathe out. For example, "I feel the pressure of my feet against the floor; I feel the pressure of my back against the chair; I feel the rise and fall of my chest as I breathe in and out; and now I feel calm and relaxed."

   This step allows your mind to let go of auditory input (what you hear) so that it can focus on what you feel.

By now, you will have begun to relax. This method works by causing the mind to let go of the normal conscious state in a step-by-step fashion. One by one your senses (sight, hearing, and touch) disengage. Your heart rate slows down. Your blood pressure decreases. Your body becomes relaxed. Your mind shifts its focus to the inside of your body.

With practice you will be able to relax quickly using this method. Practice this relaxation method at least once a day. Twice a day would be even better.

You could take a relaxation-training class. Such classes are usually inexpensive. A class may help you learn to relax more quickly. Consult the yellow pages. Find out if there is an affordable relaxation class in your area.

◆ **EXERCISE** How did you feel after you tried the relaxation method described above?

_____

_____

_____

_____

_____

❧ Maintaining a Schedule ❧

In order to maintain an effective recovery program, you must maintain a schedule. You must schedule time for growth and development at each recovery level. You need to schedule time for all of the basics. You must schedule mealtimes, so that you do not skip meals or eat poor meals on the run. You must schedule time for exercise, and you must schedule time for rest and relaxation. You must schedule time for sleep.

Here is an example of a schedule format that covers the basic considerations.

Daily Schedule

	Breakfast	Lunch	Dinner	Exercise	Relaxation	Sleep
Time	7:00 A.M.	12:30 P.M.	6:00 P.M.	7:00 P.M.	10:00 P.M.	11:00 P.M.
Day	Daily	Daily	Daily	M, W, F	Daily	Daily

◆ **EXERCISE** Make a daily schedule that covers all four basic considerations (meals, exercise, relaxation, sleep). Use the form provided on the following page.

Note: Build a little flexibility into your schedule; cut yourself some slack. There will be times when you can't stick to your schedule. Just do your best. Also, since schedules often need to be modfied due to life changes, you should feel free to write revised schedules in the extra blanks provided on the next page.

	Breakfast	Lunch	Dinner	Exercise	Relaxation	Sleep
Time						
Day						

	Breakfast	Lunch	Dinner	Exercise	Relaxation	Sleep
Time						
Day						

	Breakfast	Lunch	Dinner	Exercise	Relaxation	Sleep
Time						
Day						

	Breakfast	Lunch	Dinner	Exercise	Relaxation	Sleep
Time						
Day						

	Breakfast	Lunch	Dinner	Exercise	Relaxation	Sleep
Time						
Day						

12

Skills

Recall from Chapter 10 how the Niagara Falls metaphor allows you to compare the new choices you must make in your life to the anchors in your boat that you can throw onshore if a trigger occurs that causes you to plunge into the river. This chapter teaches you some new way to help you stay sober. Learning these techniques means having more choices, or more anchors in your boat.

Let me start by sharing a very important concept with you—a concept so important that it forms the basis for the entire chapter:

What you think about most of the time
causes how you feel most of the time.

If you think positive thoughts most of the time you will feel good most of the time, and if you think negative thoughts most of the time you will feel bad most of the time. Thinking negative thoughts keeps you stuck in the addiction process or the relapse process (stuck in the river), because negative thoughts lead to painful feelings, and painful feelings are triggers because they increase your tension level. Thinking about how much pleasure you once got out of using alcohol or other drugs can also cause feelings that turn into triggers. Thinking about old alcohol or drug experiences that were pleasurable will cause you to feel a craving to pick up a drink or a drug, and a craving is the strongest possible trigger.

In this chapter, you will learn some ways to deal with negative thoughts that keep you stuck in addiction. You will learn how to think positive thoughts that make you feel self-empowered.

❧ Maintain a Positive Mental Attitude ❧

What you focus on mentally is what you are thinking about at any given time. You have certain mental images in your mind and listen to certain mental sounds. That is what thinking means. Thinking can be like replaying old videos and old tapes. These videos and tapes are recordings of your life experiences. You likely think in images and sounds. Most of the time you are unaware of what you are replaying in your mind, but you can learn to become aware of these things. What kind of videos and tapes do you replay in your mind most of the time?

As a person with an addiction to alcohol or other drugs, chances are you focus on negative thoughts most of the time, because you replay mental images and videos that you associate with alcohol or drug use. You may focus on mental images and mental videos that show situations in the past that led to feelings that triggered your desire to pick up a drink or a drug. You may replay mental tapes you associate with feelings that trigger your addiction. For example, you may replay an old mental video or tape about something someone once did or said that left you feeling intensely angry. Since intense anger is a major relapse trigger for most if not all people in recovery from addiction, replaying old tapes like that will increase your chances of relapsing. Thinking about and choosing to replay these images, videos, and tapes consistently means that you consistently maintain a negative mental attitude.

The mental images, videos, and tapes you replay also act as cues. These mental images, videos, and tapes—these cues—cause the feelings that trigger your addiction.

You must learn how to change your mental attitude. You must change what you think about most of the time. You must pay attention and notice the negative mental images, videos, and tapes you replay in your mind, and then you must change them. You must replace them with positive mental images, videos, and tapes that cause you to have positive feelings. You must choose mental images, videos, and tapes that will cause you to feel relaxed, calm, confident, or assertive. Think of this as one of your new choices in how to respond to triggers that make you want to pick up a drink or a drug.

You can change what you think about most of the time, and changing what you think about most of the time will change how you feel most of the time.

The techniques you will learn in this chapter will help you change how you think by helping you change your mental focus. They will help you maintain a positive mental attitude.

Message from Bill

I didn't realize how much time I spent thinking negative thoughts. When I started paying attention, I found I consistently thought about things that made me depressed, anxious, or angry. I thought about what people had said or done in the past that hurt me. I replayed old mental tapes, too. I could remember every word someone said, especially if the words led to feelings that triggered a desire to use alcohol, speed, or downers, which were my drugs of choice. Most of the time I wasn't aware that I was focusing so much on the negative. The mental images, movies, and tapes played out just below the surface. Sometimes I was aware of my negative mental focus. At these times, I can remember purposely holding on to the images and sounds because they made me want to pick up a drink or a drug. I used to focus on negative images and tapes about 50 percent of the time. Eventually, I did pick up. What a wake-up call that was!

◆ **EXERCISE** What does it mean to change your mental attitude?

_____

_____

_____

◆ **EXERCISE** Chances are you often think negative thoughts. You focus on mental videos and mental tapes that lead to some of your major triggers. Identify a mental video or tape you listen to frequently that causes feelings that trigger a desire to use your drug of choice. Describe that video or tape.

_____

_____

_____

_____

∾ Learning the Techniques ∾

You have learned how focusing consistently on mental images that you associate with alcohol or other drugs keeps you stuck in your addiction. Now you will learn some techniques that will help you change your mental attitude.

SUGGESTION 1 | *Look at Special Photos or Pictures*

Do you have a special photo you carry in your wallet or purse that makes you feel good when you look at it? Maybe you have a photo of your significant other or of your children. Maybe you have a picture from nature that makes you feel good or a picture of a religious subject. Maybe you do not have a special photo or picture. If you don't have a special photo or picture that you carry, you should get one. Make sure it's one that causes you to feel good when you look at it. Then when a trigger occurs, look at the photo or picture. And as you look at it, relax your posture and slow down your breathing. You will automatically start feeling whatever good feelings you associate with the special photo or picture.

◆ **EXERCISE** Make a list of special photos or pictures you could use to deal with addiction triggers, then obtain such a photo or picture and keep it on your person.

_____

_____

_____

◆ **EXERCISE** Think of something in the past that led to a feeling that turned into a relapse trigger. Thinking about it will probably make you feel some of the desire to use your drug of choice again. When you begin to feel that way, follow the steps below:

A. Look at your special photo or picture.

B. Relax your posture.

C. Slow down your breathing.

◆ **EXERCISE** On a scale from one to ten, what was your level of desire to use your drug of choice when you felt triggered? What was it after using this suggestion for how to change your mental attitude?

_____

_____

SUGGESTION 2 | *Listen to Relaxing Music*

Listening to relaxing music often changes how you feel. It has sometimes been said that music "soothes the wild beast." Some people compare their anger to a wild beast. Does it sometimes feel that way to you? If anger is one of your major triggers, as it is for most people who are in recovery from chemical dependency, listening to relaxing music would be a very useful thing to do when anger threatens to plunge you into the relapse process. You may find relaxing music to be a good way to quiet the wild beast inside of you and help you maintain a positive mental attitude. Listening to "gangsta rap" will probably have the opposite effect—it will wake up the wild beast. Listening to relaxing music may also be a good option to use to interrupt and change any other negative feelings, such as anxiety, fear, or frustration.

◆ **EXERCISE** What kind of music do you find relaxing? Slow ballads, classical, New Age? Make a list.

_____

_____

_____

◆ **EXERCISE** Find a CD or audiotape that you consider to be relaxing. Play the CD or tape. How does the CD or tape make you feel?

_____

_____

_____

A. Sit next to a tape player or CD player. Put your relaxing tape or CD in the player. Don't start the tape or CD just yet.

B. Now think of something that made you angry in the past. Notice the level of your anger, using a scale from one to ten.

C. When you begin to feel some anger, start the tape or CD and listen to the relaxing music. Listen to the music for five to ten minutes.

What was your anger level after listening to the tape or CD for five to ten minutes?

_____

Message from Juanita

My name is Juanita. I live in L.A. I used a lot of heroin. I almost died from a heroin overdose, not just once but twice. When I finally got clean and sober, I found out that anger was my worst relapse trigger. My brain kept focusing on thoughts that made me angry, so I was triggered almost every day and had to fight like crazy to keep from copping. It felt like I was hanging from my fingernails, from a rock right down at the brink of the Niagara Falls. I reached a point where I couldn't fight the current anymore, and I plunged over the falls. I copped some heroin and relapsed—big time. Somehow, I managed to get clean again. This time around, I learned some ways to change my focus. I learned to pay attention to what I was thinking; then I learned how to change my thoughts. I had maintained a negative mental attitude most of my life, so it wasn't easy to change. It took practice. I had to continue to pay attention to what I thought about, and I had to keep applying the techniques I learned. I'm still practicing these skills. I suppose I'll have to practice them the rest of my life, but that's okay with me. I'm able to control my anger better than I ever thought I could, as well as other feelings that trigger me to want to score for my drug of choice. I have more clean time than ever before, too.

SUGGESTION 3 | *Use Humor to Interrupt Triggers*

Humor is a powerful way to interrupt triggers, a good way to get out of the river, and a good anchor. Even when you are close to the falls, humor can get you out.

A man named Norman Cousins suffered from a disease that caused him a lot of pain. Cousins didn't want to use pain medication. He believed it would have a negative effect on his recovery. He felt powerless over the pain; the feeling of powerlessness made him angry. As a way to deal with the pain, Cousins borrowed old comedy movies from the library. He discovered that watching a humorous movie for two hours not only provided him with two hours of pain-free time but also relieved his anger!

◆ **EXERCISE** Watch a funny movie. Doing so is a good way to deal with triggers. Borrow a funny video from the library, rent one from a rental shop, or buy one at a discount store. Watch the video. How does watching a humorous video make you feel?

NOTE: Avoid watching a video that focuses on alcohol or drug use.

_____

_____

_____

_____

◆ **EXERCISE**

A. Put your funny movie in the video player. Don't start the player just yet.

B. Now think of something in the past that made you feel angry, frustrated, or fearful, or that led to one of your other addiction triggers. Rate the intensity level of the feeling on a scale from one to ten.

C. Now start the movie. Watch at least ten minutes of it.

After watching the movie for ten minutes, what was the intensity level of the feeling that threatened to plunge you into the river? What was the intensity level after twenty minutes? After sixty minutes? What was the intensity level of the feeling after watching the entire video?

_____

_____

◆ **EXERCISE** Listen to a humorous audiotape or CD. Doing so is another effective tool for maintaining a positive mental attitude. Borrow or buy a humorous audiotape or CD, and listen to it. How does listening to it make you feel?

NOTE: Avoid listening to an audiotape or CD that focuses on alcohol or drug use.

_____

_____

_____

_____

_____

◆ **Exercise**

   A. Put your humorous audiotape or CD in a tape deck or CD player. Don't start the tape or CD just yet.

   B. Now think of something in the past that made you feel angry, frustrated, or fearful. What is the intensity level of the feeling on a scale from one to ten?

   C. When you start feeling some of the anger, or frustration, or fear, start the tape or CD and listen to it for at least ten minutes.

    After listening to the humorous tape or CD for ten minutes, what was the intensity level of the feeling? What was it after twenty minutes? What was it after listening to the entire recording?

_____

_____

◆ **EXERCISE** Is humor a good anchor for you, a good way to get out of the addiction process or relapse process? What other ways can you use humor as an anchor?

_____

_____

SUGGESTION 4 | *Use Physical Exercise to Interrupt Triggers*

Exercise is another good way to interrupt triggers; it is another effective anchor. Of course, before starting an exercise program you should check with your doctor.

    There are many types of exercise to choose from. Choose an exercise program that is affordable. Choose one that you can do easily without a lot of equipment, and choose one that you feel you will be most likely to use. As was mentioned in the previous chapter, exercise releases chemicals in the brain called *endorphins* that elevate your mood. When you are in a good mood, you automatically think positive thoughts. Therefore, exercise is another good way to help you maintain a positive mental attitude.

    There are many forms of exercise that you could use to interrupt addiction triggers or relapse triggers. Some examples are listed below.

▪ Pump iron	▪ Walk	▪ Run
▪ Go for a bike ride	▪ Clean house	▪ Do yard work
▪ Do push-ups	▪ Chop wood	▪ Do deep knee bends
▪ Go to an aerobics class or yoga class		

Some of the types of exercise listed above may appeal to you, or none of them may appeal to you. You must think of types of exercise that you would like to do.

◆ **EXERCISE** List at least two types of physical exercise you would be willing to do.

_____

_____

◆ **EXERCISE** Do one of the physical exercises you listed the next time you feel triggered to use your drug of choice. What effect did it have? Did it interrupt the trigger? Was it a good anchor?

_____

_____

_____

_____

SUGGESTION 5 | _Make a Gratitude List_

It is easy to forget the good things you have in your life, especially in times of stress. When you feel stressed, your mental attitude often becomes negative.

Maintaining awareness of the good things in your life creates a positive mental attitude; it makes you feel grateful. If you stay aware of some of the good things in your life, you will be less likely to pick up a drink or a drug when a trigger happens. Making a gratitude list that you can look at will help you stay aware of the good things. It will allow you to make a useful comparison. You can compare the things on your gratitude list to whatever is triggering a desire to pick up a drink or a drug, and that will help you keep things in perspective. It will help you see what is really important in your life and what is not.

A gratitude list will help you maintain a positive mental attitude. Below is a list of things that anyone should be grateful for:

- Being alive
- Having eyes and ears
- Having food to eat

- Being able to breathe
- Being able to talk

These are pretty basic for most of us, and chances are you are or have all of them. But there must be many other things you have that you are grateful for, too. You will surprise yourself as you begin taking account. As your sober time grows, so will your list.

Oprah Winfrey once suggested a variation on the gratitude list. She recommended making a list at the end of each day of three to five things you're grateful for that are _specific_ *to that day*—that is, not general items such as food on the table, or a car that runs, or good health, etc. Rather, list things such as the following, for example:

- I love the new haircut I got today.

- My spouse surprised me by cooking dinner tonight.

- I finished that big project at work on time.

- I watched a beautiful sunset.

- I felt really strong at the gym today.

Making this kind of gratitude list helps you to stay in touch with life's blessings on a daily basis.

◆ **EXERCISE** Make a list of things you are grateful for now, and make three copies of the list. Keep one copy on your person, keep a copy on your nightstand, tape a copy to the wall next to the bathroom mirror. Each time you feel triggered into the addiction process or relapse process read your gratitude list. Add to your list at any time.

I am grateful for...

_____

_____

_____

_____

_____

_____

Message from Bill

I wrote a gratitude list on the back of a business card and carried it in my wallet. But sometimes I couldn't get to my list—when I was driving my car, for example, or when I was in a room full of people and didn't want to look conspicuous. At those times, I made a mental list of the things I was grateful for. I'd just ask myself, "What am I grateful for, right now?" The list would begin to unfold in my mind. That technique got me out of the river every time I used it. It was a good anchor, and continues to be one.

SUGGESTION 6 | *Use Self-Commands to Interrupt Triggers*

You can use brief self-commands to interrupt triggers. A self-command is a word or short phrase that helps you quickly change negative feelings into positive feelings. Self-commands make good anchors; use them to pull yourself out of the river.

Here are some examples of self-commands you can use to interrupt anger triggers:

- Change your breathing!

- Alcohol and other drugs equal pain!

- Picking up a drink or a drug is never justified! Don't pick one up!

- Stop!

When you use one of your self-commands, you must do it with feeling; you must put energy into it. You don't have to yell, but you should use a strong, assertive voice. You can simply *think* the command in your head if circumstances make it inappropriate to say it out loud. If you utter the self-command silently, you can still do it with feeling. Inside your mind, it should sound loud.

◆ **EXERCISE** Copy the self-commands listed above onto something small enough to fit in your wallet—on the back of a business card, for example.

◆ **EXERCISE**

    A. Look at your list of self-commands. Choose one to use as a tool to interrupt triggers that threaten your sobriety.

    B. Now recall something from your past that led to a feeling that triggered a desire to use alcohol or other drugs. Notice the intensity level of the trigger on a scale from one to ten.

    C. When you start feeling some of the feelings produced by the trigger, look at the self-command you chose.

    D. Using a strong voice, say the self-command; say it with feeling.

◆ **EXERCISE** Using a scale from one to ten, rate the effect your self-command had on your addiction trigger or relapse trigger.

◆ **EXERCISE** Think of two or three other self-commands you could use, and write them down. Don't forget to add them to the list you carry with you.

_____

_____

_____

You have learned some ways to maintain a positive mental attitude. You have learned some ways to interrupt triggers that lead to a desire to use your drug of choice. As stated at the beginning of the chapter, these suggestions represent new choices. Refer to the list of choices you made in Chapter 10, and add the new techniques you have just learned to the list.

Message from Tommy

My name is Tommy. I'm from Washington, D.C.

I knew I had a drug habit, and I knew I wanted to recover. I'd start the day in a positive frame of mind. I'd say to myself, "Today I'm not going to be stupid. I'm not going to go over the falls." Then some little thing would happen, or maybe a lot of little things would happen in a row, and before I knew it, wham! Over the falls. I needed skills. I needed a lot of anchors. I learned some of the techniques in this chapter; then things got better. Finally, I had things to do that would work. With my new techniques, I could get out of the river before it was too late. Then I learned some more techniques and added them to the ones I already knew. Later, things got even better. The more techniques I learned, the better things got. I've been clean and sober for three years. Without my skills and techniques, I'd still be using cocaine—that is, if I was still alive.

13

What to Avoid

It is important to know how to interrupt cues and triggers when they occur so you can quickly get out of the relapse process. It is also important to know what things and situations to avoid in the first place. Certain things and situations are cues. Recall from earlier in the book that cues are often things you see, hear, or smell that create the feelings that lead to relapse. Recall also that the feelings are the relapse triggers. Whenever possible, you should avoid people, places, things, and situations that you know produce triggers. This will reduce the number of cues, and it will reduce the number of triggers created by the cues.

∽ Avoid Alcohol and All Other Drugs ∽

Of course you must abstain completely from alcohol and all other drugs—not just from your drug of choice, but from all nonprescribed mood-altering drugs. That is a given. You must abstain altogether from barbiturates, tranquilizers, marijuana, heroin, speed, amphetamines, and mushrooms.

Prescription Drugs

If you are taking prescribed medication, make an appointment with your physician and explain your situation. Tell your physician that you are in recovery from an addiction. Ask if the drug he or she is prescribing is a mood-altering drug. If it is, ask your physician to substitute a different drug—one that is not potentially addictive.

The only reason to take prescription medication is if you must have it to help you deal with a physical or mental problem. If you are taking medication for a physical or mental problem, do not stop taking the medication without consulting your physician. Use your medication only as prescribed. Read the warnings on the prescription labels.

Marijuana

Don't be fooled by the myth that marijuana is safe. Marijuana is a drug. People in recovery who use marijuana in the mistaken belief that they can use it safely in place of their "real" drugs of choice end up relapsing.

Message from Bob

I'm Bob. I was addicted to alcohol first, then to heroin. When I first started my recovery, I thought I could get away with smoking a joint now and then. After all, I reasoned, I never had a problem with marijuana. I didn't even like it. My preference was heroin, you know, the champagne of drugs. I was the typical junky snob.

At first I used marijuana once in awhile, usually before bed after a stressful day. I used marijuana for about a month without any bad results. Then I started using a little more. After about three months I was smoking two or three joints a day. Before the end of the fourth month I started skin-popping heroin. Two weeks later I was mainlining again. If you're serious about recovery, don't use marijuana.

◆ **EXERCISE** Why are you strongly urged to abstain from all drugs, unless prescribed for health reasons?

_____

_____

_____

◆ **EXERCISE** You read Bob's story. Bob's drug of choice was heroin. What happened to him as a result of using marijuana?

_____

_____

_____

∽ Avoid People, Places, and Situations Where Drinking or Drug Use Takes Place ∽

You must stop associating with people who use alcohol or other drugs. Continuing to associate with people who are still using will keep you stuck in your old addiction pattern.

Some of your family members may have drug or alcohol problems. Other people you cannot avoid also may have drug or alcohol problems. In such cases, you can only work your recovery program all the harder. But whenever possible, avoid people who are still using alcohol or other drugs.

You must also avoid places and situations where drinking or drug use goes on. Seeing someone else pick up a drink or a drug is one of the most powerful cues you could ever expose yourself to. When you are at a bar or party where people are drinking and using drugs, the cues are almost too numerous to count. You have an addiction. What you see, hear, and smell at a bar or a party reinforces your addiction in the most powerful way possible. What you see, hear, and smell in places where drinking and drugging is going on produces the strongest relapse trigger you could have: a craving to pick up a drink or a drug.

Of course you must also stay away from places where you used to buy drugs. Going near street corners where you used to score crack cocaine or cop heroin will only make you have triggers to pick up again.

Message from Craig

My name is Craig. I'm from Boston. I'm addicted to alcohol and other drugs. I was actively addicted for a long time. Then some things happened that made me want to stop using. I started a recovery program, and I was doing pretty good. I'd been clean and sober for three months. But I missed some of my old friends at the bar where I used to drink and score drugs. I started hanging out there again. Things went okay for awhile. I sat at the bar and talked with my friends, and drank orange juice. It was like that for a month or so; I mean I didn't even have an urge. I was going to three twelve-step meetings every week. I even had a sponsor, so I was doing some things right.

Then one night I was sitting in the bar talking with my friend. My friend got up to use the restroom. He left his beer on the table, across from me. It was almost a full bottle of beer. My orange juice was sitting on the table in front of me. There was music playing on the jukebox, the same kind of music I'd listened to at that same bar when I was still drinking and using drugs. I was surrounded by all the same sights and sounds and smells.

There were relapse triggers coming at me from all over the place, and I didn't even know it.

As I waited for my friend to return, my mind was in the kind of state it gets in when you're staring out the window and not really seeing anything. You know, when your brain is sort of in neutral. That's when my hand reached out across the table, right over top of my orange juice, and picked up the bottle of beer my friend had left on the table. My hand closed on the neck of the bottle. I raised the bottle off the table, bent my elbow, and brought the bottle within an inch of my lips. Then, all of a sudden I became aware of what I was doing. Just as I tipped the bottle forward to take a drink, I stopped. I couldn't believe I'd performed the whole action without even being conscious of what I was doing! I slammed the bottle down on the table and got up and ran out of the place. I didn't even wait to say goodbye to my friend. I haven't been in any bar since.

◆ **EXERCISE** Have you ever been at a place where there was alcohol or drug use that caused you to feel triggered? If so, write about the experience.

_____

_____

_____

_____

◆ **EXERCISE** For entertainment, you may have depended on places where alcohol or other drugs are used. Where else could you go for entertainment?

_____

_____

_____

_____

◆ **EXERCISE** Are some people you associate with still stuck in addiction? Are you willing to change who you associate with?

_____

_____

_____

∽ Avoid Media Images That Promote Alcohol and Drug Use ∽

The mass media can definitely shape behavior. This is obvious. The media present role models who use chemicals to change how they feel. The media present images of alcohol and drug use over and over again. Watching movies and television programs that depict alcohol and drug use can trigger a relapse. Reading books or newspaper articles with themes involving alcohol or drug use can have the same result. Popular songs that glamorize alcohol and drug use may also create relapse triggers. You are strongly urged to reduce your exposure to this kind of programming. Carefully select what you watch, what you read, and what you listen to.

◆ **EXERCISE** Think of the last time you watched a TV program or movie that depicted alcohol or drug use. How did that make you feel? Did it make you feel like picking up a drink or a drug?

_____

_____

_____

_____

◆ **EXERCISE** You may depend on television and movies for entertainment. What else could you do for entertainment?

_____

_____

_____

_____

_____

14

Advanced Methods and Techniques

Back in Chapter 12 you learned some specific techniques that will help you stay on the recovery road and out of the land of relapse. Now it's time to learn some advanced techniques. These new techniques will help you deal with triggers that arise from persistent cues that come from inside your mind, rather than from your environment.

⤳ Relapse Cues ⤳

Cues and How They Relate to Triggers

A *cue* is usually something you see or hear. A *relapse cue* is something you see or hear that causes a relapse trigger, a feeling. Some cues are memories of things you have seen or heard. They are *memory cues*. A cue is a signal to do something. An orchestra conductor cues each musician with a signal that tells them when to start or stop playing. A red light at a corner is a cue to stop. The sound of an ambulance siren is a cue to pull over to the curb. The smell of food cooking is a cue that might tell your mouth to start producing saliva. A relapse cue signals your body and brain to produce a relapse trigger, a feeling. Both painful feelings and pleasurable feelings have the potential to cause you to want to pick up a drink or a drug.

Memory Cues

Memories of things that happened to you can act as cues, and they can be as strong as or stronger than cues that happen in the present. Remembering something you saw or heard might cue you to feel the same feelings you had when it happened. Memories of painful things can make you feel bad feelings again; memories of pleasurable things can make you feel good feelings again.

Memories of things that produce negative feelings like fear or frustration act as relapse triggers. Chances are you have many such memories—memories that cause you emotional pain when they pop into your mind, memories that act as cues. They keep your tension level high.

Recalling these memories keeps you stuck in the relapse process. Some memories that act as cues for the feelings that trigger relapse are very stubborn. They pop into your conscious mind often, and it is hard to keep from focusing on them. But you can learn how to deal with memory cues that in the past kept you stuck in the relapse process; you can learn how to let go of them once and for all, so that they no longer produce the feelings that trigger your addiction to chemicals.

◆ Scenario One

Suppose someone said something in the past that hurt your feelings, causing you to become depressed, and suppose that feeling of depression triggered a desire to use your drug of choice, causing you to plunge into the Niagara River. Suppose some time has passed; you are walking down the street and happen to see that same person who hurt your feelings. How do you suppose you would react? Do you think you would feel depressed all over again? Chances are you would. Seeing the person who hurt your feelings would be a relapse cue. The person's face would act as a cue, causing you to recall what was said or done that produced the feeling of depression. You would experience the feeling of depression again, and that would trigger a desire to use your drug of choice. The person's face would act as a relapse cue until you did something to change the cue.

◆ Scenario Two

Suppose someone said something in the past that caused you to feel depressed, and you responded by getting drunk or high. You never again saw the person face to face, but walking down the street a few days later a big, bright memory of his face pops suddenly into your mind. Would the memory of the person who hurt your feelings cause you to feel depressed all over again and trigger a desire to use your drug of choice? It would! In other words, the memory would act as a cue. It would act as a memory cue, and the feeling of depression would act as a relapse trigger.

Dealing with Stubborn Memory Cues

When you recall a memory, you see it like a picture or videotape projected on a screen inside your mind. The quality of the brightness of the image attached to a particular memory is very important when it comes to recalling the memory. The brightness of the image that makes up a visual memory may range from very bright to very dim.

Visual memories often produce feelings. These feelings may be strong or weak, depending on how bright or dim the image of the memory looks to you when you see it on the screen inside your mind. Bright memories usually cause strong feelings; very bright memories may cause very strong feelings. Dim memories may cause weak feelings; very dim memories often cause very weak feelings.

Most visual memories fade out and become dim and uninteresting with the passing of time, but sometimes memories remain very bright for a long time, especially if they are the result of powerful events that made you feel very strong feelings in the first place. Old, faded memories won't give you trouble. There is not enough brightness left to interest your brain.

The faded-out memories slip out of sight, down into the murky bottom layers of the mind, because their lack of brightness makes them too uninteresting to remain on the surface. These old, heavy, faded-out memories almost never pop back up to the surface.

Memory cues that remain very bright are the ones that will give you trouble, especially the ones you associate with strong negative feelings such as fear. To use another metaphor, the brightness of the memory makes the cues lighter, which causes them to float closer to the surface of your mind. Even bright memories won't give you trouble all of the time, but they are always lurking just below the surface. They slice through your conscious mind like sharks cutting the surface of the water with their dorsal fin.

Trying to force down a big, bright memory won't work. It is like forcing a beach ball underwater. What happens when you let go? The beach ball pops back to the surface. In fact, it often pops completely out of the water! That's what happens when you force down a big, bright memory; it pops back up as soon as you let go, and for a while it looks even bigger and brighter.

The following exercise offers one way to deal with a stubborn memory cue. This method reduces the brightness of the image representing the memory. You can use it to reduce the brightness from any stubborn memory cue that keeps you stuck in the addiction process. The technique changes the memory cue. It extinguishes it. It puts out the memory cue's light, so to speak. Then the memory sinks below the surface, way down deep where it belongs, and it stays there. Practice the technique below with all of your stubborn memory cues.

◆ **EXERCISE** Make a list of your stubborn memory cues, the ones that create feelings that trigger your desire to use your drug of choice. An example of a stubborn memory cue might be one of the following:

   ▣ A big, bright memory of someone who rejected you when you were a child. When you think of the person, you feel a strong feeling of rejection that makes you want to pick up a drink or a drug.

   ▣ A big, bright memory of someone who did something that caused you to feel strong fear. When you think of that person you feel afraid all over again, and that feeling leads to a craving to use your drug of choice.

   ▣ A big, bright memory of something that happened that caused you to feel dis appointed. You think of the past event, feel disappointed, and then want to pick up your drug of choice.

   ▣ A big, bright memory of yourself doing something that resulted in a personal loss. You feel stupid and embarrassed all over again, and those feelings trigger your addiction.

Now make a list of your stubborn memory cues.

_____

_____

_____

_____

_____

_____

_____

_____

◆ **EXERCISE**

NOTE: This is a difficult technique to master, but an important one.

Select one of the memory cues you listed, and then follow the steps below. If you are alone when you are using this technique and need to close your eyes, you may open them long enough to read the next step. Ideally, you should have someone read the steps to you, perhaps a counselor. Or you might want to tape-record yourself reading the steps so that you can play the tape back and listen to the steps while keeping your eyes closed. Leave thirty seconds or so of silence between each step.

Once you have mastered this technique, you will have a way to deal effectively with any memory cue that threatens to keep you stuck in your addiction. Some of your strongest triggers may be the result of memory cues attached to things that happened to you in the past. If you suffered severe trauma in the past, you may be unable to completely heal from your addiction to alcohol or other drugs until you resolve the trauma. This technique is designed to help you resolve trauma.

1. Pretend you have a TV screen in your mind. Think of the memory cue you want to change. Project it as a picture on the screen, and notice the brightness of the picture.

2. How strong is the memory cue? Rate the strength of the cue on a ten-point scale.

3. Using your imagination, very quickly increase the brightness of the picture until the screen goes blank and the picture disappears, the way the picture on a TV screen disappears when you twist the brightness knob all the way up.

4. Let the picture fade back in. Notice that the picture has lost some of its clarity. Also, notice that the cue has lost some of its strength. Rate the strength of the cue.

5. Now increase the brightness of the picture quickly, as before, until the screen goes blank again. Let the picture fade back in. Notice that the picture has lost more brightness, and the feeling produced by the cue is even less intense. Rate the intensity on a ten-point scale.

6. Repeat step five three more times, or until the feeling produced by the cue rates a three or less on a ten-point scale.

∾ Change Your Posture, Breathing, and Voice to Manage Cues and Triggers ∾

Your posture, along with how you breathe and use your voice, can affect whatever emotional state you happen to be in at a given moment in time. Every feeling you experience is often expressed in these three aspects of your behavior. Lets say a cue occurs that produces intense anger. It is almost impossible to maintain a strong feeling of anger without also maintaining an angry posture, breathing pattern, and voice.

The following is almost always what you do with your body when you are angry:

- You maintain a rigid posture.

- You breathe rapidly in your upper chest.

- You speak rapidly in a loud, high-pitched voice.

This posture, breathing pattern, and way of using your voice reinforces anger. In fact, this pattern *creates* your anger. Using your posture, breathing pattern, and voice in this way sends a specific message to the brain. It tells your brain to make stimulating chemicals associated with angry behavior. It tells the brain to stimulate the adrenal glands, which respond by sending large amounts of adrenaline into the bloodstream.

You are not normally aware of your posture, how you breathe, or how you use your voice, but you can learn how to be aware of these things. If you learn how to be aware of these three parts of your behavior, you will have a powerful way to change how you feel. You will have a powerful way to change any feeling that threatens to plunge you into the addiction process or relapse process into a feeling that will move you toward recovery instead.

Changing your posture, breathing, and voice can change how you feel. To do so, follow the three steps described below. You can use this technique with any triggering feeling. For example, it will also work with fear, anxiety, or frustration. It will work with any feeling that involves a posture, breathing pattern, and way of using the voice that are similar to those of anger. We are using anger as an example.

When a trigger such as anger occurs:

First, relax your posture. Lean to one side, or sit down.

Next, slow your breathing, and breathe more deeply, down into your belly.

Then, slow your rate of speech, and reduce the volume and pitch of your voice; speak more softly and use a deeper tone.

Changing your posture, breathing, and voice in the ways described above can change how you feel. It will make you feel more relaxed and calm. It will send a different message to the brain. It will tell the brain to stop making chemicals associated with angry behavior and instead to make chemicals associated with relaxation. Making these changes in your posture, breathing pattern, and voice interrupts the angry feeling and reduces the likelihood that it will trigger a desire to use your drug of choice.

Message from Frank

I'm Frank, a recovering addict from Nashville. I thought this technique was too simple. I thought everything had to be difficult and complicated in order to be effective. But when I tried it I discovered that sometimes the best way is the easy way. Changing my posture, breathing, and voice is the easiest way for me to change any feeling that threatens my recovery. It pulls me out of the river fast. It was an easy technique to learn, but I found I had to practice it often.

I started by paying attention to my breathing. When I felt a trigger, I told myself to slow down my breathing, and to breathe from my belly, not up in my chest (which is how I breathe when I'm angry, or afraid, or frustrated). After I got good at changing my breathing and could do it fast, then I started paying attention to my posture, too. Then I started paying attention to how I was using my voice. Sometimes just changing my breathing was enough. When I changed my breathing, it caused my posture and voice to change too.

◆ **EXERCISE** Describe how you use your posture, your breathing, and your voice when you are angry or fearful or frustrated.

_____

_____

_____

◆ **EXERCISE** Describe the three steps you can take to change how you feel by changing your posture, breathing, and voice.

1. _____

_____

2. _____

_____

3. _____

∽ Recite a Brief Poem ∽

This technique works best if you breathe slowly and deeply as you recite the poem. Look through a book of poetry and select a poem that you makes you feel relaxed, or in some other way empowered. Memorize the poem.

◆ **EXERCISE** Write down the poem you have selected. Each time you notice a trigger, recite the poem to interrupt the trigger.

_____

_____

_____

_____

_____

_____

_____

∽ Read a Joke Book or a Book of Cartoons ∽

Has anyone ever said or done something funny in your presence when you were feeling intensely angry or frustrated or fearful? Did their actions magically reduce the intensity of your feelings or cause them to go away completely? If so, then you know the power of humor to help you deal with your relapse triggers. Keep joke books and cartoon books handy, and use them as tools to deal with triggers.

Message from Angie

My name is Angie. I'm from the Midwest. I've been in recovery for over a year, and I'm doing a lot better. Early in my recovery, I found out how much humor could help me overcome triggers to drink or use. I had a friend in the program who was a champion joke teller. I knew I could make good use of my friend's skills. I figured I could call her when I felt triggered to drink or pick up a drug, then ask her to tell me a joke. If she could make me laugh, I knew it would act as an anchor to yank me out of the relapse process. My friend agreed to help. From then on, whenever I felt triggered and I was near a phone, I'd call my friend and ask her to tell me a joke. It worked better than I thought it would, even when I was in white water right down near the brink of the falls.

◆ **EXERCISE** What kind of joke book or cartoon book would be helpful to you?

_____

_____

◆ **EXERCISE** You can also use funny situations that happened in the past. Can you remember something funny that happened in the past that makes you laugh every time you think of it? If you can, write it down. Then you can read it to yourself when you feel triggered to drink or use other drugs.

_____

_____

_____

_____

_____

❧ Take a Timeout ❧

You are learning new ways to respond to triggers. But sometimes you will feel like you are on "trigger overload." Things can pile up and seem overwhelming. At such times you may need to take a timeout. Usually taking a timeout means taking an overnight break from a situation that leads to triggering feelings; for example, a situation that causes you to feel frustrated or anxious.

Taking a timeout is not running away. Just like in a sports game, taking a timeout allows you to think things through, and to calm down. Sometimes you may need to get out of the situation entirely for a brief period.

Sometimes a short timeout is enough. You could go away for an hour or two. You could take a walk or go to a movie. You could go for coffee with your Pathways to Sobriety mentor or with your twelve-step program sponsor (you will learn about Pathways to Sobriety mentors later in the workbook). Sometimes you may need to get away for a day or two. Think this over carefully. Talk about it with a friend, or with your counselor, mentor, or sponsor before you make a decision to take a timeout that will last longer than a couple of hours.

A timeout does not signify defeat. Taking a timeout is another choice; it is another anchor to throw onshore, another way to get out of the river. You could add "timeout" to your list of choices.

Remember that you are now working a recovery program. Be sure to communicate your intentions to your loved ones and friends when and if you decide to use a timeout. Not to keep them informed would, of course, cause your loved ones and friends undue worry.

◆ **EXERCISE** What does it mean to "take a timeout"?

_____

_____

◆ **EXERCISE** Would taking a timeout be a good choice for you? Why?

_____

_____

_____

_____

◆ **EXERCISE** If you needed to take a timeout, where would you go? If you needed to take a mini-timeout, where would you go?

_____

_____

_____

◆ **EXERCISE** Who would you talk to that could help you make a decision to take a timeout?

_____

_____

∾ Go to a Pathways to Sobriety Meeting ∾

You will learn more about the Pathways to Sobriety program in Appendixes B and C, located at the back of the workbook. Appendix C tells you how to start a Pathways to Sobriety meeting. Even if you participate in another self-help program, participating in Pathways to Sobriety could increase your chances of staying clean and sober. The meetings will help you learn to deal effectively with triggers and will reinforce what you learn from _The Pathways to Sobriety Workbook_. Pathways to Sobriety members give each other support, understanding, and friendship. Pathways to Sobriety members know what you are going through.

◆ **EXERCISE** Is there a Pathways to Sobriety meeting in your area? If so, where is it and when does it meet?

_____

_____

_____

∾ Establish and Use an Empowerment Cue or an Aversion Cue ∾

You have learned that you have an addiction to alcohol or other drugs. You know that you learned your addiction by using your drug of choice over and over. This kind of learning process is sometimes called _conditioning_. Your addiction is an example of _stimulus/response conditioning_.

The trigger, always a feeling such as fear or frustration, is what fires off the addiction process and plunges you into the river. The trigger is the _stimulus_. Picking up and using a drink or a drug is the response to the trigger.

There is another part to the conditioning process: the _reward_. You will not form a habit unless you are rewarded for the response. A reward is a feeling of pleasure. The reward for your addiction behavior is the feeling of pleasure you experience when you use alcohol or other drugs.

Each time you use alcohol or other drugs and are rewarded by feeling pleasure, your addiction grows stronger. It is _reinforced_. When an addiction is reinforced often enough, it becomes so strong that even when you use alcohol or other drugs to feel pleasure and it fails to work, you still want to repeat the same behavior by using alcohol or other drugs. If you hadn't been rewarded often when you first started using alcohol or drugs to feel pleasure, you would not have developed an addiction. If you felt more pain than pleasure, your drug-using behavior would not have become an addiction. Now you are learning that your addiction behavior results in pain more often than pleasure; you are learning that the pleasure no longer outweighs the pain. That is one of the reasons you have a desire to change and to stop using alcohol or other drugs. That's why you are using this workbook.

Now you want to change. You want to recover from your addiction. But you still may find yourself feeling a strong desire to pick up a drink or a drug, even though you have sincerely promised to stop. That is the nature of an addiction. You know you are addicted to something when you find yourself wanting to use it even when you have made a conscious decision not to.

The tools you will learn in this section take advantage of the same conditioning process that your brain used to create your addiction. You will learn some tools that will help you develop a new behavior called "recovery from alcohol or drug addiction."

You learned about cues in Chapter 10 and at the beginning of this chapter. You learned about cues (signals) that cause triggers (certain feelings) that fire off the addiction process. Now you will learn about another class of cues. You will learn about cues that lead to feelings that can empower you. I call these _empowerment cues_.

An empowerment cue is a tool that helps people interrupt feelings that act as addiction triggers, such as anger, fear, frustration, or depression. There are three varieties of empowerment cues: visual, auditory, and kinesthetic.

A *visual cue* is something you can see. A photo of someone you like and admire as a positive role model, such as a loved one or a social leader like Gandhi, is an example of a visual empowerment cue. For some people, looking at such a photo causes them to have strong positive feelings such as confidence or compassion.

An *auditory cue* is something you can hear. The sound of a rousing symphony like Beethoven's *Ninth* is an example of an auditory empowerment cue. Listening to the *Ninth,* especially the choral section at the end, makes some people feel empowered.

A *kinesthetic cue* is something you can feel. Any object you can hold that gives you a positive feeling when you touch it is a kinesthetic empowerment cue. For example, some people carry in their pocket or purse a special trinket given to them by someone they like and admire. They experience positive feelings when they touch the object. Some people in twelve-step programs carry their first-year sobriety medallion or pin. When they have a desire to pick up a drink or a drug, touching the medallion or pin acts as a powerful kinesthetic empowerment cue that helps to interrupt the trigger.

Establishing an Empowerment Cue

One of the disadvantages of using a medallion as an empowerment cue is that you may lose the medallion or for some other reason may lack access to it when you need it. Using the technique described below, you can learn how to connect an empowerment cue to a specific location on your body, such as your wrist. The advantage of this kind of empowerment cue is that you cannot lose the cue and you will always have access to it.

This empowerment-cue technique is not as strange as it may sound at first. Most people find this technique fascinating as well as useful. They are often amazed at how well it works, and they really appreciate the feeling of self-empowerment the technique gives them.

Note: You may want to have someone help you with this technique. To read an example about how another person can help you learn this technique, see the "Message from Bill" on the next page.

Follow these steps:

1. Decide which wrist you want to establish the cue on. The right wrist is often best.

2. Next, recall an experience that made you feel empowered—for example, when you felt relaxed, confident, or proud. In your imagination, see, hear, and feel everything that went on.

   At the peak, when the empowered feeling is the most intense, grasp your wrist using your thumb and index finger. Squeeze your wrist firmly for fifteen to twenty seconds, then let go. Relax. Let go of the memory.

3. Now recall the event once more. As soon as the feelings peak again, grasp your wrist with the same amount of pressure as before, at the exact same spot.

Hold for fifteen to twenty seconds, then let go. Establishing the empowerment cue a second time reinforces the original cue. The process should be repeated as many times as needed in order to establish a strong empowerment cue. The cue must be strong (on a scale from one to ten, it must be at least an eight). Otherwise, the stimulus will end up being too weak; the nervous system will fail to link up the internal image with the response. Make sure to reset the cue point at the same spot, applying the same amount of pressure with the finger and thumb each time you reset it. If the same location is not used, or if the pressure is varied, the brain will get different messages, and the linkup between the cue and the memory may not take place. At best, it will end up diluted and weak.

4. This is the testing step. In order to make sure the cue is strong enough, you must test the cue.

Recall a time when you experienced a feeling that is one of your addiction triggers, for example anger or frustration. When the feeling peaks, fire the empowerment cue by squeezing the cue point on the wrist, using exactly the same pressure as was used to establish the linkup in the first place. The cue point should be held until you begin to sense a change in the way you feel—from the negative feeling to the more positive, empowering feeling. Generally, thirty to sixty seconds is adequate. You may have to grasp the empowerment-cue point a little longer before letting go, depending on the strength of the empowerment cue and the strength of the competing relapse trigger. At the end of thirty to sixty seconds, you should begin to notice a change. For example, you should notice a change in your breathing. Your breathing may slow down or shift from your chest to your belly. You may also notice a decreased heart rate. If the trigger is an angry feeling, you will begin to feel less angry. If frustration is the trigger, you will feel less frustrated.

Message from Bill

I helped a recovering addict establish an empowerment cue on his wrist as part of a demonstration in a group. He had a serious problem with anger and rage, and anger was his strongest addiction trigger. He had no problem recalling a memory he associated with intense anger that also triggered him to use his drug of choice. He focused on the memory. His breath became rapid and ragged and moved to high up in his chest, and his posture grew rigid. The muscles in his face and neck quivered and pulsated. His face got bright red. The rest of the group grew uneasy watching him. I had already helped him establish a strong empowerment cue on his wrist by connecting it to a memory of something from his past that had made him feel very relaxed. The empowerment-cue memory was in no way associated with alcohol or other drugs. As soon as he told me he was feeling very intense anger, I told him to fire the stimulus. Within sixty seconds he returned to normal. The anger subsided and the desire to use his drug of choice dissolved.

Establishing an Aversion Cue

In order to make major behavior changes when the desired change is difficult and stubborn, it is useful to have both the carrot and the stick. The carrot is the reward you get when you make the change. An empowerment cue is the carrot. An *aversion cue* can also be understood as a resource to help yourself change, except that an aversion cue leads to a painful emotional response instead of a pleasurable response. An aversion cue is the stick.

The process used to establish an aversion cue is essentially the same as that used to establish an empowerment cue. If the empowerment cue was established on the right hand, as suggested, then the aversion cue should be established on the left hand. In fact, set up the aversion cue on *the large knuckle of the index finger* of the left hand. This makes it easier to separate the two cues in your mind, so that there is no confusion regarding the use of the two cues. Follow the steps below.

1. Think of a time in the past when you experienced an addiction trigger and anticipated feeling intense pleasure as a result of using your drug of choice, but ended up with a lot of emotional or physical pain instead. Instead of feeling a pleasurable high, you lost something of value. Maybe you went to jail and lost your freedom, or maybe you lost some teeth in a bar fight. You should choose an experience that was so bad you ended up saying to yourself, "I just have to find a different way to respond to my addiction triggers!"

2. At the peak, when you are reexperiencing the painful feelings of the original event, firmly squeeze the large knuckle on your left index finger using the thumb and index finger of your right hand. Maintain firm pressure for approximately thirty seconds, then let go. Relax. Let go of the memory.

3. Repeat steps one and two at least two more times, just to make sure the aversion cue is strong enough to overpower a strong trigger to pick up a drink or a drug.

4. Now test the aversion cue. Think of something that would generate a craving to use alcohol or other drugs. At the peak of the craving, squeeze the aversion-cue point, using the same pressure at the exact same location on the large knuckle of the index finger on the left hand. If the craving to use alcohol or some other drug has been interrupted, you may assume you have succeeded in establishing the aversion cue.

If the craving is still active, reestablish a stronger aversion cue and retest. Continue practicing the technique until you have established a stimulus that will extinguish any addiction cue.

Once established, the aversion cue can be fired any time you feel a strong desire to use alcohol or other drugs. When you fire the cue (always using the same pressure, at the same point on your index finger), you will tend to reexperience the same painful feelings. Using your aversion cue will cause you to stop and think, "Do I want to use alcohol or other drugs in this situation and end up with that consequence again? Do I want to put myself through that pain again?"

◆ **EXERCISE** Think of a time in the past when you used your drug of choice expecting a lot of pleasure, but ended up feeling so much pain that you said to yourself, "I just have to find another way to change how I feel!" Write about it here.

_____

_____

_____

_____

_____

_____

_____

_____

◆ **EXERCISE** Now that you have established a strong aversion cue, make a list of six to eight major cues that might typically lead to a trigger to use your drug of choice. List them below. Take each cue, one at a time, and extinguish them using your aversion cue.

1. _____

2. _____

3. _____

4. _____

5. _____

6. _____

7. _____

8. _____

SPACE FOR NOTES...

_____

_____

_____

_____

_____

_____

_____

_____

_____

_____

_____

_____

_____

_____

_____

_____

_____

_____

_____

PART FOUR

Changing Your Mind

15

Values

This chapter begins the last part of the workbook. It represents a whole new phase of healing from addiction to alcohol or other drugs. It deals with the parts of the whole self that we are not aware of at all most of the time, or are only partially aware of most of the time.

Until now, most of the focus has been on helping you change your addiction *behavior*. Changing your behavior is the work of your conscious mind. You had to use your conscious mind in order to acquire the skills and techniques you've learned so far in the book. This chapter and the ones that follow focus on helping you heal at a deeper level. You will learn how to make changes in your subconscious mind, and doing so will make your healing from addiction more complete.

∾ The Power of the Subconscious Mind ∾

You have already learned about the power of your subconscious mind. For example, you now know that your addiction behavior pattern is stored in your subconscious mind, and that other automatic habits and programs are also stored in your subconscious mind. You have learned that your subconscious mind holds information, in the form of memories, about everything you have ever seen, heard, tasted, smelled, felt, or experienced.

But other things are stored in your subconscious mind as well. All of the higher parts of your whole self are stored in your subconscious mind, including your skills, your values and goals, your beliefs, your sense of mission, and your transcendental feelings of connectedness. These parts of the whole self represent your higher self, and together they help to determine your behavior. In Chapters 15 through 20, you will learn how to change these parts of your subconscious mind. Changing these parts will make it easier to change your addiction behavior and will make it easier to keep your behavior changed.

Changing at the subconscious level of the whole self will take you to a higher level as a human being. Doing so will lead to a transformation of your whole self.

In this chapter and the next one, you will become aware of your values and goals. You will learn how to access your values and prioritize them, and you will see the effect values have on behavior. You will see how your use of alcohol and other drugs was an attempt to satisfy your values, and how your goals (if you were able to set goals at all) often were in conflict with your values. This new awareness will help you to develop new clean and sober behaviors and to set different goals—goals that will satisfy your values in positive, growth-producing ways.

In Chapter 17, "Beliefs," you will be surprised to discover what you believe about yourself and your world. You will find out how you learned your beliefs. You will learn to identify and sort your beliefs based on whether they support your recovery from addiction to alcohol or other drugs or instead send you back along the road to the land of relapse. You will learn how to discard old negative beliefs that keep you stuck and learn new positive beliefs that will support your new clean and sober lifestyle. You will see very clearly how powerfully your beliefs, along with your values and goals, impact the rest of your whole self.

In Chapter 18 you will learn how to use your conscious mind to elicit your life purpose—your mission—and put it down on paper. After writing down your mission statement, you will learn a strategy to help keep it fresh in your conscious mind. From then on, you will feel strongly encouraged to make sure all of the other parts of your whole self match up well with your mission statement. Then, more and more, you will begin to see your recovery as a wonderful journey towards fulfillment, and less and less as merely an attempt to move away from the painful consequences of addiction.

In Chapter 19 you will learn about the importance of finding ways to satisfy the needs of the transcendental part of the whole self. You will be encouraged to explore some ideas and resources that will help you choose how to satisfy the need to feel connected in a positive way to others and to the rest of the cosmos.

In Chapter 20 you will learn about the importance of forgiveness. You will learn a method that will help you forgive those who have harmed you and a method to help you forgive yourself for the harm you have done to others.

❧ Values, Addiction, and Recovery ❧

Values don't simply influence behavior; *values determine behavior.* Your values are one of the driving forces behind your addiction to alcohol or other drugs.

You are probably not aware of your values. Most people aren't. Yet values have a strong impact on every area of your life. Values influence what you believe about yourself, others, and the world. Values influence what goals you set and pursue as well as what skills you develop, and they directly affect how you behave and where you choose to live.

Your values have played an important part in your addiction and will play an important part in your recovery. You became addicted to alcohol or other drugs because you believed these chemicals would cause you to experience valued feelings such as pleasure. You became addicted to your drug of choice because you believed it would make you have the kinds of feelings you value.

❧ Valued Things and Valued Activities vs. Valued Feelings ❧

Most people place value on things, activities, and emotional states (feelings). Valued things and valued activities are so closely related that we will treat them as though they were the same.

It is easy to know the difference between valued things and valued feelings. You can put valued things and activities in a box. You cannot put valued feelings in a box. For example, you can put money, a valued thing, in a box. You could put a car, also a valued thing, in a box if the box were large enough. Likewise, you could jog (an example of a valued activity) in a box, if the box were big enough. You can even put a relationship in a box, if you stretch your imagination a little.

But you cannot put a valued feeling in a box. For example you cannot put freedom, a valued feeling, in a box no matter what size the box.

Valued Things/Activities

You value certain things. Everyone does. For example, you value money—who doesn't? You value the other people in your life, for example your friends, spouse, or children. The things you value and treasure are like vehicles that move you toward your valued feelings and away from painful feelings. Valued feelings are good feelings, like love or confidence. Painful feelings are negative feelings, like fear or depression. Painful feelings are often relapse triggers. One of the things you valued most was alcohol or other drugs. Perhaps until you began your recovery from addiction, you had come to value alcohol or other drugs above all other things.

Valued things also include things you like to do. Jogging, communicating, or writing down thoughts in your journal are examples of valued activities. You use things you like to do to experience valued feelings.

Examples of Valued Things/Activities

1. Car

2. Money

3. Helping others recover from addiction

4. Writing poetry

5. Job

◆ **EXERCISE** Look at the list of examples above. Circle the valued things/activities that apply to you.

◆ **EXERCISE** List at least three more of your valued things/activities.

_____

_____

_____

_____

Valued Feelings

Freedom, security, and love are examples of things we want and value. This class of values is important to everybody. There are three valued feelings all people must have in order to be happy. Psychologist William Glasser called them the "three A's of happiness." They are achievement, acceptance, and affection.

When you are unhappy it is because your valued feelings have gone unsatisfied, or because someone or something has threatened or violated one of your valued feelings.

You are chemically dependent. When you feel triggered to use your drug of choice, it is because

1. one or more of your valued feelings has been threatened or attacked, causing you to feel pain; or

2. you believe using the drug will cause you to experience pleasure, one of your highly valued feelings, or at least will make the painful feeling go away.

Your values determine how you act, and they influence how you spend your time and energy. You were not born with a set of values. You learned them. You learned some of your values from teachers and peers, some from movies and books, some from whoever raised you. You learned your values from your life experiences.

As an alcoholic or drug addict, you learned to treat alcohol and other drugs as valued things. You did so for two reasons. One reason is because the drug you used made you feel drunk or high (two examples of valued feelings). The other reason is because, in the beginning, the drug gave you relief from painful feelings like fear, anxiety, or depression. You learned to use drugs to satisfy your most valued feelings, whatever they were. You also learned to repeat certain behaviors associated with drug or alcohol use, when those behaviors led to your valued feelings. For instance, the excitement you experienced when you went to a dangerous place to score drugs was a kind of high in itself, wasn't it, if excitement was one of your valued feelings?

Now you are learning that using alcohol or other drugs, or engaging in behaviors associated with their use, is not a good way to experience valued feelings. You are learning that, in the long run, using alcohol and other drugs causes more pain than pleasure—pain for yourself and pain for others—and you are trying to find other ways to experience valued feelings. You will need to clarify your values, so that you can become aware of the benefits of other valued feelings such as a feeling of achievement or affection. You are trying to stop the insane business of chasing the pleasure of the alcohol or drug high.

Examples of Valued Feelings

1. Making a contribution
2. Feeling free
3. Love/Being loved
4. A feeling of accomplishment
5. Serenity

◆ **EXERCISE** Look at the examples listed above. Circle the valued feelings that apply to you.

◆ **EXERCISE** List at least three more of your valued feelings.

_____

_____

_____

Message from Donna

My name is Donna. I'm an addict from Cincinnati. When I was using, I had no idea what my values were. I found out later that my most valued feeling was the high feeling I got from my drug of choice, which happened to be cocaine. But I treated the cocaine high as though it were a positive value. I wasn't aware of how short-lived the high was—toward the end, when I was using more and more and barely copping a high at all anymore, it seemed as though the rush came and went in the blink of an eye. But finally I became aware of how long the pain of the consequences lasted, and I became aware of how long the pain lasted for those I hurt. Like most addicts, I hurt myself and my family most. When I finally stopped using, I found out I had some true values, some positive values. I found out I had some values I could use that didn't result in pain for myself and others.

How Valued Things, Valued Activities, and Valued Feelings Interact

Valued things, valued activities, and valued feelings interact with each other. The feelings you value cause you to look for things and activities in your environment that will satisfy your valued feelings. If you value euphoria more than other feelings, you will search for things and activities to satisfy the desire to experience that valued feeling. Were you searching for euphoria when you found alcohol, cocaine, marijuana, heroin, or some other drug?

You became an addict, in part, because you chose the wrong ways to experience a valued feeling. That means you now have to make different values choices. You must identify your values, let go of the negative values that support your addiction, and then learn how to focus on values that will support your recovery and help you avoid relapse.

Look at the table on the next page. It illustrates how certain valued things and activities are related to certain valued feelings.

People often value the things or activities listed in the left-hand column below because they believe they will lead to the valued feelings listed in the right-hand column below.

These valued things/activities...	...might lead to these valued feelings
Car	Feeling free
Money	Security
Relationship	Affection
College degree	A feeling of achievement
Family	Acceptance
Job/career	Contribution

❧ Identifying Valued Things and Activities ❧

You will start the process of clarifying your own values by identifying and making a list of things and activities you value.

You must come up with a list of valued things and valued activities *other than* alcohol or other drugs, and other than activities that revolve around alcohol or drug use. Of course, your list of valued things and valued activities should not include things or activities that would harm yourself or others.

◆ **EXERCISE** Simply ask yourself the following question: "What things or activities would I like to have or do that would make me feel one or more of my valued feelings?"

Then write your answers down on the worksheet on the next page. A few examples are given to help you get started.

❧ Identifying Valued Feelings ❧

Once you have made a list of your valued feelings, you can begin to identify and make a list of the valued feelings you hold. The following exercise will help you accomplish this task.

◆ **EXERCISE** For this exercise, you will need a table and fifteen to twenty small pieces of paper. Each one should be about two inches square. Use a pencil so you can erase.

1. Ask yourself, "As I continue my new clean and sober lifestyle, how do I want to feel every day for the rest of my life?" Your first answer might be, "Loved. I want to feel loved every day of my life." Whatever your first answer is to this question, write it down on one of the pieces of paper. Write down whatever valued feeling comes to mind.

Valued Things/Activities Worksheet

1. High school diploma (valued thing)

2. Good job (valued thing)

3. Talk to kids, help them stay off drugs (valued activity)

4._____

5._____

6._____

7._____

8._____

9._____

10._____

11._____

12._____

13._____

14._____

15._____

16._____

17._____

18._____

19._____

20._____

2. Then ask yourself, "What other feeling is important to me?" Your next answer might be, "I'd like to feel excited every day in whatever I do." Whatever your second answer may be, write it down on another piece of paper. Don't bother trying to put your values in any kind of order. You'll do that later. Just get them all down.

   Now ask yourself, "What other feeling is important to me?" You third answer might be, "Peaceful. I want to feel peaceful, at least some of the time, every day." Whatever your third answer is, write it down on another piece of paper.

3. Continue asking yourself, "What other feelings are important in my life?" until you have at least ten different feelings. Write each feeling on a separate piece of paper. Place them all in a pile. Spend at least twenty minutes on this part of the exercise.

4. Keep going until you cannot think of any more ways you'd like to feel. Then, following the instructions below, arrange your valued feelings according to which ones are most important to you.

   A. Pick up the pieces of paper that you wrote your values on. Take the first two pieces, whatever they say, and place them face up on the table.

   B. Let's say the values written on the first two pieces of paper are "love" and "freedom," respectively. Ask yourself, "What is more important in my life: love or freedom?" If the answer is "love," place the piece of paper containing the word "love" at the top of the stack, in the first position. Right underneath it, place the one with the word "freedom."

   C. Take the third piece of paper from the pile. Let's say it says "respect." Ask yourself, "What is more important in my life: love, freedom, or respect?" Let's say you answer, "Respect is more important to me than freedom. But love is still more important than respect." Then you will know you need to place "respect" second, between "love" and "freedom."

   D. Continue arranging and rearranging your values according to what you feel is most important. Use all the pieces of paper you wrote your values on.

   E. Now look at the arrangement. Ask yourself, "Are there any changes I want to make?" Keep rearranging your values until you know they are in the proper order. You will know by how the arrangement looks, sounds, and feels. If you feel no need to change the arrangement, consider this part of the exercise to be complete.

Finding Your Breaking Point

There is one other important thing you need to know about your values. There is a breaking point somewhere within their order of importance. It could be at number six or seven, or maybe number eight or nine. Whatever that place is, it is the point at which you would say, "Stop! You can't take that away from me! I can't live without that value!"

◆ **EXERCISE** Here is how to find your breaking point. Start with the last value in your arrangement. Now ask yourself, "If I had all of the other good feelings, could I get along okay without this one?" If the answer is, "Yes," go to the next one up the ladder of importance. Ask the same question. Keep asking, "If I had all the other good feelings, could I get along okay without this one?" When you hear yourself say, "No! Absolutely not!" That is your breaking point.

Now you know exactly what your values are and which ones are most important to you. You can use this knowledge to help yourself focus more effectively on what you really want out of life, and on what you want to avoid. You can use this knowledge to help yourself see more clearly why you will benefit from stopping the use of chemicals once and for all.

Your breaking point has another important meaning. When any of your values at or above your breaking point are threatened, or you think they are being threatened, you are very likely to feel triggered to use alcohol or other drugs.

◆ **EXERCISE** Copy your list of values onto the worksheet on the next page, so you will have a permanent record of them that you can refer to. List your values in their order of importance to you, and identify your breaking-point value by placing a star (*) next to it.

❧ Putting It All Together ❧

Review your list of valued things/activities and your list of valued feelings. On the worksheet located on page 180, write your top five valued feelings under the heading "Valued Feelings." List them in order from most important to least important.

After you have listed your valued feelings, look at your list of valued things/activities. Writing on the worksheet, match up your valued feelings with the things and activities you believe would lead to your top five valued feelings. As you complete the worksheet, you may find yourself coming up with new valued things/activities—that is, items that didn't occur to you when you were making your list the first time but that you now identify as things/activities that might lead to your valued feelings. If so, add them to your original list, and include them in the worksheet here.

Example:

Valued Feelings	Valued Things/Activities
1. Freedom	Running my own business
	Reliable car
2. Security	Good income
	Live in safe neighborhood

Valued Feelings Worksheet

1. _____

2. _____

3. _____

4. _____

5. _____

6. _____

7. _____

8. _____

9. _____

10. _____

11. _____

12. _____

13. _____

14. _____

15. _____

16. _____

17. _____

18. _____

19. _____

20. _____

Valued Feelings	Valued Things/Activities	
1. _____	_____	_____
_____	_____	_____
2. _____	_____	_____
_____	_____	_____
3. _____	_____	_____
_____	_____	_____
4. _____	_____	_____
_____	_____	_____
5. _____	_____	_____
_____	_____	_____

∽ Consequences of Relapsing into Active Use of Alcohol or Other Drugs ∽

Now you know what your top five valued feelings are, and you know what things you need do in order to experience your most important valued feelings. Here is your final exercise. It is in two parts.

Write down your top three valued feelings and the corresponding valued things/activities once more. Then write down what will happen to each of these if you relapse back into active use of alcohol or other drugs.

Valued Feeling and Corresponding Valued Things/Activities	What Will Happen If I Relapse
1. _____	_____
_____	_____
_____	_____

2. _____   _____

   _____   _____

   _____   _____

3. _____   _____

   _____   _____

   _____   _____

◆ **EXERCISE** You have learned that you have used alcohol or other drugs and engaged in alcohol- and drug-using behaviors in order to achieve valued feeling states. What new, non-alcohol-using and non-drug-using behaviors could help you experience those valued feelings? (For example, if one of your valued activities is to earn your high school diploma because you want to experience a feeling of accomplishment, a behavior that could lead to that valued feeling might be to enroll in a GED class.)

_____

_____

_____

_____

_____

_____

_____

❧ Conclusion ❧

Congratulations. You have just completed a major recovery task. You have learned what your values are and how those values determine your behavior. You have also learned that you need to find new behaviors to experience your values.

Review this chapter often. It will help you stay on the road of recovery. As you continue along the road, refer often to your lists of values. Update them and rearrange them as things and circumstances in your life change. Remember, you and your recovery are works in progress. Expect change—it's part of life and growth. See it for what it is; and it is good!

16

Goals

You have decided to stop using chemicals and to work a recovery program to avoid relapsing back into active alcohol or drug use. Staying drug-free must always be your number-one goal. Your main goal should be to continue your recovery from your addiction. But now you must set other goals, too. You must set goals around each of the eight parts of the whole self. The goals you set will lead you to your main goal: ongoing, contented sobriety.

∾ What Is a Goal? ∾

A goal is usually more than a wish or a dream. Wishes and dreams are usually vague ideas about the future. A goal is a clearly defined, reachable, future destination. It is the result of a carefully designed plan.

The Six Elements of a Goal

A goal related to overcoming addiction:

1. should be a clear statement about something you really want;

2. should be positive and move you forward in your recovery and toward your mission;

3. should be reachable and clearly specified in writing;

4. should include a time frame;

5. should include a method that has immediate action steps;

6. should include a way to measure progress.

If a goal does not include these six elements, it is not a goal; it is a wish or a dream.

∾ Steps to Successful Goal Setting and Achievement ∾

Goal setting and goal achievement encompass four steps. You must make four decisions and then follow through on them.

STEP 1 | *Define the Goal*

First you need to decide on a reachable goal. Ask yourself if the goal you want to set is reachable; if in doubt, ask others for their opinion. You must be specific. Ask yourself exactly what you want to accomplish. Let's say you decide you want to lose weight. Saying that your goal is simply to lose weight is not specific enough; you must specify the amount of weight you want to lose. Let's say you decide to lose twenty pounds; twenty pounds is specific.

STEP 2 | *Set the Time Frame*

Now you must decide exactly when you want to lose the twenty pounds. Let's say you decide on a six-month time frame. Let's assume today is the first of January. If today is the first of January, then the first of July should be your target date, exactly six months from today.

STEP 3 | *Plan the Method*

Next you must decide on a method and then take immediate action. Let's say to lose weight you decide:

A. To limit your intake of carbohydrates to 200 grams per day, increase your intake of protein to 60 grams per day, and limit fat intake to 60 grams per day (the figures given are used only as examples; they're not meant to be dietary guidelines);

B. To exercise three times a week for forty-five minutes;

C. To implement the following steps (this is the action step; actually, it is a series of action steps):

　1. You *go* to the store and buy a carbohydrate-gram counter;

　2. You *use* the carbohydrate-gram counter as a guide for meal preparation;

　3. You *join* a health club and *complete* your first workout.

STEP 4 | *Measure Your Progress*

Now you must decide how to measure your progress. If you don't know whether or not you are moving towards your goal, you will lose interest. Then you may give up. If you give up, you will fail.

You must think of the best way to measure your progress. You could check your belt notches; that's one way to see if you are losing weight and moving toward your goal. But you could lose inches by exercising and still not lose weight; so that may not be a good way to measure your progress. You could use a scale. You could weigh yourself the day you start your program, then weigh yourself once a week and see exactly how many pounds you've lost. A scale would give you an accurate way of measuring your progress. There would be no guesswork.

Now you can write a clear, specific goal statement that looks and sounds like this:

"I will lose twenty pounds by the first of July, six months from today. I will limit my intake of carbohydrates to 200 grams per day, increase my intake of protein to 60 grams per day, and limit my fat intake to 60 grams per day. I will exercise for forty-five minutes three times a week. I will weigh myself once a week to check my progress."

Now you have a clearly defined destination. You have a plan, and you have taken action. Now you have a real goal, not just a vague wish or dream for the future.

Here is a summary of the four steps involved in setting and achieving goals:

1. Decide on a specific goal and write it down.

2. Decide on a specific time frame.

3. Decide on a method and take immediate action.

4. Decide on a way to measure your progress.

You can apply this goal-setting and goal-achievement formula to any goal. If the goal is reachable, you will probably succeed.

◆ **EXERCISE** What is a goal?

_____

_____

_____

◆ **EXERCISE** What are the six elements of a goal?

_____

_____

_____

_____

_____

_____

◆ **EXERCISE** List the four steps to successful goal setting and goal achievement.

_____

_____

_____

_____

Message from Bill

In a previous message I said that in the past I didn't have any goals. Now I have goals. Maintaining my recovery from chemical dependency (and from my anger addiction) is still my main goal, but I have other goals, too. I set goals around all eight parts of my whole self. My goals move me ahead on all eight recovery principles.

Goals have to do with the future. But when I set a goal, I don't go and live there with it in the future. I think of the goal I want to set, then I set it; that means I write it down, following the four-step process outlined above. Then I focus back on the here and now.

I have to have something to look forward to, something to plan for; but it has to be meaningful. So when I set a goal it has to connect with one of my higher values; it has to satisfy my recovery mission and move me forward. If it doesn't connect to a higher value, I'll lose interest. I never set a goal that conflicts with my values. When I've done that in the past, I've usually failed; or if I attained my goal, I felt disappointed instead of glad.

❧ Recovery Goals and the Eight Parts of the Whole Self ❧

To begin the process of setting your own goals for recovery, start by thinking about the eight parts of the whole self. The eight parts of the whole self are the framework for the recovery goals you must set. Your goals should lead to improvement in each part. Here is a summary of how to define goals in relation to each of the eight parts:

1. **Biological (physical) goals**—goals for the health of your body and emotions

2. **Environment goals**—goals about where you will live and who you will live with

3. **Behavior goals**—goals about your actions and words

4. **Skill goals**—goals about learning new things and acquiring new tools

5. **Value goals**—goals about expanding your values

6. **Belief goals**—goals about letting go of limiting beliefs and adopting new beliefs that support your recovery

7. **Mission goals**—goals that move you toward your personal mission

8. **Transcendental goals**—goals that help you feel connected to others, to the world, and to the rest of the cosmos in a positive way

Consider the biological part of the whole self. Ask yourself, "What must I do to improve the biological (physical/emotional) part of myself?" Using the word *must* instead of *could* makes it more likely you will follow through. Using the space provided below, list two or three things you must do to improve that part of yourself.

Then go on to the next part. Ask yourself, "What must I do to improve the environmental part of myself?" Then write down two to three things you must do to improve that part. Follow this procedure for each of the eight parts of the whole self. To get you started, two examples are listed below for each part. Your job is to come up with two or three more goals for each part. Spend at least five minutes on each part.

It is important to understand the nature of goals and the power goals have in your life. Goals are things you want to move toward that you believe will lead to the feelings you want and deserve. Goals help you satisfy your positive values. You want to stay happily free of alcohol and other drugs, so you must be goal-oriented. Goals keep you on track and move you along on your mission.

◆ **EXERCISE**

Biological (Physical/Emotional) Goals

1. Stop smoking by my next birthday.

2. Attain my ideal weight by July 1st.

3. _____

4. _____

5. _____

Environment Goals

1. Listen to relaxing music for fifteen minutes a day over the next three months.

2. Make two new sober friends within two weeks from this date.

3. _____

4. _____

5. _____

Behavior (Action/Words) Goals

1. Notice when I am speaking too loudly and immediately reduce the volume.

2. Become aware when I'm breathing too rapidly due to stress, and slow down my breathing.

3. _____

4. _____

5. _____

Skills Goals

1. Learn how to relax under stress in less than two minutes.

2. Teach relaxation skills to three people in thirty days.

3. _____

4. _____

5. _____

Values Goals

1. Read my values list every morning before I leave the house.

2. Discover five more of my valued feelings within two weeks.

3. _____

4. _____

5. _____

Beliefs Goals

1. Identify two more of my negative beliefs and change them within thirty days.

2. Adopt two positive beliefs about other people by the end of this month.

3. _____

4. _____

5. _____

Mission Goals

1. Memorize my mission statement within one week.

2. Recite my mission statement once at night and once in the morning starting tonight.

3. _____

4. _____

5. _____

Transcendental Goals

1. Within the next seven days, visit the philosophy or spirituality section at the public library or at a large bookstore and explore available titles having to do with the transcendental field.

2. Read at least one book that will increase my understanding of transcendental thought.

3. _____

4. _____

5. _____

∾ Moving Toward Your Goals ∾

In the past you were motivated to use alcohol or other drugs to move away from painful feelings such as anxiety or frustration or to intensify pleasurable feelings such as excitement or relaxation. As you start out along the road to recovery, you may sometimes feel that you do not have the resources to move away from painful things and conditions. Goals will help you move toward positive feelings and things. One of the reasons you decided to stop using alcohol or other drugs in the first place was to avoid the pain that your addiction caused you and your loved ones in the past. Now you will have positive goals to move toward. They will help you feel better about yourself and the world, and they will help you avoid relapsing back into active alcohol or drug use.

You have taken the time to set some goals so that you can now begin to move toward something meaningful. Now you can spend more time and energy moving toward the conditions and things that you want in your life. This does not mean you should completely forget about the pain of the past. It does not mean you should become complacent. You must stay aware of the pain and chaos that will occur if you fall back into active chemical use.

But you must learn to focus more time and energy on your goals. Achieving goals will help you go beyond the mere avoidance of the painful results of continued chemical use. Your goals will help you find the kind of fulfilled and happy clean and sober life that you deserve.

As soon as you set a goal, things start happening. Your brain automatically gathers its resources to take you to your goal. *Your brain will take you anywhere you want to go, but you have to tell it exactly where you want to go. To do this, you have to put it in writing.*

Goals will keep you moving toward your mission. Your mission will help you see that recovery is more than the mere absence of alcohol and other drugs, more than the absence of pain.

❦ Setting a Goal to Maintain Your Recovery ❦

You have decided to stop using alcohol or other drugs to change how you feel, and you want to stay stopped; therefore, you must make it a goal and you must write down your goal. Your goal statement should include the benefits of stopping and staying stopped as well as the negative results of relapsing back into alcohol or drug use. When writing your goal statement, use language that makes you feel you have no choice but to stop using alcohol or other drugs immediately, and to stay stopped.

◆ **EXERCISE** Follow these instructions:

1. Write down a clear, concise goal statement (less than twenty words), including a time frame. Example: "I will stop using chemicals to change how I feel, and I will maintain my recovery from chemical dependency, beginning this date: _____."

_____

_____

_____

_____

_____

_____

_____

2. Write down three specific benefits that you believe would make the effort worthwhile. Examples: "More freedom of choice, improved health, improved relationship with my significant other."

Benefits:

_____

_____

_____

_____

_____

3. Write down three specific losses that you know would cause you severe emotional pain if you don't stop using alcohol or other drugs once and for all. Examples: "I will lose my job, because my boss will fire me. Eventually I will lose my health, maybe even die a premature death. I will lose my present relationship or miss out on developing a relationship with someone. I will lose my children."

Losses:

_____

_____

_____

_____

_____

4. Look at the losses you listed. Close your eyes and visualize experiencing the losses. Get in touch with the pain. Example: Imagine yourself without a job or separated from your loved ones. Spend one to two minutes doing this step.

5. Look at the benefit list, then close your eyes and visualize experiencing the benefits. See an image of yourself responding to relapse triggers in a different, clean and sober way, and enjoying each of the benefits. Spend three to five minutes doing this step.

6. Review step four once daily in the morning; follow immediately by executing step five. Repeat steps four and five again in the evening before going to sleep.

17

Beliefs

Addiction to alcohol or other drugs isn't just a behavior problem. Addiction is but a symptom of a real problem that goes much deeper. Addiction is also a *belief* problem. You could even say that your beliefs control your addiction to chemicals.

～ What Are Beliefs? ～

Beliefs are ideas that you have learned about yourself and your world and that you have accepted as true or false, right or wrong, or good or bad. But beliefs are not necessarily facts. Beliefs are not things. They are more like strong feelings. Most of the time you are not aware of your beliefs, because they are stored in your subconscious mind.

Beliefs are the ideas that guide your life. Your beliefs give your life direction and meaning. They are convictions; therefore, beliefs are related to trust. You trust in something when you believe in it. A belief is a feeling you have about whether something is true or false, good or bad, or right or wrong.

Beliefs can be divided into two classes: *beliefs that have a positive effect on your recovery* and *beliefs that have a negative effect on your recovery.*

Positive Beliefs

Positive beliefs, as we refer to them in this discussion, can empower you. They can open doors of possibility and they support you. Positive beliefs make you feel that you are worthwhile, that others are worthwhile, and that the world is worthwhile.

Positive beliefs tend to brighten your outlook. They give you confidence by helping you see the future in an optimistic light. Positive beliefs make you feel good about yourself, others, and the world. Positive beliefs cause positive feelings, and *positive feelings keep you out of the addiction process or relapse process.*

Negative Beliefs

Negative beliefs are toxic. Negative beliefs tend to limit you. They may disempower you. They can even slam shut the doors of possibility. They work against you by making you feel your life is not worthwhile. They make you feel others are not worthwhile, and they make you feel the world is not worthwhile. Negative beliefs cause you to make decisions and to act in ways that keep you stuck in the addiction process; that is why we say negative beliefs are toxic.

Negative beliefs tend to darken your outlook. They increase your fear and take away your confidence by causing you to see the future in a pessimistic light.

Negative beliefs make you feel bad about yourself, other people, and the world. Negative beliefs usually cause negative feelings; *negative feelings are triggers for your addiction.*

How You Acquired Your Beliefs

You were not born with your beliefs—you learned them. You learned your beliefs from your parents, from your teachers, and from your peers. You learned them from the mass media (television, radio, newspapers). You learned some of your beliefs as a result of things that happened to you. Since beliefs are learned, that means you can give up old beliefs and learn new ones. But sometimes it is hard to let go of old beliefs, even when they no longer work for you.

Why You Must Change Some of Your Beliefs

It is important to stay out of the river and away from the falls. You have learned some techniques for interrupting triggers and getting out of the river. You learned how to change your breathing to interrupt triggers quickly. You learned other techniques so you wouldn't go over the falls again. Those skills help you avoid negative results. But you need to make major belief changes, too. What if you were to continue believing that using alcohol or other drugs is a good way to change how you feel? What if you were to continue believing that alcohol and other drugs mean pleasure? Those are the kinds of beliefs that can keep you stuck in your addiction. Those are the beliefs that can keep you in the river.

To fully heal from addiction you must change your character. Since your beliefs are a major part of your character, you must give up the negative beliefs that keep you stuck in your addiction and replace them with beliefs that support your recovery.

A man was asked to take part in an experiment about the power of belief. The experiment used hypnosis. The man was hypnotized and went into a deep trance. A trance is like being very relaxed but still awake. While the man was in the trance, he was told he would be touched on the arm with a piece of hot metal, but he was actually touched with a piece of ice. A blister formed at the point on his arm where he believed he had been touched with hot metal.

Beliefs have a powerful influence in your life. The power of your beliefs can affect all other recovery levels, even the biological level.

∾ Beliefs and Addiction ∾

Your addiction to alcohol or other drugs is likely fueled by negative beliefs. Negative beliefs can function like the gasoline and oil that run a car. That is a strong statement. But stop and think about it. Would you have developed an addiction if you hadn't believed alcohol or other drugs were a good way to change how you feel? Your beliefs are the foundation for your addiction. Your beliefs are more than likely the concrete upon which your addiction is built, and it is your beliefs that probably keep you stuck.

In order to heal from addiction, you must identify the beliefs that may be keeping you stuck, then you must change those beliefs. You must change your beliefs about the meaning of alcohol and other drugs. You must give up the belief that using alcohol or other drugs means nothing but pleasure and, instead, adopt the belief that using alcohol or other drugs generally means pain. Changing your basic beliefs about alcohol or other drugs will make it easier to stop your addiction behavior, because *your beliefs contribute in a very powerful way to your behavior.*

Message from Manny

My name is Manny. I'm from Detroit. I'm an alcoholic. I really wanted to stop drinking, but I kept tripping over my negative beliefs. I didn't know how much they kept me stuck in my addiction to alcohol. I didn't even know that I had a choice in the matter. When I found out it was my negative beliefs that kept sending me back into the relapse cycle and found out that I did have a choice and could change my beliefs, I was finally able to put together some sober time. I learned how to identify my negative beliefs, then learned how to get rid of them and adopt new beliefs that weren't so self-defeating. That's when I started making real progress in my recovery.

◆ **EXERCISE** What are beliefs?

_____

_____

_____

◆ **EXERCISE** What effect do beliefs have on your behavior?

_____

_____

_____

◆ **EXERCISE** What do your beliefs have to do with your addiction?

_____

_____

_____

_____

◆ **EXERCISE** How did you acquire your beliefs and why must you change them?

_____

_____

_____

_____

∾ How to Change Beliefs about Alcohol and Other Drugs
That Keep You Stuck in the Addiction Process ∾

◆ **EXERCISE** First, you must _identify the beliefs you have about alcohol and other drugs that keep you stuck._ Look at the list of beliefs below. Some of them may be familiar. Circle the beliefs that you hold to be true.

Alcohol and other drugs mean pleasure.

If I stop using my drug of choice, I won't be able to deal with stress.

If I stop using my drug of choice, I won't feel comfortable in social situations.

What other beliefs do you hold about anger that keep you stuck in your addiction? List at least five.

_____

_____

_____

_____

◆ **EXERCISE** Now pick a negative belief from your list and *make a decision to change it.* Recognize the belief for what it is: a *limitation.* Recognize that negative beliefs stand in the way of permanently stopping the alcohol or drug use that in the past caused harm to other people and to yourself. You could even plug the negative belief you want to change into the motivation strategy you learned in Chapter 8.

I have made a decision to change the following belief:

_____

_____

_____

_____

◆ **EXERCISE** Now think of a positive belief that you want to adopt to replace the negative one. You may have targeted the belief "Alcohol and other drugs mean pleasure" as the one you want to change. Now you might write down, "I can learn how to feel pleasure without using alcohol or other drugs" as the new belief to take the place of the old, negative belief.

Here are some examples of beliefs that will help you stop using alcohol or other drugs once and for all:

I can learn new ways to feel pleasure without using alcohol or other drugs.

I can learn how to feel confident without using alcohol or other drugs.

My staying clean and sober is the only way to keep on track toward a contented, happy life for me and for my loved ones.

This is the new belief that I will use to replace the old, negative belief:

_____

_____

_____

_____

◆ **EXERCISE** Now write down three things you've already lost because of the negative beliefs you've held about alcohol or other drugs. Examples: "Loss of freedom, loss of career advancement, loss of a love relationship."

Three things I have lost due to my negative beliefs about alcohol and other drugs:

_____

_____

_____

◆ **EXERCISE** Now write down three potential future losses you will suffer if you continue to hold the negative belief. Examples: "Further jail or prison time, more lost career opportunities, further rejection by others."

Three things I will lose in the future if I don't let go of the negative belief:

_____

_____

_____

◆ **EXERCISE** Write down three specific benefits you know you'll gain by changing that negative belief. Examples: "Improved health, career advancement, potential for an exciting new relationship."

Three ways I will benefit if I do change the belief:

_____

_____

_____

◆ **EXERCISE** Now recall the old negative belief that you want to change, and look at the losses you listed. Close your eyes and visualize the three losses you've already suffered, and get in touch with the pain. Look at the future losses you listed and visualize yourself experiencing those future losses. Exactly how does all this make you feel? Spend at least three minutes on this step.

How I feel about my past losses, and how I will feel in the future if I do not change that belief:

_____

_____

_____

_____

_____

_____

◆ **EXERCISE** Now recall the new positive belief and look at the benefits list. Close your eyes and imagine the future benefits of replacing that old negative belief with the new positive belief. Notice how adopting the new belief will make you feel. Spend at least three minutes on this step.

How the benefits of changing that negative belief will make me feel in the future:

_____

_____

_____

_____

_____

The best time to go through this process is just before you go to sleep at night. Repeat the process every night for a period of five to seven days. Then you can start another cycle using a different negative belief.

∼ Acquiring Positive Beliefs about Yourself, Others, and the World ∼

Positive beliefs are beliefs that make you feel good about yourself, others, and the rest of the world. Positive beliefs are positive statements, whether they are true or not in a strict scientific sense. Positive statements about yourself are called *affirmations*.

Positive Beliefs about Yourself

◆ **EXERCISE** Read the positive self-affirmations listed below. Read them to yourself every morning before you start your day and each night just before you go to sleep.

I am a worthwhile person.

I deserve to be happy.

I deserve love.

I deserve respect.

I have a purpose.

◆ **EXERCISE** Make a list of other self-empowering positive beliefs or affirmations that will help you heal from your addiction.

These are other self-empowering positive beliefs or affirmations I want to acquire:

_____

_____

_____

_____

_____

_____

If possible, tape-record your self-empowering beliefs; then listen to the tape several times a day.

Positive Beliefs about Others

It is important to hold positive beliefs about yourself; it is equally important to hold positive beliefs about others.

◆ **EXERCISE** Read the positive beliefs about others listed below. Circle the beliefs you already hold.

Most people are basically good.

Most people are willing to help you when you need their help.

Most people can be trusted.

◆ **EXERCISE** List at least three other positive beliefs you hold about others.

_____

_____

_____

_____

◆ **EXERCISE** List at least three positive beliefs you would like to hold about other people but don't right now.

_____

_____

_____

_____

Positive Beliefs about the World

It is important to have positive beliefs about yourself and others. You also need positive beliefs about the world. Negative beliefs about the world will keep you stuck in your addiction to alcohol or other drugs.

◆ **EXERCISE** Look at the positive beliefs about the world listed below and circle the beliefs you already hold.

The world is mostly a friendly place.

The world has meaning.

I am a meaningful part of the world.

I have an important part to play in the world.

◆ **EXERCISE** List at least three other positive beliefs about the world you would like to hold.

_____

_____

_____

_____

∾ Beliefs about Death ∾

The fear of death weighs on the minds of most human beings, but it has been found that people addicted to alcohol or other drugs often feel the weight of the fear of death more heavily than other people. Intense fear of death may be one of the basic triggers for your addiction. Intense fear of any kind is a major trigger for most people's addictions.

Intense fear of death is directly related to negative beliefs about death. Until you give up your negative beliefs about death, you will never be rid of the fear of death. Until the fear of death is put to rest, that intense negative feeling will always be a major relapse trigger.

Negative Beliefs about Death

◆ **EXERCISE** Look at the negative beliefs about death listed below. Do you hold any of these beliefs? Circle the negative beliefs you hold about death.

Death is the end. There is nothing after that.

Death is the final insult.

After the struggle, death is your reward.

Death is a time of punishment and pain.

Life has no purpose; death has even less purpose.

◆ **EXERCISE** Do you hold other negative beliefs about death? Write them down.

_____

_____

_____

◆ **EXERCISE** How do your negative beliefs about death make you feel?

_____

_____

_____

Positive Beliefs about Death

◆ **EXERCISE** Look at the positive beliefs about death listed below. Circle the ones you now hold, if any.

Death is not the end; it leads to greater growth.

Death is a great resting time.

The soul survives the death of the body.

This life is a school. If I learn what I need to learn, I will go to a higher grade when I die.

◆ **EXERCISE** List at least three positive beliefs about death you would like to hold.

_____

_____

_____

◆ **EXERCISE** How would positive beliefs about death make you feel?

_____

_____

_____

_____

Message from Jim

My name is Jim. My addiction to cocaine cost me more than I like to admit. I lost five years of my freedom. I lost my family; I almost lost my life. I'm still on parole, but I'm starting to get my act together.

I didn't know how much I feared death. Of course, I denied that I was afraid of death at all. I was a real tough guy, you see. But death was one of my major fears. I didn't dwell on it all the time, at least not consciously. But, once in a while, it would pop up to the surface. Then I'd find myself thinking about it. Then I'd get depressed. Then I'd head for the dope man's house.

My belief was, you live a little while. You go through a lot of pain, maybe you cop a little happiness, then you die. And that was that—period. No applause, no reward. They stick you in the ground to rot. You as a personality disappear forever like a puff of smoke in a windstorm. That's what I used to believe about death. No wonder I got depressed every time thoughts of death came into my mind.

Finally, I saw how my negative beliefs about death were keeping me stuck in my cocaine addiction. So I decided to change my beliefs about death. I didn't care whether my new beliefs were "right" or "wrong." I didn't care whether they were "true" or "false." I chose some new beliefs that reduced my fear of death. It took a little while to get used to the new beliefs. But when they started to feel "true," my feelings about death changed. My fear of death grew smaller and smaller, and that had a positive effect on my recovery.

18

Life Mission

You have decided to stop using alcohol and other drugs, and to stay stopped. You have sorted out your values. You have set some goals related to each of the eight parts of your whole self. You have decided to change old beliefs that keep you stuck. You have now come to the next important step in your recovery from addiction. In this chapter you will learn the importance of identifying your life mission. You will discover and write down your personal mission statement, and you will learn how to use it to help you maintain a clean and sober lifestyle.

∿ What Is Your Life Mission? ∿

Your mission is what you believe to be the meaning of your life. It is what you believe you were born to be and to do. It is what you believe to be the main reason that you are alive. Your life mission is what is left when everything else that you find important about your life has been stripped away from you.

Your mission *must benefit others*. It must bring good into your life, and it must bring good into the lives of others.

It is useful to believe that you were born with a mission but have forgotten what it is. Now you must rediscover your mission. Rediscovering your mission may be difficult, because your mission is buried deep in your subconscious mind. Now you must resurrect it by pulling it back up into consciousness the way the sun pulls flowers up from the earth in springtime.

It is useful to think of your mission not as a choice, but as a mandate. Think of your mission as something you *must* do.

People who lack conscious awareness of their mission
and have lost many of the things they value
are likely at high risk for losing the will to live.

Your mission statement is potentially your most powerful tool. It could pull you out of the addiction process or relapse process when everything else fails, and it could help keep you out of the process at other times. It can be a powerful anchor in the bottom of your boat. It can help you reach shore no matter how far you are from the bank.

Message from Allen

My name is Allen. I'm a recovering alcoholic. I had no idea I had a purpose, a life mission. In fact, I was sure I didn't have a purpose and that no one else had a purpose either. That was the main reason I was stuck in my addiction to alcohol for so long. To me, life was meaningless. Believing that, I couldn't make sense out of anything. Even good feelings didn't make sense to me, and I sure couldn't make sense out of the pain in my life. I was an atheist, and of course that didn't help; as an atheist I was sure nothing had a purpose. Nothing had meaning to me. I believed everything happened by chance, like a dice game. That was before I heard of Einstein and his famous statement. He said, "God doesn't play dice with us," or something close to that. I don't think I could have discovered my life mission if I hadn't first given up being an atheist. Finally I did. Then I discovered my purpose. I discovered my mission and wrote it down. Then things started making sense; then I could make sense even out of the pain.

❧ The Story of Viktor Frankl ❧

The story of Viktor Frankl is often used to illustrate the power of having a personal mission. Viktor Frankl was a Jewish psychiatrist who spent four years in a Nazi concentration camp. Conditions in the camp were so horrible that they were almost beyond the comprehension of anyone who hadn't actually gone through it. The ratio of survival in the camp was one in twenty; for every person who survived, nineteen others died.

The Nazis did everything they could to strip away Frankl's humanity. They starved him, beat him, and humiliated him unmercifully. But the Nazis could not break this courageous man, no matter what they did.

Allied soldiers liberated Frankl's camp at the end of the war. When they saw how horrific things had been, they were amazed to find Frankl and a few others still alive. The soldiers looked at the conditions in the camp. They saw the pathetic condition of the few survivors, and could not believe their eyes. When the soldiers interviewed Frankl, they could see that Frankl had been treated no better than those who died. The soldiers asked Viktor Frankl how he managed to survive when so few others were able to.

Frankl said, "I survived because I had a mission."

At first the soldiers did not understand. They asked for clarification.

Frankl said, "I survived because I had a mission. My mission was, first, just to survive this camp; then to tell the whole world what happened here, so that no one would ever have to go through anything like this again."

That was Frankl's personal mission statement. That is what kept Frankl alive.

Frankl said he stayed focused on his mission. He said his mission made it possible to make sense out of what was happening to him; it made it possible to make sense even out of the pain.

Frankl said he used his mission to manage his feelings; he used it to fight against fear and despair. He used his mission to control the anger and rage he felt at the hands of the Nazis. He said he knew he couldn't do or say anything in anger to his captors; they would kill him if he did.

Frankl said most of the prisoners who died didn't have a mission. Therefore, they couldn't make sense out of the pain. Some of them did or said angry things to the Nazis, and the Nazis killed them. Other prisoners became so depressed they lost all hope, and just gave up and died. Many committed suicide.

After his release from the concentration camp, Viktor Frankl went on to develop a new form of therapy. He called it *logotherapy*, from the Greek word *logos*, which Frankl interpreted as "meaning." Frankl believed that people suffering from emotional or addictive disorders would experience spontaneous healing once they became aware of their life mission. Frankl taught that people who have a conscious sense of purpose and mission live longer, happier lives.

∿ How to Discover Your Life Mission ∿

Frankl did not know what his life mission was going to be until he went to the concentration camp; he may not even have known he had a mission. At first he couldn't make sense out of the pain he experienced in the camp anymore than the other prisoners could. As conditions at the camp got worse, Frankl's condition got worse. His body and mind began to break down. He, too, began to lose hope. Then out of deep despair Frankl asked himself a simple question: "What is the meaning of my life? What is my mission?" The answer was: "My mission is to survive this camp and then tell the whole world what happened here, so no other human being will ever have to go through anything like this again."

You must ask the same question Frankl asked. You must ask yourself: "What is the meaning of my life?" The answer to this question is your life mission.

∿ Why Should You Write Down Your Mission Statement? ∿

You read Viktor Frankl's story above. You saw how he used his mission statement as a way to manage his feelings, especially his anger. Frankl focused his attention on his mission all of the time; he was always aware of it and could always remember it. He kept it always in his consciousness so that he would not forget it.

The reason you are writing down your mission is so that you will remember it. You will forget it if you don't write it down. If you forget your life mission, you will be unable to use it to help yourself make sense out of what is happening in your life and to help you recover from your addiction to alcohol or other drugs.

◆ **EXERCISE** Write down your mission statement. Here are the ground rules:

1. Begin with your commitment to remain abstinent from alcohol and other drugs.

2. Your mission statement should be brief (twenty-five words or less).

3. Your mission statement should cause you to have strong positive feelings about yourself, other people, and the world.

4. Your mission statement should reflect your highest values.

5. Your mission statement must benefit other people as well as yourself.

6. Your mission statement should make you feel a sense of urgency. Reading it should make you feel that you must fulfill your mission.

Here are two examples of life-mission statements that others have written.

"My life mission is to continue to recover from my addiction and to behave in a way that pulls out the best from myself and others."

"My life mission is to stay alcohol- and drug-free and to help others who are also struggling to recover from their addiction."

Bill's Mission Statement

Bill Fleeman, the author of this workbook, spent a lot of time thinking about his mission statement before writing it down. It was not an easy task. When he finally got it down, he felt at the time that it was exactly as he wanted it to look and sound. He felt certain it would be the final version. About a year later, Bill found it necessary to rewrite his mission statement. He had continued to change and grow and found he had to change his mission statement so that it would reflect the change and growth he had experienced. Another year went by. Bill changed and grew a little more, so he had to change his mission statement again. The changes he made each time did not result in a completely different mission statement. The result of each change was an expansion of the original mission statement. Bill has said his mission statement will probably continue to change, at least in small ways, as he continues to change and grow.

Each morning before he starts his day, Bill recites his mission statement. His current mission statement appears below. Notice that Bill's mission statement also addresses his and other people's anger issues.

My life mission is to live a clean and sober, nonviolent lifestyle, and to help as many other human beings as possible find their clean and sober pathway to peace.

Once you have completed your mission statement, make several copies of it. Keep a copy of your mission statement in your pocket or purse. Keep a copy of your mission statement next to your favorite chair; tape a copy to the bathroom mirror. Read your mission statement at least once in the morning and once at night. Read it every time a relapse trigger occurs. If possible, record your mission statement on audiotape. Listen to the tape one or more times a day.

Write your mission statement in the space provided on the next page. Use pencil so you can erase. Take your time. This is a very important part of the healing process, so take it seriously. You will have to write several drafts before your mission statement is really complete. If you think you are done after just one or two attempts, that's okay, but keep thinking about it and changing it as needed.

My life mission is to stay clean and sober and...

_____

_____

_____

_____

_____

_____

_____

_____

⮹ Mission Support ⮹

Now that you have discovered your mission and have written it down, you will need to develop some mission support. Your mission support should be made of positive feelings. In order to stay on your mission, you need to maintain a positive emotional state. You need to have good feelings, consistently. Of course you can't feel good all of the time, but in order to stay on your mission you must feel good as much of the time as possible. Positive feelings help you stay on course; they help you keep moving in the direction of your mission. Negative feelings will send you off course, away from your mission. Anger is a negative feeling, so anger will knock you off your recovery path. Confidence is a positive feeling; confidence will keep you on course.

◆ **EXERCISE** In this exercise you will make a list of the positive feelings that will support your mission. You may refer to your values list from Chapter 15. Your valued feelings are the kind of positive feelings you will need to include on your mission-support list. You can list your valued feelings to get started on your mission-support list.

In the space provided on the following page, write down the positive feelings that will help you stay on track toward your life mission. Try to list at least twenty positive feelings.

Mission Support

1. _____

2. _____

3. _____

4. _____

5. _____

6. _____

7. _____

8. _____

9. _____

10. _____

11. _____

12. _____

13. _____

14. _____

15. _____

16. _____

17. _____

18. _____

19. _____

20. _____

Message from Bill

When I discovered my mission, things happened that made me aware of its power. One very dramatic thing happened. It was when I was working as a counselor in a drug and alcohol inpatient treatment unit.

I woke up feeling sick one morning. I was feverish and had a headache. I felt bad all over. Thinking I might feel better later, I went to work anyway. Later I felt worse instead of better and decided to go home early. On my way out, a client stopped me in the hallway. He said he was depressed and needed to talk. He said he was having strong cocaine cravings. He said if he didn't talk to somebody, he was afraid he was going to pack up his belongings and leave treatment.

At first, I thought, "Why me?" I was about to tell him to go talk to one of the other counselors, but then I changed my mind. A small voice inside whispered, "Hey, Bill! How come you're taking up space on this planet? What is your purpose, your mission?" I unlocked my office, and the depressed client and I went in and sat down. I listened to the client's story and gave him some feedback. After about forty-five minutes I ended the session.

As the client walked out the door, he said he felt better after talking to me. He said he was still having cravings but they weren't as strong, and he said he would stay on the unit. As I cleared my desk and prepared to leave, I made a remarkable discovery: All my symptoms were gone! I felt my forehead. It was cool to the touch. My fever was gone! So was my headache. I no longer felt ill. The client had said he felt better; I felt better! And I felt great the rest of the day and night.

Why had my symptoms disappeared, I wondered? What happened to my fever and headache? At first it puzzled me, then I figured it out. My personal mission, in a nutshell, was to help people. Though I was ill and didn't at first want to stop on my way out the door and meet with the client, my mission popped into my conscious mind. Becoming aware of my personal life mission caused me to set aside my desire to go home and instead led me to decide to spend a little time with the client who had sought my help.

During the counseling session, I became totally focused on helping the client. All my mental and emotional energy was focused on that goal. My mission called on every other part of my whole self to help, including the biological part. Even my immune system made an all-out effort. It removed all of my symptoms so that I would have the physical energy I needed to get through the session.

19

The Transcendental
Part of the Self

In Chapter 6, you learned that the transcendental part of the self is defined as a positive feeling of connectedness to other people, to the universe, and to the rest of the cosmos. You also learned that in order to maintain a clean and sober lifestyle and be *happy*, you must change and grow in every part of your whole self, including the transcendental part.

Although *The Pathways to Sobriety Workbook* is not a religious document, and participation in the Pathways to Sobriety self-help program does not require a belief in a higher power, the workbook and self-help program do recognize that the whole self includes a part that could be labeled *transcendental* or *metaphysical* (or even *spiritual*). Unless you already have a transcendental belief system that supports your recovery, you are strongly encouraged to take a close and serious look at your transcendental part and to adopt a belief system that supports your new clean and sober lifestyle. Even if you *do* have a transcendental belief system in place that is working to support your recovery, you are still encouraged to read this chapter and to complete the exercises in it. Doing so may give you new insights that will help you maintain a contented clean and sober lifestyle.

∾ The Importance of the Transcendental Part ∾

To be happy means to be contented, joyous, or serene. It can also mean to be blissful, satisfied, or merry. There are many other words that describe what it means to be happy. Whatever word you choose to describe what happiness means to you will depend on your own unique personal history and experience.

Together, all of the eight parts of the self determine whether you will be happy or unhappy as you continue to work your recovery program and continue to change and grow. But the primary determinant of your happiness is, logically, the very highest level—that is, the transcendental or metaphysical level. The quality of this part of your whole self, therefore, will largely determine the quality of all of the other parts of your whole self.

People who find meaning at the transcendental level are likely to have a positive personal mission, to possess useful empowering beliefs, to have uplifting values and worthwhile goals, to develop good emotional-state management skills, to exhibit sober behavior, to choose a supportive environment, and to feel physically and emotionally well. People who have a healthy orientation at the transcendental level seem to enjoy more choices, in general, and naturally choose people, places, and things that reinforce their recovery.

Although people who develop positive beliefs at the transcendental level may experience ongoing physical and emotional pain, even very intense pain on a daily basis, they seem to be able to deal with it more effectively. In general, people who focus on their transcendental part in a balanced way often experience less conflict in their lives, and less pain.

People who have never been addicted to alcohol or other drugs are often those who have a well-developed sense of connectedness at the transcendental level. People who consistently pay attention to this part of the whole self are much more likely to enjoy contented recovery. Indeed, addiction to alcohol or other drugs is often a response to the feelings of helplessness and hopelessness that arise when a person cannot find meaning at the transcendental level of the whole self. People who are addicted to alcohol or other drugs are often trying to experience a feeling of connectedness to others, to the universe, and to some abstract "something" outside of themselves. For some alcoholics and drug addicts, use of alcohol and other drugs is a kind of "transcendental search," as well as an attempt to assuage the emotional pain that results from feeling totally disconnected and alone. Remember Bill's story? He was addicted to alcohol and other drugs, as well as to anger and rage, and was an atheist from age seven until he began his recovery many years later.

The transcendental part of the whole self is related to all of the other parts, but it is related more closely to the higher levels. It is more closely related to the mission part than it is to any other part of the whole self.

A well-defined transcendental focus can cause your brain to organize your resources differently, can lead to a completely different personal identity, and can encourage you to adopt different beliefs. It will probably cause you to reorder your values and to set goals that you would not otherwise set or even entertain. It can encourage you to develop sharper skills and can make it easier to change your behavior. As you learned in Chapter 6, the condition of your transcendental self can even affect your physical and emotional health.

What Kind of Transcendental Belief System Should You Adopt?

The Pathways to Sobriety Workbook and self-help program suggest that full recovery from alcohol or drug addiction generally requires the inclusion of positive beliefs at the transcendental level. But it is not the job of *The Pathways to Sobriety Workbook* or program to choose your transcendental or metaphysical path. It is up to you to choose a belief system that serves you best. Pathways to Sobriety makes only one suggestion: *that you choose a transcendental or metaphysical orientation that supports your recovery from addiction*. Otherwise, instead of supporting your new clean and sober lifestyle, it will work against you. Bear this in mind: Whatever transcendental philosophy you may choose as a way to experience and express this important part of the whole self will be closely connected to your mission, yet take you beyond it.

The way people get in touch with their transcendental self differs from culture to culture and from individual to individual. All cultures have rituals that help people get in touch with their transcendental part. In some cultures, people learn rituals from the village shaman. In other cultures, people learn their rituals from ministers, priests, or rabbis. In most cultures, people come together periodically to share rituals with one another. They attend festivals. They go to churches or temples. Almost always, the desired goal is to experience a feeling of connectedness to other people, to the universe, and to the rest of the cosmos.

Speaking of rituals, people addicted to alcohol or other drugs often share a set of rituals associated with their drug of choice. The rituals revolve around obtaining and preparing the drug, handling the drug, and using the drug. For example, heroin addicts make an elaborate ritual of preparing and shooting up. Crack-cocaine addicts have their special rituals. So do alcohol addicts. Loss of the rituals associated with their drug of choice becomes part of the withdrawal syndrome that recovering people experience, especially during the early days of recovery. It is important, therefore, to replace the rituals associated with the use of alcohol or other drugs with rituals that support abstinence. Developing rituals associated with the transcendental part of the self will help you replace the old self-destructive rituals.

You may already have found your transcendental path. If that is the case, then you will only need to continue on that particular path. If you have not yet found a satisfying path, then you will want to focus on finding one.

⤳ Nonreligious Transcendental Philosophy ⤳

As stated elsewhere in the workbook, *spiritual* or *spirituality* doesn't have to mean *religious* or *religion*. *The Pathways to Sobriety Workbook* uses the word *transcendental* instead of *spiritual* because it is less likely to offend those who are uncomfortable with the word *spiritual*. Sometimes, and for the same reason, the word *metaphysical* has been used.

There are people who do not belong to any of the great religions. They are not Christians, Jews, Buddhists, Muslims, or Hindus, yet they adhere to beliefs and ideas that are clearly spiritual. Their beliefs and ideas make them feel connected in a meaningful way to other people and to the rest of the universe even though they may not believe in the traditional idea of a supreme being. They hold to a form of nonreligious spirituality. They sometimes call themselves *humanists* because they believe strongly in the dignity and worth of all human beings and often work hard at helping others.

One way to begin the process of developing a healthy transcendental self is through reading. Go to the library, or go on the Internet, and read about transcendentalism. Another way to begin your transcendental exploration is by learning about some of the "New-Age" approaches. You could take a class on the subject at your local college. You could join a discussion group. You can probably think of many other ways to acquire information that would relate to your transcendental exploration. You are strongly urged not to omit this part of the recovery process. Unless you pay attention to the transcendental part, which some believe to be the highest and most powerful part of the whole self, you may be unable to achieve the kind of happy and contented sobriety that you deserve.

Message from Duane

Hi. I'm Duane. I'm in recovery from my addiction to alcohol. I grew up on a reservation in South Dakota. I went to a Christian church on the reservation. I started drinking when I was twelve. I quit school and quit church when I was sixteen. I left the rez and went to live in Seattle, Washington. I was a construction worker till my drinking got so bad I couldn't hold a job. I wound up on skid row. I went to jail a couple times. Nothing serious, drunk and disorderly mostly. I lost everything there on those Seattle streets— I mean everything. I went to a couple of rehabs. The second one worked. About a year later, I was still sober but I sure wasn't happy. I felt alone. In a room full of people, I still felt alone.

I ended up going back to the reservation to visit my relatives. My family was proud that I'd sobered up. One of my cousins was in recovery too, but he looked like he was happy. My cousin could see that I wasn't happy. We had a talk and my cousin asked me about my spiritual condition, which Pathways to Sobriety calls the transcendental part of the whole self. I didn't want to talk about that. But he pressed me. He told me I would never be happy in recovery and would probably go back to drinking sooner or later unless I worked a spiritual program. I told my cousin I'd never go back to the church where I went as a kid. I had too many resentments against it. He said I didn't have to. He told me he'd been practicing the old Lakota ways and suggested I try out the old ways too. He said maybe it would help me feel connected. I thought about it. Finally, I started studying some of the spiritual practices of my ancestors. It was hard, because all the prayers and rituals were in the Lakota language and I didn't know very much Lakota. The school I went to as a kid on the rez didn't allow us to speak Lakota words. We were punished if we did. All that changed not long ago, so now it's okay. Anyway, I had a lot of catching up to do when it came to the language. I started going to the sweat lodge to pray. I learned the Lakota words as I went along. I learned a special prayer that I say every morning before I start my day. It helps me stay aware of the importance of the spiritual or transcendental part of my recovery. Soon my friend will guide me on my first vision quest. I'm still learning about Lakota spirituality. But now that I feel more connected to Wakan Tanka (Great Mystery), I feel connected to other people too, and to the rest of Wakan Tankas's creation. Now I'm happier in recovery.

◆ **EXERCISE** Duane chose to explore and adopt the beliefs of his Lakota ancestors, rather than returning to the spiritual belief system he grew up with. Will you explore other beliefs, or will you return to the transcendental or spiritual belief system you may have grown up with?

_____

_____

_____

_____

◆ **EXERCISE** If you decide to explore other transcendental beliefs, how will you begin your search?

_____

_____

_____

_____

◆ **EXERCISE** Duane chose daily prayer as one way to help himself stay aware of the importance of the transcendental part of his recovery from addiction. What ritual will you use?

_____

_____

_____

_____

Message from Bill

I haven't, as yet, embraced any of the world's major religions. I am in a continual process of building my personal transcendental belief system out of what I learn from many different systems. That's how I have to do it.

Recently, as I was putting the finishing touches on this workbook and getting ready to submit the manuscript to the publisher, I had the privilege of watching a group of Buddhist monks spend four days and use millions of tiny grains of sand of different colors to create a mandala—a beautiful, intricate circular design about four feet square. The mandala represented the world. Upon completion of the mandala, the monks destroyed it by sweeping all of the sand into a pile. Then the monks led a procession down to a lake and poured the sand into the waters.

The monk's interpreter explained that the destruction of the mandala symbolized the impermanence of all things. The interpreter said the monks had concentrated on thoughts of peace while creating the mandala. Pouring the sand into the waters of the lake symbolized the monks' desire for their thoughts of peace to flow out to the rest of the world.

I was impressed by the entire ceremony. But I was even more impressed by what I had seen in the faces of the monks both during the building of the mandala and after its destruction. It was the peace I saw in their faces that impressed me most.

20

Forgiveness

∼ The Importance of Forgiveness ∼

Forgiveness is the final step in the recovery process.

The word *forgiveness* means to "cease to resent"; it means to "pardon" or "release."

Horrible things may have been done to you during your life. Some of the things you have done to others while you were drinking or using other drugs may have been as bad, or worse, than what was done to you. But you can learn how to heal from your addiction by learning how to forgive those who harmed you and by learning how to forgive yourself. Forgiveness helps make the pain of the past go away.

Forgiving others and forgiving yourself can remove the barrier that otherwise could continue to stand in the way of the total healing from addiction that you deserve. Forgiveness will help you let go of the feelings of humiliation, resentment, guilt, and shame that would otherwise threaten to plunge you back into the river and over the falls.

Once you forgive, the power of the memories of what was done to you and what you have done to others will likely be greatly diminished.

Once you forgive, you will be amazed. You may find out how the caged bird feels when it is released and why it sings. You may move with increased energy toward your goals. You may discover the joy that can be found in service to others. You may make a giant leap on the path of your mission. You may learn the meaning of serenity. You may feel connected to others, to the world, and to the higher power of your understanding as never before. You may feel transformed.

But forgiving is not an easy thing to do. The first and hardest part of forgiveness is getting past the negative beliefs about forgiveness—the beliefs you have about forgiveness that have a negative effect on you. Look at the examples of negative beliefs about forgiveness listed below.

Examples of negative beliefs about forgiveness:

- Forgiveness means allowing people to walk over me.

- I could never forgive those who caused me so much pain.

- Those who hurt me don't deserve to be forgiven.

- I don't deserve to be forgiven.

- I can't forgive myself.

◆ **EXERCISE** What does the word *forgiveness* mean?

_____

_____

_____

◆ **EXERCISE** Why is forgiveness so important?

_____

_____

_____

◆ **EXERCISE** This exercise will help prepare you to forgive others and yourself. Review the belief-changing techniques you learned in Chapter 17. Think of at least two positive beliefs about forgiveness that would help you begin to forgive.

Examples:

- If I forgive others, I will someday end up thinking better thoughts about myself.

- If I forgive myself for what I have done to others, I will be able to move further along the road to happy and contented sobriety.

_____

_____

_____

_____

You must forgive those who harmed you in the past, no matter how much you may have suffered as a result of what was done to you. No matter how great the pain, no matter how deep the scars on your body or in your mind, you must find it in your heart to forgive those who harmed you. You must let go of your resentment and hate.

In order to forgive, you do not have to *forget*. In fact, it is often not possible to forget. You can repress, but you probably cannot forget what has been done to you or what you have done to others. When you forgive, however, you will likely stop spending so much time thinking about those who harmed you and about what they did. Once you forgive, chances are that your overall tension level will decrease and you will feel less anxiety as you go about your daily life. You will probably have fewer cravings for alcohol or other drugs. You will also likely have more positive energy for dealing with the stressors that occur every day in the here and now.

As you forgive all those who have harmed you, remember this: You are not forgiving them for *their* good; you are forgiving them for *your own* good.

◆ **EXERCISE** Make a list of people who have harmed you or toward whom you hold strong feelings of resentment or anger. Briefly state what the person did to you and how it made you feel.

Example:

Name: My father.

What the person did: He came home drunk and beat me up.

How it made me feel: I felt unloved.

Name: _____

What the person did: _____

How it made me feel: _____

Name: _____

What the person did: _____

How it made me feel: _____

Name: _____

What the person did: _____

How it made me feel: _____

Name: _____

What the person did: _____

How it made me feel: _____

Name: _____

What the person did: _____

How it made me feel: _____

◆ **EXERCISE** Find a quiet place to sit. Read the statement below to yourself, filling in the blank with the name of the person you have made a decision to forgive. There may be more than one person you need to forgive, but start with one person. When you feel you have really forgiven that person, write the next person's name in the blank.

> *"I forgive you, _____, not because I have forgotten what you did to me. I forgive you not just because I want to be free of the pain you inflicted on me. I forgive you so that I may be free of the resentment and anger that pain has caused in my life and that has contributed to the pain I have caused others. I forgive you so that I may recover from my addiction."*

After you complete the exercise, call someone you trust. If you have a Pathways to Sobriety mentor or friend, call and tell them what you have just accomplished. Share it, in a general way, at your next Pathways to Sobriety meeting. Open yourself up to positive feedback from the group.

You may need to repeat this exercise more than once. You may need to repeat it many times before you *feel* you have truly forgiven those who harmed you. Repeat the exercise once or twice a day, until you really *feel* you have forgiven them.

๛ Forgiving Yourself ๛

Now you will focus on forgiving yourself. Don't stop short of your main goal now. It would be like climbing the mountain only to stop a few yards from the summit and, turning your back, deprive yourself of the wonderful view from the top. You have come this far. So don't stop now; go all the way to the mountaintop.

As you did with the exercise on forgiving others, find a quiet place to sit. Read the statement below to yourself. When you finish, share what you have accomplished with your Pathways to Peace mentor or friend, or with someone else you trust.

◆ **EXERCISE** Make a list of people you have harmed because of your addiction. Next to each name, briefly state what you did or said to the person. You can refer back to the list you made in Chapter 7 of the people you have harmed and include those names on your list. If you feel you have done major harm to more than five people, you can list them on a separate sheet of paper.

Example:

Name: My wife

What I did: I came home drunk, and during an argument threatened to hit her with my fist.

The result: My wife broke down and cried.

Name: _____

What the person did: _____

How it made me feel: _____

Name: _____

What the person did: _____

How it made me feel: _____

Name: _____

What the person did: _____

How it made me feel: _____

Name: _____

What the person did: _____

How it made me feel: _____

Name: _____

What the person did: _____

How it made me feel: _____

◆ **EXERCISE** Find a quiet place to sit, then read the statement below to yourself.

> *"I forgive myself for hurting _____, not because I feel what I did is excusable in any way, and not because I feel I do not deserve the consequences I suffered for what I did or the consequences I may suffer in the future because of my use of alcohol or other drugs. I forgive myself so that I may heal from the guilt which would cause me to relapse back into active addiction."*

Repeat this exercise at least once a day until you really *feel* you have forgiven yourself.

In Chapter 7 you were asked to become willing to forgive. You did some exercises about apologizing to people you had hurt. Review the work you did. Are there some loose ends you need to tie up? Do you need to follow up your forgiveness exercise with some more amends work? If so, now is the time.

Forgiveness is an ongoing process. Be patient with yourself. If the anger and hurt keep coming back, you know you're not done. Work at it. You'll know when you're done—your pain will greatly decrease and may even go away completely.

Message from Beth

My name is Beth. I'm a recovering addict. I know how important forgiveness is.

I was thirty before I began my recovery. I was a hurtin' unit, as they say; I was full of rage. My father had abused me, if you know what I mean. I was in kindergarten when he did it the first time. My mother found out when I was twelve. She wanted to kill him; instead, she took me away. I was angry at my father for what he did; I was angry with my mother for taking me away. I was so confused! I took my anger out on everybody. Finally, I saw I was addicted to anger. Fortunately, I also saw that I could change my behavior. I changed some of my behavior fast. But I wanted to be happy, not just nonviolent, so I knew I had to forgive. I forgave my father in an unsent letter, because he was dead by then; I forgave my mother face-to-face; finally, I forgave myself. Forgiving myself was the hardest part. Having forgiven others as well as myself, I started growing fast—I mean fast!

Sometimes my life is still no bed of roses. But there are moments now that are wonderful! Most of the time I feel good about myself, and most of the time I feel good about other people. That's totally different than it used to be.

∾ Self-Contract ∾

When you began this workbook you signed a self-agreement. You have now completed the workbook. But completing the workbook is only the beginning. You should continue to apply what you have learned for the rest of your life.

Now it is time to sign a self-contract. A contract is stronger than an agreement. An agreement indicates that you will *try* to fulfill the points of the agreement to the best of your ability at the time it is written; a contract is a promise—a total commitment. A self-contract means you won't just try; it means you will fulfill all the points. Period.

Self-Contract

Now you understand the nature of addiction. Now you have a program that will help you stop using alcohol or other drugs once and for all. Now you have no excuses. Now you are ready for a self-contract.

Look at the self-contract below. Sign it when you're ready. Do not enter into it lightly. You will want to have someone you like and admire witness your signature.

I, _____, am now totally committed to living an alcohol- and drug-free life from this day on, as of this date, _____.

1. I have admitted that I was addicted to alcohol or other drugs. I have stopped using all nonprescribed drugs, including alcohol, and have accepted responsibility for my addiction.

2. I now choose people, places, and things that support my recovery.

3. As a person with an addiction, I now understand that, for me, use of alcohol or other drugs is never justified.

4. I have learned and will continue to learn clean and sober ways to manage my emotions.

5. I continue to identify and discard negative beliefs and values that have a negative effect on my recovery, and continue to discover positive beliefs and values that support my recovery.

6. I now set and move toward meaningful goals that reflect my new positive values and beliefs.

7. I have now discovered, or I choose to believe, that my life has a special purpose that can only be fulfilled if I remain clean and sober.

8. I am now fully committed to remaining abstinent from all nonprescribed drugs, including alcohol. I now live according to a set of beliefs, values, and goals that support my recovery, while helping others find their pathway to sobriety.

I understand that violating this contract is a violation of myself.

Date: _____

Signature: _____   Witness: _____

21

Conclusion

Congratulations! You have just completed a major task. The workbook you have just finished required a lot of study and effort. But your job has just begun. In order for you to maintain your recovery, you must maintain the changes you have made, and you must make even more changes. You must continue to grow and work to follow all eight principles of your recovery.

You may already be a member of Pathways to Sobriety; if not, you are strongly encouraged to join a Pathways to Sobriety group in your area as soon as possible. You will need a Pathways to Sobriety mentor to help you along.

Message from Damon

My name is Damon. I'm from British Columbia. My addiction to alcohol and cocaine took me where no man or woman wants to go—prison. Maybe you haven't had to pay for your addiction with your freedom. Yet. Most addicts don't end up in prison. Sometimes they get locked up overnight for DWI or maybe for a few days or a few weeks on a simple assault charge. Usually, though, most addicts don't do prison time.

But that's what my addiction to chemicals cost me. My freedom—five years' worth! This message is for anybody who will listen, but especially for those sitting in a little cage with steel bars on the window.

I started using drugs before I was even old enough to need to shave my face, first alcohol then cocaine. I lost everything to drugs except my life. I've been clean and sober since I started a recovery program the last year I spent locked up. Yes, I was still using alcohol and drugs even in prison. Can you believe that? It's true. If you are a real addict like me, you'll find a way to score no matter where you are. About a year after I got to prison, I got busted in the yard for possession of crack. They sent me to a cell block where I was locked down twenty-three hours a day. They called it the SHU. That stands for special housing unit. It was special alright. My cell had a little cage attached to the back of it that was made of heavy-gauge steel wire. I could go out in that cage and pace back and forth for an hour a day like a monkey at the zoo, if it wasn't raining or snowing.

The good part of being in the SHU was that I was given a crash course on chemical dependency that I had to complete in order to get back into the general population. At first I resisted. Then I thought, What the hell, I might as well do it. I finished the course and stayed clean till I got released on parole three and a half years later. I've been back in society for two years. I've got five and a half years of clean time now. I'm still on parole, but I'm free! Recovery is still hard at times but not as hard as doing time. And it keeps getting easier. And I'm reasonably happy. I want you to know that too. Now here's the rest of my message.

You're an addict. If your drug of choice happens to be alcohol, you're still an addict. Don't kid yourself into thinking alcohol isn't a drug. You're starting to work a recovery program, and you are facing the meanest dude on the street. He will do whatever he can to do you in. He will try every day to hurt you in every way. He will attack you from every side. He will take shots at you if you look away. If he gets the chance, he will dump poison into your brain. He will come in the night to steal your soul. His goal is to destroy you—completely. He has already done a number on you. If you're reading this from behind bars, look where he sent you! I'm not talking about the judge who sentenced you, man. I'm talking about your addiction. He is the meanest dude on the street. Yet if you can still move your eyeballs, you might stay alive.

But watch that dude every second. Never turn your back on him—never! If you're someplace and things don't look right, he's there waiting for his chance. Especially watch your back. He likes to sneak up and sucker punch you from behind. That's his style, you see. He doesn't like eye contact. He hates it when you face him.

Don't just watch for him, listen for him too. Listen for his footsteps on the street after dark, sneaking up on you out of the shadows. He'll whisper in your ear about the good old times. Don't listen. Shout him down!

You've also got to let your gut help you keep track of him. If you're somewhere you shouldn't be and your gut doesn't feel right, that's him! That's him alright. When that happens, get out of there fast. Run, don't walk!

You can smell him too. So let your nose help you keep track of him. If you're someplace that doesn't smell right, he's there. And he doesn't smell good. Kinda funky, you know?

The same dude who is after you was after me. He hurt me real bad. He had me right down on the concrete at times, beating the hell out of me. In fact, he almost killed me! He almost killed me in bars, in crack houses, in jails, in cars. But I foxed that dude! That's why I know you can too.

Listen up, man. I'm giving you a gift. It's called hope. If you take my gift, you gotta give it to somebody else someday. If you don't, the one who almost killed you and me will come and take it back.

Appendix A

Your Story

The pages that follow are meant to help you begin the difficult task of writing down your story. Writing down your story will increase your understanding of yourself and help you more fully heal from your addiction to alcohol or other drugs.

Don't worry about spelling or grammar. Just get your story down on paper. The pages are blank except for headings provided to help you organize your thoughts as you write. However, you don't have to make the events of your life fit exactly within the headings. They are there only to make the task a little easier. Nor does your story have to follow the sequence that has been suggested. Bill used a chronological sequence when he wrote his story. He started from the beginning and worked his way toward the present according to what he remembered. A chronological sequence is probably the easiest way to keep things straight. You can use the same method Bill used, or you can do it a different way. The important thing is that you end up with a deeper understanding of yourself and a happier recovery.

My Childhood

_____

_____

_____

_____

_____

_____

_____

_____

My First Use of Alcohol

_____

_____

_____

_____

_____

_____

_____

_____

My First Blackout

_____

_____

_____

_____

_____

_____

_____

_____

My First Drug Use

_____

_____

_____

_____

_____

_____

_____

_____

My First Major Consequence

_____

_____

_____

_____

_____

_____

_____

_____

When Things Got Worse

_____

_____

_____

_____

_____

_____

_____

_____

_____

Geographical Cures

_____

_____

_____

_____

_____

_____

_____

_____

Failed Attempts to Quit

_____

_____

_____

_____

_____

_____

_____

_____

_____

First Rehab

_____

_____

_____

_____

_____

_____

_____

_____

When I Reached Bottom

_____

_____

_____

_____

_____

_____

_____

_____

_____

_____

Things I Did and People I Hurt

_____

_____

_____

_____

_____

_____

_____

_____

When My Recovery Began

_____

_____

_____

_____

_____

_____

_____

_____

My Future: How I Want to Be

_____

_____

_____

_____

_____

_____

_____

_____

Where I Want to Be

_____

_____

_____

_____

_____

_____

_____

_____

_____

_____

What I Want to Accomplish

_____

_____

_____

_____

_____

_____

_____

_____

How I Want to Be Remembered

_____

_____

_____

_____

_____

_____

_____

_____

_____

SPACE FOR MORE NOTES...

_____

_____

_____

_____

_____

_____

_____

_____

_____

_____

_____

_____

_____

_____

_____

_____

_____

_____

Appendix B

The Pathways to Sobriety
Self-Help Program

∾ Overview: What Is Pathways to Sobriety? ∾

Pathways to Sobriety is a self-help program for people in recovery from addiction to alcohol or other drugs. Members meet in groups once a week, or more often, to help each other understand addiction and to help each other stop using alcohol and other drugs once and for all.

Anyone with an addiction can participate in Pathways to Sobriety. Participation in community-based Pathways to Sobriety groups is free.

∾ The Pathways to Sobriety Mission ∾

The Pathways to Sobriety mission is to help addicted people stop using alcohol or other drugs once and for all; to help them discover and pursue their highest values; to help them reach their goals; and to encourage them to help other addicted people find their pathways to sobriety.

∾ Pathways to Sobriety Members ∾

Pathways to Sobriety members come from all walks of life and from all over the world. They are men and women of every race and religion and of all ages. Some are married; some are divorced or separated; some have never been married. Some Pathways to Sobriety members have been in prison because of their addiction to alcohol or other drugs. Some members are told they must attend Pathways to Sobriety; some are encouraged by others to attend. But most members attend Pathways to Sobriety on their own. They came to Pathways to Sobriety because they lost things they valued and because they want to change. Some members lost their wives or husbands; some lost their children; some lost their jobs; some lost their freedom.

Some members also attend twelve-step self-help groups. They find the two approaches to recovery compatible.

All Pathways to Sobriety members had problems due to their addiction to alcohol or other drugs. All had harmed others; all are trying to change; all are trying to put the past behind them and to create a better future for themselves.

∾ The Pathways to Sobriety Mentor Program ∾

Pathways to Sobriety has a mentor program. A mentor is a wise teacher or trusted advisor. A mentor is sometimes called a "role model." A role model is someone who sets an example. A role model can set a good example or a bad one. A Pathways to Sobriety mentor is expected to set a good example.

The Pathways to Sobriety mentor program strengthens the power of the group. Pathways to Sobriety mentors help new members. But they are not counselors and they do not charge fees.

Appendix C

How to Start a Pathways to Sobriety Group in Your Area

You have completed *The Pathways to Sobriety Workbook*, and now you want to reinforce what you have learned for yourself and share what you have learned with others. You probably want to participate in a Pathways to Sobriety group in your area. If there are no groups in your area, you will want to start one.

✎ First Steps in Starting a Group ✎

Finding a Place to Meet

Starting a group is not difficult. First you need a place to meet. Contact the pastors of some churches in your area. Ask them if they would donate space. Human-services agencies that do drug- and alcohol-abuse counseling might help you find space.

Getting the Word Out

Next you need to get the word out. Contact your local newspaper. Ask them to put an announcement in their calendar of events; there is usually no charge. Shoppers' guides will usually place an announcement for you at no charge. In the announcement, simply say that a Pathways to Sobriety group is forming. Mention that the group is free. Make sure to include the location as well as the day and time of the meeting. Include your phone number in the announcement, and ask people to call for details.

Also contact radio stations and local TV stations. They often offer free public-announcement services. Another good way to get the word out is to place flyers on supermarket bulletin boards. You could even ask to start a Pathways to Sobriety group at the local jail. County probation offices are also good resources for finding a location and for spreading the word.

Refreshments and Other Expenses

You may want to provide free coffee at the meeting. If so, pass a basket for a small donation (one dollar or less) to help with costs. Passing the basket can also help cover other small costs that may go along with running the group.

Meeting Times

Evenings from 7:00 to 8:00 P.M. are usually the best meeting times for most people. It is difficult to get people to commit to a Pathways to Sobriety meeting on weekends or during daytime hours during the regular work week.

It will take time and effort to get a Pathways to Sobriety group up and running in your area. It may take a small amount of money. But the result will likely be more than worthwhile. You will have an opportunity to help yourself. You will have an opportunity to help other people who, like you, want to stop using alcohol or other drugs once and for all. You will have an opportunity to help people who are stuck in addiction because they don't know where to turn. You can help. You have a new understanding of the nature of addiction. You have new skills. You can help provide a place they can turn to.

Pathways to Sobriety Materials

In order to start a Pathways to Sobriety group, you need a few materials. You need at least one *Pathways to Sobriety Workbook*. See the back of this book for information on ordering workbooks.

On pages 238–240 of this workbook you will find the Pathways to Sobriety Meeting Facilitator's Guide. When you start your group, use the guide to assure a successful meeting. Simply keep it in front of you and read from it.

On pages 241–243 of this workbook you will find reproducible versions of The Pathways to Sobriety Principles, The Pathways to Sobriety Rules, and The Pathways to Sobriety Definition of Addiction. As you will discover when you read the facilitator's guide, these three lists should be read at the opening of every Pathways to Sobriety group meeting. You may make copies of these pages for this purpose. You may want to have these pages laminated in plastic, in order to keep them in good condition.

However, you are asked not to copy any other parts of the workbook. *The Pathways to Sobriety Workbook* is copyrighted material. Each group member should purchase his or her own workbook. When a member cannot afford to purchase a workbook, the group should use money from "the basket" to purchase a workbook for the member.

Pathways to Sobriety Group-Structure Guidelines

Each Pathways to Sobriety group is composed of a volunteer primary facilitator, a volunteer secretary/treasurer, a volunteer assistant, and participants.

Primary Facilitator's Responsibilities

- Locates meeting space.

- Gets the word out (publicity).

- Asks for a volunteer to serve as secretary/treasurer.

- Opens and closes the meetings.

- Sets up meetings, assisted by volunteers.

- Keeps the physical space in proper order.

- Passes the basket for donations at end of meetings.

- Communicates with Pathways to Sobriety main office.

- Serves one to three months as facilitator.

- Obtains and "trains" alternative facilitators.

Secretary/Treasurer's Responsibilities

- Records donations collected at meetings and from book sales.

- Maintains group treasury (bank account or just an envelope).

- Purchases workbooks and other resource materials.

- Makes workbooks available for purchase by members.

- Provides indigent members with workbooks at no cost, using donations collected from passing the basket and proceeds from book sales.

- Presents brief financial report to group once per month.

- Sends small quarterly donation from group treasury to PTS main office.

- May act as cofacilitator at request of primary facilitator.

- May act as facilitator when primary facilitator is absent.

Volunteer Assistant's Responsibilities

- Helps facilitator set up meetings.

- Makes the coffee.

- Requests funds for coffee from secretary/treasurer.

- May act as facilitator when primary facilitator and secretary/treasurer are both absent.

- Be on time.

- Comply with group rules.

◈ **Pathways to Sobriety Meeting Facilitator's Guide** ◈

The Pathways to Sobriety Workbook is the official guidebook for all Pathways to Sobriety programs. The workbook should be used as the primary educational tool for the groups. Pathways to Sobriety group participants need to learn about the contents of the workbook in order to help themselves and each other recover from addiction and learn how to live a happy clean and sober life.

At least some time should be spent reading from the workbook during each group session. Ideally, a group will read a part of each chapter during the hour the group meets. Twenty to thirty minutes should be devoted to reading the workbook during the first half hour of the meeting. Groups should cycle through one reading of the entire workbook every four to eight months. Reading of the material should be voluntary. If a participant does not wish to read, he or she may simply say "I pass" or "I would rather not read today." No one should feel they are being forced to read.

After reading from the workbook during the first half of the group session, the second half should be opened up for comments from the participants. The facilitator should help the group focus their comments on the contents of the workbook. Once the reading from the workbook has been completed, participants should also be encouraged to talk in a general way about personal issues that pertain to recovery from addiction. When discussion veers from the main purpose of the Pathways to Sobriety program and message, the facilitator should use the Pathways to Sobriety principles, the rules, and the definition of addiction to help the group refocus.

Using the workbook and the materials as the primary focus of the meetings will keep the group process from breaking down into "blame and complain" sessions.

IMPORTANT: Because Pathways to Sobriety is a nonreligious program, groups should refrain from using prayer as part of their format. A secular relaxation method may be used to begin and end a group meeting.

Meeting time is approximately one hour.

1. Open the meeting. Start by introducing yourself to the group:

   "Hi everybody. My name is _____, and I'm here because I'm addicted to _____ [name your drug of choice]."

   Then, starting on your right or left, go around the group and have everyone else introduce themselves by first name and tell why they are at the meeting.

2. Guide members through brief relaxation exercise to help them reduce their stress level. Take about thirty seconds. Speak slowly, using a soft tone. Use the script provided below.

   "Take a deep breath in, then a deep breath out, and relax your posture. Continuing to breathe in a relaxed way, slowly and deeply, reflect on how important it is to learn to relax in this way. Practice this skill several times a day, until it becomes a part of you. Use this technique whenever you feel stressed or whenever you feel a trigger to use your drug of choice."

3. Ask a member to read The Pathways to Sobriety Principles.

4. Ask a member to read The Pathways to Sobriety Rules.

5. Ask a member to read The Pathways to Sobriety Definition of Addiction.

6. Ask a member to read the section in the Introduction titled "Pathways to Sobriety: A Solution" (page 1).

7. Make any announcements that would be of interest to the group.

8. Go directly to whatever workbook chapter the group is studying. Go around the room, starting on your left or right, and ask for volunteers to read a page or two from the chapter. Do not stop to do the exercises in the group, unless the group has decided to do so. Ask the participants to complete the written work on their own time, before the group meets again. Continue reading until at least half of the chapter has been completed. Then ask members if they have any questions about the material just read. If so, encourage members to help each other find the appropriate answers. When confusion occurs, refer to the workbook, or to the principles, the rules, or the definition of addiction.

9. Ask members if they have any problems or issues having to do with recovery that have come up over the past week and that they would like some feedback about from the group. Start on your right or left, and give each person a chance to comment. Participants who do not wish to comment may simply say "I pass" or "I don't want to comment tonight." Those who wish to comment should be allowed two to five minutes to speak. Then go to the next person. Do not allow a few individuals to take up most of the time. Participants may comment more than once if everyone else has been given an opportunity to comment.

10. Approximately two minutes before ending the meeting, pass the basket for rent and coffee donations. (This is voluntary. No one should be made to feel they have to donate, and no one should put more than a dollar or two in the basket.)

11. Close the meeting with the following meditation:

Everyone sit back and get into a more relaxed posture again. Take a slow, deep breath. Maintaining that relaxed posture, continue to breathe slowly and deeply. Be aware for a moment or two of all the addicted people all over the world, and of what they have lost because of their use of alcohol or other drugs. Some of them have lost their families; some have lost their jobs; some have lost their freedom, or their self-respect. Some have even lost their lives.

Be aware also of the thousands of people all over the world who have been hurt by things addicted people have said or done to them, and recognize that they don't deserve the pain they are going through.

Be aware that it doesn't have to be that way for us anymore. We can meet together as we have today and help each other find new clean and sober ways to deal with the same old triggers—new ways that do not cause harm to ourselves or others.

Above all, recognize that everybody in this room deserves to be happy, as long as it is not at someone else's expense.

Have a good week, everybody. See you next week.

12. Before leaving the meeting site, make sure everything is in order (lights off, water taps off, etc.).

If You Need Assistance

If you need help starting or facilitating a group, or if you wish to order additional Pathways to Sobriety workbooks, contact Pathways to Sobriety. We will be glad to do what we can to assist you.

Pathways to Sobriety
PO Box 259
Cassadaga NY 14718
(800) 775-4212
E-mail: transfrm@netsync.net

∾ *The Eight Principles of* ∾
the Pathways to Sobriety Recovery Program

First Principle

We admit we have abused or have been addicted to alcohol or other drugs. We have stopped using all nonprescribed drugs, including alcohol, and now accept responsibility for our addiction.

Second Principle

We understand that our environment can either support our recovery or work against it. Whenever possible, we choose people, places, and things that support our recovery.

Third Principle

As people recovering from addiction, we now know we can never justify using alcohol or other drugs, or other addictive behaviors, to change how we feel.

Fourth Principle

We are now learning new clean and sober techniques that help us to manage our emotions.

Fifth Principle

We discovered that the negative beliefs and values that helped support our addiction were counterproductive. Now we discard those negative beliefs and values and are discovering new, positive beliefs and values that support our recovery.

Sixth Principle

When we were addicted, we lacked meaningful goals. Now we set and move toward meaningful goals that reflect our new, positive values and beliefs

Seventh Principle

We have discovered, or have chosen to believe, that our lives have a special purpose that can be fulfilled only if we remain clean and sober.

Eighth Principle

Being fully committed to remaining abstinent from alcohol and all nonprescribed drugs, we now choose to live according to a set of beliefs, values, and goals that supports our recovery, and to help others find their pathways to sobriety.

© 2004 Pathways to Sobriety

∾ The Pathways to Sobriety Rules ∾

Here are the Pathways to Sobriety rules.
The rules assure the safety of the members.

Pathways to Sobriety members:

1. Agree not to discuss information outside the group
that is shared in meetings or among members;

2. Agree not to be violent at meetings;

3. Agree not to attend meetings under the influence of alcohol or other drugs;

4. Agree not to bring weapons to the group.

© 2004 Pathways to Sobriety

∾ The Pathways to Sobriety ∾
Definition of Addiction

What is addiction?

Imagine a line stretching from wall to wall across a room.

The left-hand wall represents limited use of chemicals.

Problem use is located somewhere near the center of the line.

The right-hand wall represents full-blown addiction to alcohol or other drugs.

© 2004 Pathways to Sobriety

Pathways to Sobriety
Books, Videos, and Master Programs
Available for Purchase

Teen and Spanish Pathways to Sobriety Workbooks

The Pathways to Sobriety Workbook may soon be available in teen and Spanish-language versions.

Niagara Falls Metaphor Video

The video graphically compares relapse to a trip down the Niagara River and over the falls, as described in Chapter 9 of the workbook.

Pathways to Sobriety Program Master Package

The master package includes *The Pathways to Sobriety Workbook* in a loose-leaf binder and the *Niagara Falls Metaphor Video*. This package makes the workbook available to large numbers of users at a fraction of the cost. Your school, institution, organization, or agency may use the master to produce an unlimited number of copies, *for in-house use only*.

On-Site Introductory Seminars Also Available

Pathways to Sobriety can come to you and introduce the Pathways to Sobriety program to your community or organization.

◆ ◆ ◆

For prices, more information, or to order, call:

Pathways to Sobriety • PO Box 259 • Cassadaga NY 14718 • (800) 775-4212
E-mail: transfrm@netsync.net

Resources for Physical Fitness & Pain Relief

ShapeWalking
Six Easy Steps to Your Best Body

by Marilyn Bach, Ph.D., and Lorie Schleck, M.A., P.T.

Millions of Americans want an easy, low-cost fitness program. *ShapeWalking* is the answer. It includes aerobic exercise, strength training, and flexibility stretching and is suited for exercisers of all levels.

ShapeWalking is ideal for people who want to control weight; develop muscle definition; prevent or reverse loss of bone density; and target tone the stomach, buttocks, arms, and thighs. The second edition includes over 70 photographs as well as updated exercises and resources.

144 PAGES ... 70 PHOTOS ... PAPERBACK $14.95 ... 2ND EDITION

The Complete Guide to Joseph H. Pilates' Techniques of Physical Conditioning: *With Special Help for Back Pain and Sports Training*

by Allen Menezes

Almost 80 years ago, Joseph Pilates developed a body-work system focusing on strengthening the core muscles of the abdomen and strengthening and increasing flexibility in the arms and legs. This guide to Pilates' techniques includes a complete floor program of basic, intermediate, and advanced routines, with detailed descriptions of each exercise and step-by-step photographs. There is a special section on relieving back, ankle, and shoulder pain, and insights on how Pilates work can be adapted by athletes.

208 PAGES ... 191 PHOTOS ... 80 ILLUS. & CHARTS ... PAPERBACK $19.95 ... SPIRAL BOUND $26.95

Get Fit While You Sit
Easy Workouts from Your Chair

by Charlene Torkelson

Here is a total body workout that can be done right from your chair, anywhere. It is perfect for office workers, travelers, and those with age-related movement limitations or special conditions. The book offers three programs. The One-Hour Chair Program is a full-body, low-impact workout that includes light aerobics and exercises to be done with or without weights. The 5-Day Short Program features five compact workouts for those short on time. Finally, the Ten-Minute Miracles is a group of easy-to-do exercises perfect for anyone on the go.

160 PAGES ... 212 PHOTOS ... PAPERBACK $12.95

Fusion Fitness
Combining the Best from East and West

by Chan Ling Yap, Ph.D., Foreword by Stephanie Cook

Fusion Fitness is the next step in fitness programs, a combination of the best Western and Eastern techniques including Pilates, Alexander Technique, Callanetics, yoga, and t'ai chi to create a dynamic exercise program for strength, endurance, toning, coordination, core stability, and cardiovascular fitness.

Dr. Yap explains how and why the different disciplines have been fused, and why in some cases she has combined the principles to create new exercises. The book has over 130 photos and illustrations, and 35 charts.

224 PAGES ... 62 PHOTOS 70 ILLUS. ... PAPERBACK $16.95

The Chiropractor's Self-Help Back and Body Book: *How You Can Relieve Common Aches and Pains at Home and on the Job*

by Samuel Homola, D.C.

Written by a chiropractor with over 40 years experience, this book is for people with chronic head, neck, arm, wrist, back, hip, leg, and shoulder pain; sufferers from sciatica, a weak back, arthritis, hypoglycemia, and osteoporosis. It includes information on how to handle arthritis, how to protect a weak back during sex and pregnancy, and how to tell sense from nonsense in the chiropractic care of your back pain. The book is illustrated with 43 line drawings prepared by a professional artist.

320 PAGES ... 43 ILLUS. ... PAPERBACK $17.95

Treat Your Back Without Surgery: *The Best Nonsurgical Alternatives for Eliminating Back and Neck Pain*

by Stephen Hochschuler, M.D., and Bob Reznik

Eighty percent of back pain sufferers can get well without surgery. Be one of them! From the authors of *Back in Shape*, this new guide discusses a range of nonsurgical techniques — from t'ai chi and massage therapy to chiropractic treatment and acupuncture — as well as exercise plans, diet and stress management techniques, and tips to ease everyday pain. Because surgery is sometimes necessary, you'll also get advice on how to find the best surgeon and what questions to ask.

224 PAGES ...38 PHOTOS ... 5 ILLUS. ... PAPERBACK $15.95 2ND EDITION

The Art of Getting Well
A Five-Step Plan for Maximizing Health When You Have a Chronic Illness

by David Spero, R.N.

Self-management programs have become a key way for people to deal with chronic illness. In this book, David Spero brings together the medical, psychological, and spiritual aspects of getting well in a five-step approach: slow down and use your energy for the things and people that matter — make small, progressive changes that build self-confidence — get help and nourish the social ties that are crucial for well-being — value your body and treat it with affection and respect — take responsibility for getting the best care and health you can.

224 PAGES ... PAPERBACK $15.95

Chinese Herbal Medicine Made Easy
Natural and Effective Remedies for Common Illnesses

by Thomas Richard Joiner

Chinese herbal medicine is an ancient system for maintaining health and prolonging life. This book demystifies the subject, by providing clear explanations and easy-to-read alphabetical listings of more than 750 herbal remedies for over 250 common illnesses ranging from acid reflux and AIDS to breast cancer, pain management, sexual dysfunction, and weight loss. Whether you are a newcomer to herbology or a seasoned practitioner, you will find this book to be a valuable addition to your health library.

432 PAGES ... PAPERBACK $24.95

How Women Can Finally Stop Smoking
by Robert C. Klesges, Ph.D., and Margaret DeBon

This guide reveals that what works for men does not necessarily work for women when it comes to quitting smoking. Women tend to gain more weight, their menstrual cycles and menopause affect the likelihood of success, and their withdrawal symptoms are different.

The book is in two parts. Part One guides women in choosing the best time to quit and in deciding which method to use. Part Two gives directions for managing withdrawal and weight gain, finding peer support, and controlling stress.

192 PAGES ... 3 ILLUS. ... PAPERBACK $11.95

Loving Your Partner without Losing Your Self
by Martha Beveridge, MSSW

This book explains how to maintain your sense of self in a relationship. Beveridge, an experienced therapist, shows why romantic relationships often deteriorate from intense love into day-to-day struggles that tear couples apart, and gives practical and unique strategies for transforming these struggles into deeper intimacy. These include:

- getting past the ABCs (Attacking, Blaming, Criticizing)
- recognizing the symptoms of poor boundaries (clinging, jealousy, acting single, running away)
- dealing with the smokescreen issues (time, money, sex)

256 PAGES ... PAPERBACK $14.95

Creating Extraordinary Joy
A Guide to Authenticity, Connection and Self-Transformation

by Chris Alexander, with a foreword by Deborah Waitley

Extraordinary joy is a state of deep satisfaction and continuous delight that comes when we really like who we are, how we live, and what we do. The key to this is synergy: making connections that energize and inspire us beyond the ordinary.

Using timeless teachings, images from nature, powerful exercises, and real-life examples, Chris Alexander describes the seven steps that can put synergy in your life and create the most important sort of happiness: an immoderately, exuberantly joyful life.

272 PAGES ... PAPERBACK $15.95

The Pleasure Prescription
To Love, to Work, to Play — Life in the Balance

by Paul Pearsall, Ph.D.   New York Times Bestseller!

This bestselling book is a prescription for stressed-out lives. Dr. Pearsall maintains that contentment, wellness and long life can be found by devoting time to family, helping others, and slowing down to savor life's pleasures. Pearsall's unique approach draws from the principles of ancient Polynesian wisdom and his own 25 years of psychological and medical research. Includes the Aloha Test.

288 PAGES ... PAPERBACK $13.95 ... HARDCOVER $23.95

When Violence Begins at Home
A Comprehensive Guide to Understanding and Ending Domestic Abuse
by K. J. Wilson, Ed.D.

With understanding and empathy, this guide to domestic violence addresses the needs of multiple audiences, including battered women of various ages and backgrounds, teenaged victims of violence, educators, community leaders, legal officials, and even batterers themselves. Special chapters clarify the responsibilities — and limitations — of friends and family, shelter employees, health-care providers, law enforcement officers, employers, and clergy. A listing of local and national resources directs affected people to information and people who can help.

416 PAGES ... 2 ILLUS. ... PAPERBACK $19.95

Helping Your Child Through Your Divorce
by Florence Bienenfeld, Ph.D.

This guide encourages divorcing parents to focus on what is best for their child and to forge a new alliance— as parent partners who are no longer marriage partners. Includes examples of model agreements and strategies for dealing with common problems. Drawings by children of divorcing parents illustrate the anger and hurt that children feel as a result of being pulled between parents.

224 PAGES ... 37 ILLUS. ... PAPERBACK $14.95

Free Yourself from an Abusive Relationship
Seven Steps to Taking Back Your Life
by Andrea Lissette, M.A., CDVC, and Richard Kraus, Ph.D.

A lifesaving guide for women who are victims of violence and abuse. Step One describes different kinds of abuse. Step Two is about abusers and who they abuse, with sections on children and senior citizens. Step Three deals with crises, stalking, rape, and assault. It includes an in-depth look at legal help and court proceedings. Step Four shows women how to live as survivors, with practical advice on money matters and work issues. Step Five discusses the decision to stay or leave, and Steps Six and Seven move from healing and rebuilding to Becoming and Remaining Abuse Free.

304 PAGES ... PAPERBACK $16.95

Violent No More
Helping Men End Domestic Abuse
by Michael Paymar, Trainer at the Duluth Domestic Abuse Intervention Project.

Based on the model domestic abuse intervention program in Duluth, Minnesota, *Violent No More* addresses abusive men directly, taking them step-by-step through the process of recognizing their abusive behaviors, taking a time-out when necessary, and learning how to express anger without violence. The changes are illustrated with the often-shocking stories of several previously abusive men—and of women who were abused.

304 PAGES ... PAPERBACK $17.95 ... REVISED 2ND EDITION

Keeping Kids Safe
A Child Sexual Abuse Prevention Manual
by Pnina Tobin, MPA, and Sue Levinson Kessner, M.S.

The threat of sexual abuse is constant, and it is crucial to teach children how to recognize when they are in danger and how to obtain help. *Keeping Kids Safe* contains curricula for ages 3–7 and 8–11 with scripts and workshops. Children are taught to distinguish between wanted and unwanted touches, and to say "No!" and get help. A Facilitator's Guide informs educators about myths and facts about child sexual abuse; development issues and indicators of abuse; and reporting procedures and follow-up methods.

192 PAGES ... 29 PHOTOGRAPHS ... PAPERBACK $24.95 ... SPIRAL BOUND $29.95 ... REVISED 2ND EDITION

I Can Make My World a Safer Place
A Kid's Book about Stopping Violence
by Paul Kivel • Illustrations and games by Nancy Gorrell

This book for kids ages 6–11 shows what children can do to find alternatives to violence in their lives. Kivel explains public danger (gangs, fights, and drug-related violence) and private danger (sexual assault and domestic violence) and gives suggestions for staying safe. Simple text and activities such as mazes and word searches encourage young readers to think about and promote peace. Activism is discussed, using examples such as César Chavez and Julia Butterfly. The multicultural drawings by Nancy Gorrell are playful and engaging, guiding the reader, reinforcing the text, and making difficult ideas easier to understand.

96 PAGES ... PAPERBACK $11.95

All books may be ordered at our website www.hunterhouse.com

ORDER FORM

10%	DISCOUNT on orders of $50 or more —
20%	DISCOUNT on orders of $150 or more —
30%	DISCOUNT on orders of $500 or more —

On cost of books for fully prepaid orders

NAME

ADDRESS

CITY/STATE   ZIP/POSTCODE

PHONE   COUNTRY (outside of U.S.)

TITLE	QTY	PRICE	TOTAL
Pathways to Sobriety (paperback)		@ $17.95	
Pathways to Sobriety (spiral bound)		@ $24.95	

Prices subject to change without notice

Please list other titles below:

		@ $	
		@ $	
		@ $	
		@ $	
		@ $	
		@ $	
		@ $	

Check here to receive our book catalog ☐   FREE

Shipping Costs	
By Priority Mail: first book $4.50, each additional book $1.00	TOTAL _____
	Less discount @____% (_____)
By UPS and to Canada: first book $5.50, each additional book $1.50	TOTAL COST OF BOOKS _____
	Calif. residents add sales tax _____
For rush orders and other countries call us at (510) 865-5282	Shipping & handling _____
	TOTAL ENCLOSED _____
	Please pay in U.S. funds only

☐ Check ☐ Money Order ☐ Visa ☐ MasterCard ☐ Discover

Card # _____ Exp. date _____

Signature _____

Complete and mail to

Hunter House Inc., Publishers

PO Box 2914, Alameda CA 94501-0914

Website: www.hunterhouse.com

Orders: (800) 266-5592 | email: ordering@hunterhouse.com

Phone (510) 865-5282 | Fax (510) 865-4295

PTS 03/2004